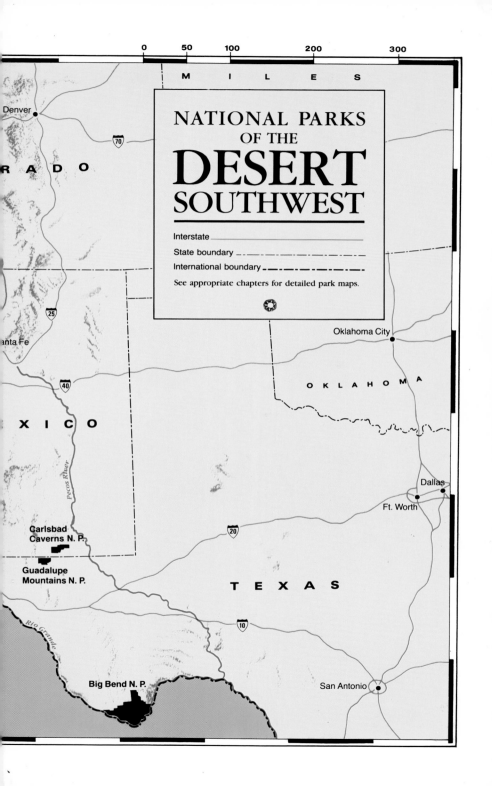

0   50   100   200   300

M   I   L   E   S

NATIONAL PARKS
OF THE
DESERT
SOUTHWEST

Interstate _____

State boundary _ _ _ _ _ _ _ _

International boundary _ . . _ . . _ . . _ . . _

See appropriate chapters for detailed park maps.

Denver

70

R A D O

25

anta Fe

40

Oklahoma City

O K L A H O M A

X I C O

Pecos River

Dallas

Ft. Worth

20

Carlsbad
Caverns N. P.

Guadalupe
Mountains N. P.

T E X A S

Rio Grande

10

Big Bend N. P.

San Antonio

THE SIERRA CLUB GUIDES
TO THE
NATIONAL PARKS
OF THE
DESERT
SOUTHWEST

Published by
Stewart, Tabori & Chang

Distributed by
R A N D O M   H O U S E

Copyright © 1984, 1996 by Stewart, Tabori & Chang, Inc.
Maps copyright © 1996 by Joyce Pendola
Illustrations and maps copyright © 1984, 1996 by Bill Russell

Library of Congress Cataloging-in-Publication Data

The Sierra Club guides to the national parks of the desert Southwest / (text by
Conger Beasley, Jr. . . . et al.; consulting editor, James V. Murfin; project editor,
Irene Pavitt). — Rev. and updated.
        p.   cm. — (Sierra Club guides to the national parks)
Includes index.
Spine title: Desert Southwest.
ISBN 0-679-76493-3 (pbk.)
1. National parks and reserves—Southwest, New—Guidebooks.
2. Southwest, New—Guidebooks. I. Beasley, Conger. II. Murfin, James V. III.
Pavitt, Irene. IV. Sierra Club. V. Title: Desert Southwest VI. Series.
F785.3.S57 1996
917.9'0443—dc20
                                                                                    96-11448
                                                                                    CIP

TEXT BY:
Conger Beasley, Jr.: Grand Canyon and Petrified Forest
Michael Collier: Mesa Verde
Frank Deckert: Big Bend
Dave Ganci: Saguaro*
Robert Gildart: Bryce Canyon and Zion
Daniel Murphy: Carlsbad Caverns and Guadalupe Mountains
Jeremy Schmidt: Great Basin*
Stephen Trimble: Arches, Canyonlands, and Capitol Reef
*New in the revised edition.

Text revisions throughout this edition by the Project Editor.

Photo credits can be found on pp. 392–393.

PROJECT EDITOR: Donald Young (Revised Edition); Irene Pavitt (First Edition)
CONSULTING EDITOR: James V. Murfin (First Edition)
DESIGNER: J. C. Suarès
PHOTO EDITOR: Amla Sanghvi (Revised Edition); Christine A. Pullo (First Edition)
COPY EDITOR: Randy Blunk (Revised Edition)
ART AND PRODUCTION: Alice Wong, Lisa Vaughn, Melanie Random,
Evangeline Yao, Christopher Young (Revised Edition)

Created by Stewart, Tabori & Chang, Inc., 575 Broadway, New York, NY 10012

Printed in Singapore

24689753

Revised Edition

Cover Photographs: The Needles District, Canyonlands (© Stewart M. Green/Tom
Stack & Assoc.); Mule deer (© Stephen Trimble); Buttonbush flower (© Joe
Branney/Tom Stack & Assoc.); Illustration and map (© Bill Russell). Frontispiece:
The Golden Throne, Capitol Reef (© Jim Shotwell/Tom Stack & Assoc.). Back
cover: Double Arch, Arches National Park (© Frank Mendonca/Tom Stack & Assoc.)

The fifty-four national parks of the United States contain many glorious natural splendors. Each year, tens of millions of Americans and growing numbers of visitors from around the world contemplate the beauty of snow-capped mountains, cascading waterfalls, groves of soaring trees, glistening surf-kissed beaches, and deep and mysterious red-rock canyons. Herds of large mammals enhance the setting in some parks, and uncounted numbers of other animals, birds, crawly things, and plants occupy their own niches as participants in nature's grand design.

The National Park System contains about 375 units, but the five volumes of *The Sierra Club Guides to the National Parks* feature only those units designated as a "national park" or as a "national park and preserve." An act of Congress is required for the establishment of a park. The world's first national park—Yellowstone—was created in 1872. The list has grown steadily, as the American people, through their elected representatives, demonstrated many times their commitment to preserving parks for the enjoyment of themselves and of generations yet to come. In 1994 alone, three more parks were added to the list.

The Sierra Club was founded in California in 1892 by the naturalist John Muir and some of his friends. One of the oldest and largest conservation organizations, the Club, which now has more than 550,000 members, has been in the forefront of many efforts to create new parks.

This series has been produced with the cooperation of the Sierra Club and with the participation of the National Park Service and Random House. Leading nature writers and photographers have contributed to the guides. This revised edition contains new chapters on the six parks established since the mid-1980s. As well, the chapters on the forty-eight other parks have been thoroughly reviewed and completely updated.

We hope you will enjoy exploring the parks, and we know these guides will enhance your experience.

—*Donald Young, Editor*

M A P S

C O N T E N T S

ARCHES
NATIONAL PARK

Delicate Arch, only 45 feet high, appears much taller.

ARCHES NATIONAL PARK
P. O. BOX 907
MOAB, UTAH 84532
TEL.: (801) 259-8161

HIGHLIGHTS: Delicate Arch • Double Arch • Landscape Arch • Fiery Furnace • Devils Garden • Herdina Park • Klondike Bluffs • Courthouse Towers • Park Avenue • Balanced Rock • Garden of Eden

ACCESS: From Moab take U.S. 191 North for 5 miles to park entrance. See map on pages 14–15.

HOURS: Daily, 24 hours, year-round. Visitor Center, 8 A.M.–4:30 P.M.; extended hours in summer; closed Christmas Day.

FEES: Charged at entrance and for camping; Golden Age and Golden Eagle passes honored.

PARKING: Adequate parking at each public-use point.

GAS, FOOD: In Moab.

LODGING: In Moab.

VISITOR CENTER: Arches Visitor Center, at main entrance, offers slide show, books, maps, and posters for sale.

MUSEUM: In Arches Visitor Center. Offers geological and historical displays.

PETS: Not permitted in backcountry roadless areas or on hiking trails. All pets outside vehicles must be on leash. Horseback riding permitted in specific backcountry areas. Permit required for all horseback trips. All riders should first stop at Visitor Center. No grazing; no rentals; no stables.

PICNICKING: At Visitor Center, Balanced Rock, and Devils Garden.

HIKING: Trails available. Carry water.

BACKPACKING: Backpack camping permitted in wilderness area with free permit, but at least 1 mile from roads and .5 mile from trails, and out of sight of the arches. No water is available.

CAMPGROUND: Devils Garden, 52 sites, both tent and trailer. First-come basis. Fires only in fire grates; gathering wood forbidden. No showers, no hookups. Fee charged.

TOURS: Through Fiery Furnace daily in spring, summer, fall. In English only; other tours depend on season and staff.

OTHER ACTIVITIES: Additional interpretive activities during high season. Sightseeing flights at airport outside park.

FACILITIES FOR DISABLED: Arches Visitor Center, campground restrooms, a campsite, and the restroom at The Windows.

For additional information, see also Sites, Trails, and Trips on pages 26–32.

ARCHES NATIONAL PARK CONTAINS THE greatest known concentration of natural stone arches. The park is a jewel—a scattering of sandstone spires perched above the Colorado River canyon on a highland that feels like a formal garden, decorated with twisted pinyon and juniper trees and natural statuary of arches, buttes, towers, and hoodoos. The La Sal Mountains—more than 12,000 feet and snow-capped most of the year—form a tantalizing background of evergreen and aspen forest.

Arches introduces the unique rock landscapes of the Colorado Plateau. Its story is straightforward: a collapsed salt dome cracked rocks on its flanks, and they eroded to fins of sandstone ideal for arch formation. Big enough to feel wild—73,379 acres—the park is small enough to be enjoyed in a day. An 18-mile paved road penetrates to its heart and leads past most major features. Easy and moderate trails lead to many arches, including the monumental buttresses of Double Arch, Landscape Arch (one of the world's longest natural spans), and exquisite Delicate Arch.

This is high desert country, ranging from 3,960 to 5,653 feet. Shrubs dominate, with cottonwoods along washes the only trees other than the tough dryland junipers and pinyons. Practically nothing grows on some shales, but hanging gardens luxuriate at seeps. Animal life is typical of rugged plateau country: deer, jack rabbit, gray fox, raven, mourning dove, white-throated swift, toad, collared lizard, rattlesnake. Dry, achingly hot in summer and sometimes frigid in winter, Arches makes a challenging home for these living things, but their evolutionary success matches the feel of the park landscape—spare, careful, quiet, and elegant.

Near this complex of fins lies Sand Dune Arch.

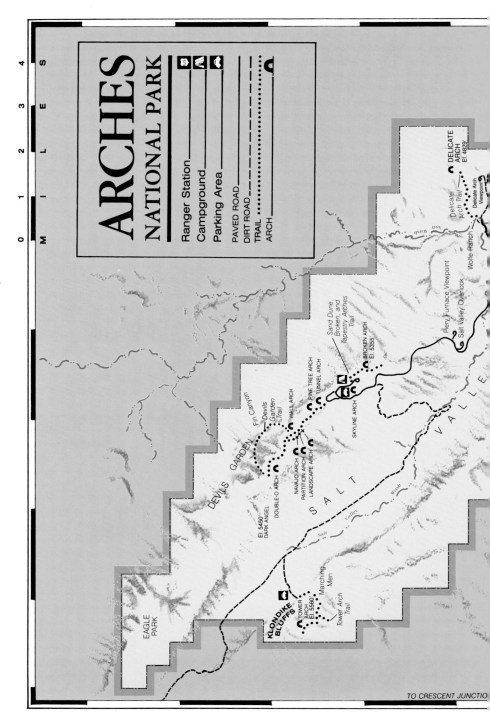

ARCHES
NATIONAL PARK

Ranger Station
Campground
Parking Area

PAVED ROAD
DIRT ROAD
TRAIL
ARCH

MILES

0 1 2 3 4
M L E S

DELICATE ARCH El. 4829'

Delicate Arch Trail
Delicate Arch Viewpoint

Wolfe Ranch

Salt Wash

Fiery Furnace Viewpoint
Salt Valley Overlook

Sand Dune, Broken, and Tapestry Arches Trail

BROKEN ARCH El. 5355'

PINE TREE ARCH
TUNNEL ARCH
WALL ARCH

SKYLINE ARCH

SALT VALLEY

Fin Canyon

Devils Garden Trail

DEVILS GARDEN

NAVAJO ARCH
PARTITION ARCH
LANDSCAPE ARCH

DOUBLE-O ARCH

El. 5450'
DARK ANGEL

Salt Valley Wash

Wash

Marching Men

EAGLE PARK

KLONDIKE BLUFFS

TOWER ARCH El. 5560'

Tower Arch Trail

TO CRESCENT JUNCTIO

FISHER TOWERS AND CASTLE VALLEY

DRY MESA

128

N

Colorado River

Salt Wash

THE WINDOWS DISTRICT

GARDEN OF EDEN

COVE OF CAVES

NORTH WINDOW
SOUTH WINDOW

COVE ARCH

Turret Arch and The Spectacles Trail

Point

DOUBLE ARCH

Double Arch Trail

TURRET ARCH
El. 5280'

Balanced Rock
El. 5120'

EYE OF THE WHALE

Rock Pinnacles

TO MOAB

TOWER OF BABEL
El. 4537'

THE ORGAN

La Sal Mountains Viewpoint

Sheep Rock

COURTHOUSE TOWERS

Park Avenue Trail

Park Avenue

Visitor Center
El. 4085'

Three Penguins

MOAB CANYON

VICINITY MAP

UTAH
COLORADO

70

128

ARCHES N.P.

Moab

46

191

Crescent Jct.

La Sal Jct.

Green River

Canyon Lands N.P.

INSET SCALE

0   10   20
M I L E S

191

15
ARCHES

A thousand years back in canyon-country prehistory, two powerful cultures had developed in the Arches region, the Fremont and the Anasazi. Arches National Park straddles the boundary between them, an open territory used from about A.D. 1000 to 1300 as a marginal agricultural and hunting area by the Anasazi from the south, and as a hunting area and shrine for magical rock art by the Fremont from the north.

The Prehistoric Frontier

Anasazi corn farmers must have regarded Arches as a barely usable frontier. The Fremont favored hunting and gathering, and probably used the park seasonally. The finest rock-art site—with Fremont, Anasazi, and Barrier Canyon-style figures—tragically was vandalized in 1980.

On this fine line of agriculture, where just enough rain fell to support life, a minor drought evidently pushed the people past an invisible threshold between success and failure, bringing regional abandonment about 1300. The ultimate fate of the Fremont remains a mystery. The Anasazi migrated farther and farther south; today their descendants live in the Hopi and Rio Grande pueblos.

The Ute Indians were living across all of western Colorado and eastern Utah when whites arrived. The Ute hunters took so well to horses in the early 1800s that they carried their hunts and raids from the buffalo plains in the east to the Navajo and Paiute country in the south and west. The Utes, too, left petroglyphs at Arches.

Trails and Trappers

Most of the whirl of nineteenth-century exploration passed north of Arches, on the same easy path that Interstate 70 and the railroad follow today. But one historic trail came up from New Mexico, bound for California, to cross the Colorado River at Moab and head north right past the present-day park. The trappers and traders called it the Old Spanish Trail, although it was used most heavily by Mexicans and Americans in the 1830s and 1840s.

One mountain man left his cryptic signature on a number of cliffs in the area, including one at Arches dated June 9, 1844. We know little about this mysterious Denis Julien, but his inscriptions in Canyonlands hint that he may have been the first to travel down the Colorado and Green rivers by boat.

Canyon Conquest

As the Mormons pushed out from Salt Lake City, they chose the

Skyline Arch c. 1935. In 1940, the rock slab to the right fell away.

present site of Moab for their Elk Mountain Mission in 1855. But the Utes whom they sought to convert rebelled, and three Mormon deaths forced abandonment that same year. Not until the late 1870s did settlers return to the east side of the Colorado River. By 1883, Moab had a post office, and the Denver and Rio Grande Railroad between Denver and Salt Lake City passed by just 30 miles north.

In the late 1800s, Arches got its first settler in the person of John Wesley Wolfe, a Civil War veteran who left Ohio for his health, and until 1910 lived with his family on the bank of Salt Walsh below Delicate Arch. His cabin still stands, counterpart in pioneer spirit to the broken spear points and petroglyphs of the vanished Native Americans.

Establishment of the Park

The father of Arches National Park was a prospector who in 1923 suggested to the managers of the railroad that they develop Klondike Bluffs as a tourist attraction. Alexander Ringhoffer guided the officials through the remarkable sandstone maze, and the impressed railroad men contacted Stephen Mather, first director of the National Park Service. Mather initiated the political process that created the small Arches National Monument in 1929. Over the years, Moab groups, led by Dr. J. W. Williams and Loren L. Taylor, pushed through major additions to the monument, and in 1971 their work culminated in the establishment of Arches National Park.

GEOLOGY

Unlikely as it seems, common salt is the creative force behind the features of Arches National Park—the densest cluster of natural stone arches on earth. A roundabout story, however, leads to this realization, and to the landscape of today's park.

Arches and Salt

The main thread of the tale began 300 million years ago, when a huge basin developed in southeastern Utah and southwestern Colorado. Oceans filled the basin, and a neighboring highland shed into it vast quantities of sediment. As the ocean shrank, salts, gypsum, and other "evaporites" crystallized from the brine under the hot rays of the Pennsylvanian period sun. This basin is called the Paradox Basin, and the 3,000 feet of salt deposits, the Paradox Formation.

The area went through hundreds of millions more years of deposition, uplift, and erosion. But the ancient salt remained a

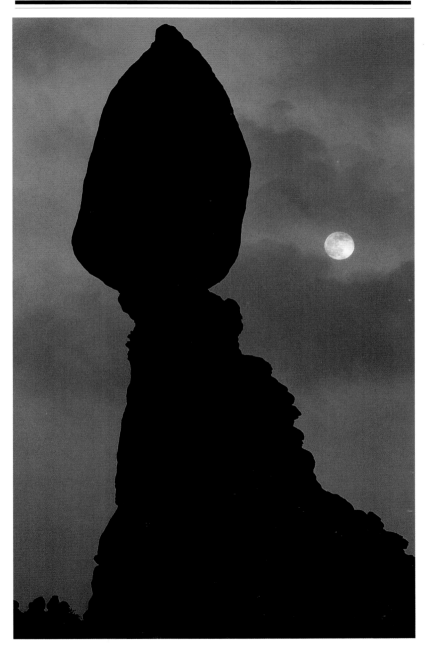

Balanced Rock, near The Windows.

major character in its story. Later formations that overlie the Paradox salt came to Arches as sediments that rippled the tidal flats of shallow seas, from rivers and lakes, and as the wind-blown sand dunes of deserts. Two hundred million years of rocks, in thirteen distinct layers, lie exposed in the park. Once you learn to recognize these formations, their names resonate with the sense of the place: Paradox, Honaker Trail, Cutler, Moenkopi, Chinle, Wingate, Kayenta, Navajo, Entrada, Summerville, Morrison, Dakota, and Mancos.

As these heavier layers piled on the lighter underlying salt, they forced the salt upward where the rock cover was thinnest, squeezing it in slowly moving "plastic" flows along areas of weakness in long parallel cores. More and more salt flowed into the rises as new sediments weighed heavier and heavier on the troughs. The rising salt domed up the overlying rocks in folds, cracking rocks along their sides.

Then, less than 10 million years ago, regional uplift further cracked the flanks of these folds in a series of joints paralleling each long salt dome. Finally, as erosion ate down through the rising stack of ancient sedimentary rocks, ground water reached the salt, dissolving out dome foundations, which collapsed. Exactly such events led to the landscape seen today in Salt Valley.

Arches and Water

Thus this rather nondescript valley slowly gave rise to the spectacular Entrada Sandstone ridges where the arches form. Water dissolves cement between sand grains in the rock, and grinds down along joints, isolating narrow "fins." Winter brings a trickle of snowmelt freezing in cracks, wedging the fins to rubble. Slabs pop off when cliffs release ancient pressures built up when they lay buried under thousands of feet of other rock. Cleansing summer thunderstorms sweep away "waste" rock to the Colorado.

And sometimes, a block wedged from a wall deepens an alcove just enough to pierce the fin, a pothole grinds through a cliff edge, and a last rockfall leaves behind a natural, free-standing stone span—an arch.

Joints along both sides of Cache and Salt valleys provided the blueprint for the groups of arches and spires: The Windows, Devils Garden, Fiery Furnace, and Delicate Arch on the east; Klondike Bluffs, Herdina Park, and Eagle Park on the west. The miniature "Monument Valley" of Courthouse Towers formed along a second major fold in the earth's surface. Underlying these Enstrada rock gardens, the Navajo Sandstone lies exposed as a rolling floor of "petrified sand dunes."

Golden eagle.

In the prairies and in tropical rain forests, ecological communities remain the same for hundreds of miles; but in the American West, abrupt changes in elevation create banded life zones, from low desert flats to tundra-crowned mountains—all visible in a single glance.

At Arches, elevation varies little—from 3,960 feet to 5,653 feet. Precipitation averages a puny 8.5 inches over the entire park. Yet vegetation changes abruptly in a single stride—from grassland to desert scrub, from oak thickets to pinyon and juniper woodland. Why so much variety?

Plant Communities: The Desert Mosaic

The biological story of Arches is grounded in rock. On Navajo Sandstone slickrock and on either side of Salt Valley along ridges studded with clusters of Entrada fins and spires, Utah juniper and Colorado pinyon pine form a sparse woodland that covers nearly half the park. Juniper is more tolerant of arid conditions than is pinyon, and because Arches is near the low-elevation limit of woodland, juniper predominates.

These trees grow in unlikely-looking cracks where moisture accumulates and underwrites life not possible otherwise. Cliffrose, squawbush, single-leaf ash, and serviceberry take advantage of the same cracks.

In areas with a few inches of sandy "soil," shrubs take over. Blackbrush dominates in Arches, its roots sunk where moisture collects just above bedrock, allowing slow uptake of water. Once sand accumulates beyond 18 inches, ground water percolates too deep for blackbrush, and grassland thrives—most notably in Salt Valley, where bunch grasses like galleta, Indian rice grass, and sand dropseed grow.

Salt Valley once may have been pure grassland. After nearly a century of heavy grazing by sheep and cattle, however, shrubs like Mormon tea and snakeweed crowd the grasses. Not until 1982 was

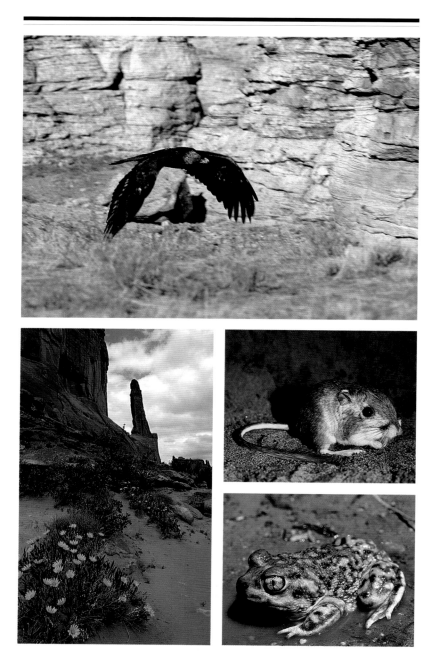

Clockwise, from top: Golden eagle. The kangaroo rat survives without water. The spade-foot toad digs beneath dry earth to find water. Mule's ears, Park Avenue.

grazing finally eliminated from the most recent additions to Arches.

Where deep wind-blown sand piles up in orange dunes, wavy-leaf oak and feathery old-man sage stabilize the loose grains. The shales of the Mancos and Morrison formations support only a sparse cover of saltbush, shadscale, and *Astragalus*. In alkali-ridden bottom lands along Salt Wash, salt-tolerant shrubs like greasewood and seepweed survive.

And where water works its magic full-time, along streams and at seeps, the plant world runs wild with luxuriance, free from desert restraints. Tamarisk (introduced from Eurasia years ago), cottonwoods, and willows line Salt and Courthouse washes. Shielded by alcoves, hanging gardens festoon seeps with columbine, monkey flower, primrose, and maidenhair fern. Here, plants need not contrive waxy coverings for tiny leaves, grow enormous spreading roots, or maintain thick fleshy stems for water storage; at seeps and streams, plants can relax.

Animal Life: Coping with the Desert

The animals of Arches National Park take advantage of each plant community in myriad ways, and they have evolved their own means of coping with desert extremes. Kanagroo rats, for example, burrow in sand dunes, relying only on the moisture that is contained in the dry seeds they eat and on an incredibly efficient water metabolism. Pinyon jays flock through pinyon groves in ridiculously noisy groups, feeding on (and caching for winter) the nutritious pine nuts. Spadefoot toads dig as deep as 20 inches below dry potholes to wait for moisture, while the hardened mud crust above them bakes in summer and freezes in winter, its ground temperature fluctuating through almost 200 degrees.

With luck, in daytime at Arches you will see an antelope ground squirrel race across the road, white tail held suavely over its back; or a collared lizard might sprint between rocks, rearing up on its hind legs to obtain top speed.

Birds liven up the sunlit sky as well. Golden eagles nest in the cliffs of Arches, soaring high on midday updrafts in search of a jack rabbit lunch. A black-throated sparrow calls from a perch in blackbrush. Trilling house finches answer from juniper snags. And from the cliffs above, the down-scale lilt of a canyon wren seems the song of the rock itself.

Night comes. Hunters range out from their dens—mountain lions after deer, gray foxes after rodents and birds, midget faded rattlesnakes after mice, coyotes after absolutely anything.

Overleaf: The fragile and wondrous Landscape Arch, spanning 306 feet, is one of the world's largest known natural arches.

Arches lends itself to relaxed, prowling drives through bonsai slickrock gardens and to easy strolls past awesome arcs of stone. The park entrance lies just 5 miles north of Moab, but it leads into a wild rock landscape that could be continents or centuries away from the pavement and plastic of town.

Park Headquarters and the Colorado River Canyon. From the Visitor Center, and the road winding up into the park behind it, you get a good look at the Moab Fault. Rocks across the valley are 100 million years older than formations behind the Visitor Center; the valley here follows a 30-mile fault that has dropped rocks on the Arches side 2,500 feet below corresponding layers on the opposite side of the canyon. This panorama makes for good practice in geological thinking.

Back toward Moab, between the Visitor Center and the Colorado River, the road follows the park boundary. Then up the Colorado for 10 miles on Utah 128, you remain just across the river from the park. This lovely drive leads to Fisher Towers, and eventually to Cisco, on Interstate 70. The wide, gentle curve of the Colorado River beneath Navajo Sandstone walls is reminiscent of what Glen Canyon must have looked like before being drowned by Lake Powell.

Park Avenue and Courthouse Towers. The main park road leaves the Visitor Center and winds through Arches for 18 miles to Devils Garden. In its first mile, it zigzags up the abrupt escarpment of Entrada and Navajo sandstones along the Moab Fault, an instant initiation into slickrock balds, hanging gardens in alcoves, and sculptured stone.

In just 2 miles, the road reaches Park Avenue, an open canyon that is lined with great skyscraper slabs of Entrada. A 1-mile trail leads down through scattered junipers to meet the road at a second parking area. Park Avenue makes a good place to begin to fine-tune your eye for distinguishing rock formations.

The Entrada has three members, and throughout the park their different natures control the course of erosion. The soft, lower Dewey Bridge Member erodes quickly. It supports many of the park's fins, which are formed by remnants of the higher, harder Slick Rock Member. Capping some monuments is the uppermost, white Moab Member. The "buildings" of Park Avenue are Slick Rock Entrada sitting on foundations of the Dewey Bridge Member. Toward the end of the walk, Navajo Sandstone (beneath the Entrada) forms the floor of the canyon—the avenue's sidewalk.

Just beyond Park Avenue is Courthouse Towers, a jumble of small buttes and towers whittled off a huge arching slab of Entrada by Courthouse Wash and its tributaries—in much the same way that the larger buttes of Monument Valley, Arizona, are remnants of a continuous mesa. Several arches, balanced rocks, and towers here have names that match their whimsical shapes— the Three Gossips, Sheep Rock, Baby Arch.

Just a bit farther, a huge expanse of cross-bedded Navajo Sandstone, "the petrified sand dunes," stretches away to the east toward the La Sal Mountains. Great buttresses of Entrada guard the mountain like circling battleships, flaring orange at sunset.

The Windows. Nine miles from the Visitor Center stands Balanced Rock, which guards the spur road to The Windows section. This is the halfway point on the road, and was the park entrance when the main approach to Arches was a dirt road winding in from farther north on U.S. 191.

Near Balanced Rock, Edward Abbey, then a park ranger, lived in a trailer and kept the journal that became the classic book *Desert Solitaire.* Near here, too, was Abbey's favorite juniper tree: "there is a kind of poetry, even a kind of truth, in simple fact . . . . If a man knew enough he could write a whole book about the juniper tree. Not juniper trees in general but that one particular juniper tree which grows from a ledge of naked sandstone near the old entrance to Arches . . . ."

Find a juniper of your own to watch. Abbey was right; they have much to teach.

Along the 3-mile side road to The Windows are buttes and hoodoos—rocks shaped like hams, golf balls, and elephants—and several of the park's finest arches. Short trails of a few hundred yards lead from the end of the Road to Turret Arch, North and South Window (together forming the Spectacles), and famed Double Arch.

These are open, approachable spans. They have formed on spurs of the highest butte in the park, and here you feel the sweep of the country—to the La Sal Mountains, to Courthouse Towers across the slickrock field of petrified dunes. This is a good place for wildflowers. Watch for larkspur, yucca, evening primrose, sand verbena, Indian paintbrush, and orange-red dock.

Panorama Point. Back on the main road, just past Balanced Rock, begins the descent toward Salt Valley. At its rounded rim is Panorama Point, where nearly the whole park is visible.

A counterclockwise 360° view during an evening storm starts at the south: Balanced Rock, The Windows, and the Garden of

TRAILS OF ARCHES NATIONAL PARK

PARK AVENUE TRAIL: Starts at Park Avenue viewpoint; ends at Courthouse Towers viewpoint; 2 miles round trip; .75 hour; 320-foot ascent; open canyon with "skyline" of sandstone fins; usually hiked one way (hikers picked up at lower trail head).

DOUBLE ARCH TRAIL: Starts at Windows parking area; ends at Double Arch; .8 mile round trip; .5 hour; 80-foot ascent; easy walk through pinyon and juniper woodland to two-buttressed Double Arch.

TURRET ARCH AND THE SPECTACLES TRAIL: Starts at Windows parking area; ends at The Spectacles; .6 mile round trip; .75 hour; 150-foot ascent; right branch of easy trail leads to Turret Arch; left branch leads to North and South Windows (The Spectacles); can stand under arch.

DELICATE ARCH TRAIL: Starts at Wolfe Ranch; ends at Delicate Arch; 3 miles round trip; 2 hours; 500-foot ascent; steep climb up natural ramps of slickrock to the arch, which is perched on the edge of a sandstone bowl, framing the La Sal Mountains; magnificent views. Hazardous drop-offs.

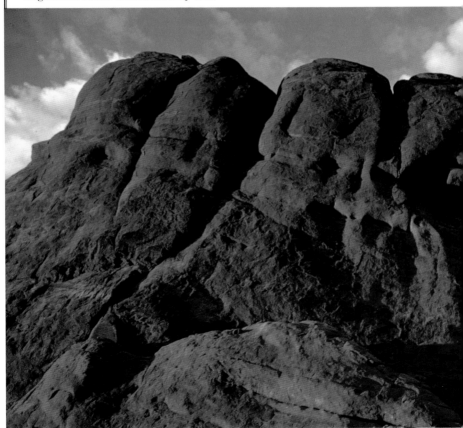

TOWER ARCH TRAIL: Starts at Klondike Bluffs parking area; ends at Tower Arch; 2.4 miles round trip; 2 hours; 80-foot ascent; primitive trail through dunes, pinyon, and juniper into high bluffs with imposing towers; return trail loops past the Marching Men.

SAND DUNE, BROKEN, AND TAPESTRY ARCHES TRAIL: Starts at parking area at 16-mile mark on park road; ends at campground; 1.5 miles round trip; 1 hour; 50-foot ascent; crosses open meadows and threads its way between high fins and through Broken Arch, with spurs to Sand Dune Arch and Tapestry Arch.

DEVILS GARDEN TRAIL: Starts at end of park road; ends at Dark Angel; 4.5 miles round trip; 5 hours; 320-foot ascent; leads to seven arches (including Landscape Arch, one of the longest natural spans in the world), and views of several more arches; overlooks Fin Canyon; best to photograph sites in early morning; primitive trail beyond Double O Arch (at 2.1 mile); carry water and food.

SEE MAP ON PAGES 14–15.

Skyline Arch in Devils Garden doubled in size in 1940. See page 17.

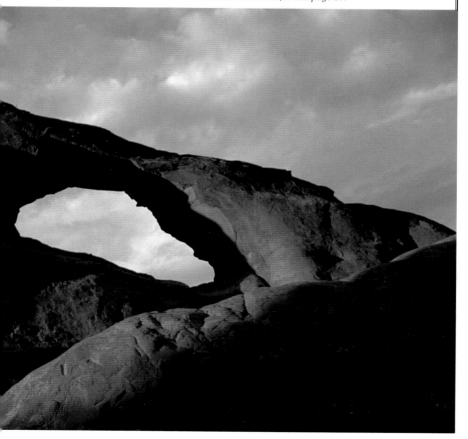

Eden—black silhouettes and blinding lightning strikes; behind them, the La Sals, with fresh snow over golden autumn aspen, wisps of rain trailing out of a cloud cap, a slash of orange Entrada at their base. The great red walls up toward Castle Valley and the Colorado River canyon; a rise of slickrock around Delicate Arch, red rock turned glistening wet silver by rain. Beyond, "biscuits" of the uppermost Entrada, the white Moab Member, form a flat field in front of the distant Book Cliffs (which look like real mountains); the forest of fins in the Fiery Furnace—a dense pack of sandstone slices; then Devils Garden running back behind, up the flank of the salt dome, more and more distant fins ending at the faraway mysterious spire of Dark Angel. The open flat bowl of Salt Valley— Klondike Bluffs sitting nicely above it on the left, presiding in style. Lightning striking due west, thunder rolling around behind it.

And then the full moon comes out from behind clouds, high and crisp over the Garden of Eden and the La Sals.

Delicate Arch and Wolfe Cabin. Twelve miles from the Visitor Center, a gravel road leads to Wolfe Cabin and the Delicate Arch Trail and viewpoint. This is one of the finest trails in the canyon country, 1.5 miles long, a 500-foot climb that can be a scorcher in midsummer, but is worth every panting step.

The trail begins at Wolfe's 1906 Bar-DX Ranch cabin, crosses Salt Wash on a suspension bridge (look for seeps and springs upstream), and winds up Entrada slickrock where junipers pose in suggestive elegance. They foretoken the elegance of the arch itself, which bursts on you from around a corner at the end of the trail with unconscious drama—perched on the edge of a graceful bezel of stone. The span of Delicate Arch reaches just 45 feet high, but appears much bigger in its setting.

It is difficult to photograph Delicate Arch; the classic view is so famous that it no longer captures the thrill of this place. For a less predictable image, try the viewpoint across the canyon, which can be reached by a short spur road from Wolfe Ranch. Beyond, wilderness in upper and lower Salt Wash makes for good backpacking.

Fiery Furnace. The Fiery Furnace is the densest array of fins in the park, named for their red glow at sunset. Deep slots separate spires in a maze that hides at least eighteen arches and one natural bridge. Tortuous routes through the Furnace make it tricky for route-finding, and most hikers see this area only when rangers lead 3-hour walks through it.

Opposite: The Organ is a red sandstone monolith in the Courthouse Towers section of the park. To many visitors it resembles a massive pipe organ.

Devils Garden. The park road enters Devils Garden, where a series of trails lead to major arches; finally, the drive ends at the campground. The first trail in Devils Garden is a short walk to Broken and Sand Dune arches. At the extreme north end of the Fiery Furnace, Sand Dune Arch hides low in a slot between two fins; a dune beneath it almost buries its abutments. Try to be there early in the morning, when the sand still preserves nighttime tracks of beetle, kangaroo rat, and gray fox.

A bit farther along is Skyline Arch, which is famous for its "before November 1940" and "after November 1940" photographs. During that winter, a large block fell from the arch, doubling its size.

The main Devils Garden Trail leads from the end of the road to Landscape Arch (.8 mile), Double-O Arch (2.1 miles), and Dark Angel (2.4 miles). Branches lead to several arches along the way, and one trail loops back through isolated Fin Canyon. Beyond Landscape Arch, the trail is more rugged.

Devils Garden contains most of the known arches in the park, more than one hundred by one count. Landscape Arch is its jewel, at 306 feet one of the world's longest known natural stone spans.

Beyond lie the quiet ramps of stone leading deeper into Devils Garden, good country for backpacking. Listen for black-throated sparrows and canyon wrens; sound carries so well that footfalls thud in soft sand at 150 yards. In its peace and grace, this truly is a garden.

Klondike Bluffs. Klondike Bluffs lies 9 miles down a dirt road across Salt Valley from Devils Garden. The first cluster of spires at Arches to be publicized, the bluffs are now the least visited area of the park accessible by car. The Tower Arch Trail runs through the high bluffs, in dune sand and through pinyon and juniper woodland, about 1.7 miles to a fine arch. A rougher return is possible past the playful Marching Men.

Not so linear as Devils Garden, Klondike Bluffs almost feels like the big, complex landscapes of Canyonlands National Park. The sense of isolation is powerful; here, if anywhere in the park, mountain lion tracks might turn up, imprinted in the kneaded sand.

Four-Wheel-Drive Roads

Rough roads lead from near Devils Garden past Klondike Bluffs and to Herdina Park, and then return to pavement near Balanced Rock. Check with park rangers on current road conditions. In Herdina Park, an arch stares through a humpback of slickrock: The Eye of the Whale.

Opposite: Double Arch, one of more than one hundred arches in The Windows.

BIG BEND
NATIONAL PARK

Rime coats trees and grass at Panther Pass.

BIG BEND NATIONAL PARK, TEXAS 79834
TEL.: (915) 477-2251

HIGHLIGHTS: Sotol Vista • Castolon • Boquillas Canyon • Lost Mine Trail • Santa Elena Canyon • Hannold Grave Homesite Fossil Bone Exhibit • Dagger Mountain • Dagger Flat • Old Sam Nail Ranch • The Basin

ACCESS: From Alpine, 108 miles to park headquarters on Texas 118. See map on pages 38–39.

HOURS: Daily, year-round. Most Visitor Centers and ranger stations, 8 A.M.–4 P.M. daily. Panther Junction Visitor Center, 8 A.M.–6 P.M.

FEES: At entrance, for visitors in vehicle or arriving in bus or on foot; for camping in developed areas.

PARKING: Ample throughout park.

GAS: At Panther Junction and Rio Grande Village.

FOOD: At Chisos Mountain Lodge, The Basin.

LODGING: At Chisos Mountain Lodge, The Basin. Call (915) 477-2291 for reservations.

VISITOR CENTER: At Panther Junction, Rio Grande Village, The Basin, and Persimmon Gap.

MUSEUM: Barton Warneck Environmental Education Center in Lajitas.

GIFT SHOP: At Chisos Mountain Lodge.

PETS: Permitted on leash, except in public buildings and on trails. Horseback riding permitted; no rentals inside park.

PICNICKING: At various areas throughout park.

HIKING: Permitted. Spring water sometimes available, but best to carry it.

BACKPACKING: Permitted with free permit. No wood fires. Carry water.

CAMPGROUNDS: Concession operates trailer park with full hookups and showers. Park has 3 campgrounds, 198 sites, no hookups.

OTHER ACTIVITIES: River trips, fishing, birding, photography.

FACILITIES FOR DISABLED: Restrooms, Panther Path Nature Trail, Window View Trail.

For additional information, see also Sites, Trails, and Trips on pages 54–70 and the maps on page 38–39 and 57.

DEEP LIMESTONE CANYONS CARVED BY THE Rio Grande; barren desert flats and rugged mesas; mountains nearly 8,000 feet high where Douglas-fir, ponderosa pine, and white-tailed deer exist in a last stronghold against encroaching aridity: this is Big Bend National Park. Containing 1,250 square miles of Chihuahuan Desert country on the Mexican border, Big Bend nestles in the downward arc of the Rio Grande that gave the region—and the park—its name. Colorful geologic formations, as well as fossils of sea creatures, dinosaurs, and early mammals, reveal much of the earth's history. Plants and animals from Mexico reach the northern extreme of their ranges at Big Bend, and some from the United States are uncommon this far south. Some species occur *only* here. More than 400 kinds of birds have been seen in Big Bend, more than in any other national park.

The beauty is often subtle but sometimes overwhelming: sweeping vistas with horizons 100 miles away, displays of desert wildflowers, the cathedral-like ambiance at the bottom of a river canyon. There is mystery and magic as well. The weird, stark appearance of the country coupled with the romance of the Mexican border gives visitors the feeling that a last frontier lingers on and that they are a part of it.

HISTORY

Beginnings

Scant evidence exists of the prehistoric big-game hunters who roamed the Big Bend region 10,000 or more years ago. In subsequent centuries, the climate gradually warmed and dried, influencing the life styles of local Native Americans. When Spanish explorers first passed through the area, they observed Indians farming along the Rio Grande as well as hunting and gathering in the desert.

Spanish and Indians

In the early 1500s, Spanish explorers moved into the area in their quest for riches. Seldom did they penetrate the Big Bend region, but preferred to detour around this harsh country, which they termed *El Despoblado*—"the uninhabited land." Spanish settlements were raided frequently by Indians who retreated to the safety of *El Despoblado*. Pressured by the Comanches, the Apaches moved into the Big Bend country from the north and assumed the role of harrassing the Spanish. By the early 1800s, the Spanish decided that riches were not to be had in the region,

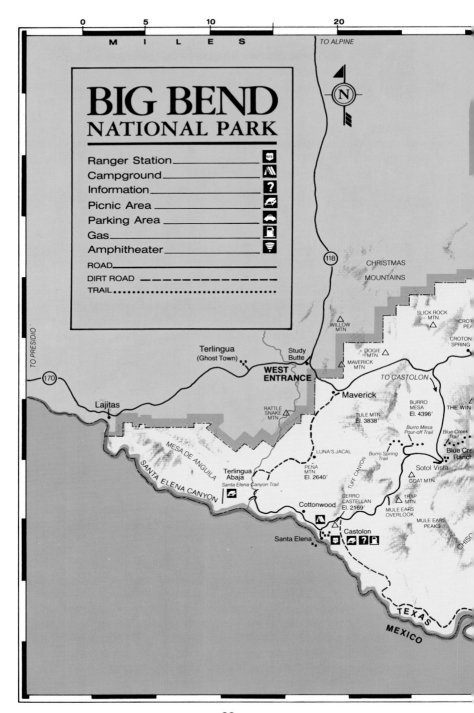

BIG BEND
NATIONAL PARK

Ranger Station _____ 🚓

Campground _____ ⛺

Information _____ ❓

Picnic Area _____ 🧺

Parking Area _____ 🚗

Gas _____ ⛽

Amphitheater _____ 🔦

ROAD _____

DIRT ROAD _____

TRAIL ....

0   5   10   20

M I L E S

TO ALPINE

N

118

CHRISTMAS
MOUNTAINS

SLICK ROCK
MTN.

CROT
PEA

WILLOW
MTN.

CROTON
SPRING

TO PRESIDIO

Terlingua
(Ghost Town)

Study
Butte

DOGIE
MTN.

MAVERICK
MTN.

WEST
ENTRANCE

TO CASTOLON

170

Maverick

BURRO
MESA
El. 4396'

THE WIN

Lajitas

RATTLE
SNAKE
MTN.

TULE MTN.
El. 3838'

Burro Mesa
Pour-off Trail

Blue Creek
Trail

MESA DE ANGUILA

LUNA'S JACAL

Burro Spring
Trail

Blue Cre
Ranch

SANTA ELENA CANYON

Terlingua
Abaja

Santa Elena Canyon Trail

PEÑA
MTN.
El. 2640'

TUFF CANYON

Sotol Vista

GOAT MTN.

CERRO
CASTELLAN
El. 2169'

Cottonwood

TRAP
MTN.

MULE EARS
OVERLOOK

MULE EARS
PEAKS

Santa Elena

Castolon

CHIS

TEXAS

MEXICO

TO MARATHON

NORTH ENTRANCE

Persimmon Gap
El. 2870'

SANTIAGO MTNS

DOG
CANYON

ROSILLOS
MOUNTAINS

DAGGER
MTN.

DAGGER
FLAT

VICINITY MAP

UNITED STATES

385

118

170

Terlingua

BIG BEND
N.P.

Boquillas

MEXICO

INSET SCALE

0   15   30
M I L E S

HORSE CANYON

La Linda

Adams
Ranch

CARMEN

DEL

SIERRA

SUE PEAKS

ROYS PEAK

FOSSIL
BONE
EXHIBIT

Grapevine
Hills Trail

PAINT GAP
HILLS

GRAPEVINE
HILLS

LONE MTN.
El. 4143'

PANTHER JUNCTION

PARK
HEADQUARTERS

Chihuahuan Desert
Nature Trail

RIDGE

LOST
MINE PK.

PUMMEL
PEAK

Lost
Mine
Trail

NUGENT MTN.

PINE CANYON

Dugout Wells

JUNIPER CANYON

CHILICOTAL
MTN.

ERNST VALLEY

Hot Springs
Historic
Walk

RIO
GRANDE
VILLAGE
El. 1850'

BOQUILLAS CANYON

Boquillas Canyon
Trail

TEXAS

MEXICO

825'

Glenn Springs
El. 2537'

Hot Springs

Boquillas

ELEPHANT TUSK
El. 5249'

NQUEZ MTN
5156'

San Vicente, Mexico

TALLEY
MTN.

COW HEAVEN MTN.
El. 3881'

Solis

MARISCAL MTN.

MARISCAL CANYON

Grande

Talley
El. 2000'

and they left. As Anglo-Americans pressed westward, the Comanches were forced south into the Big Bend and eventually drove out most of the Apaches. The great Comanche War Trail sliced through the heart of the Big Bend, and as settlers continued to move into and through the Big Bend, forts were built to protect them from the Indians. During the mid-1800s, the U.S. Army struggled to reduce the Comanche influence in the Big Bend. Indian dominance increased during the Civil War, when frontier forts were abandoned. In 1874, however, the Comanches were defeated and moved to a reservation in Oklahoma.

Explorers and Surveyors

Much of the early American exploration of the Big Bend was conducted by parties traveling on and along the Rio Grande. The first such group to traverse the entire southern boundary of the present-day park was part of the international boundary survey. The exploration was led by Marine Tyler W. Chandler and Lieutenant Duff C. Green in 1852. They traveled by land and water and chose to go arund Santa Elena Canyon and Boquillas Canyon, both of which appeared too dangerous from their peripheral observations.

Attempting to complete the boundary survey in 1881, Texas Ranger Captain Charles L. Nevill and four surveyors succeeded in navigating through Santa Elena Canyon. (At least, the Nevill *expedition* succeeded. Captain Nevill, who had nearly drowned in a boat accident upriver, chose to direct operations from the cliffs above.) Finally, in 1899, Robert T. Hill of the U.S. Geological Survey led an expedition into this land of tall tales (and, perhaps, taller realities) to squelch or confirm the rumors about this last frontier of Texas. In only three weeks, Hill and his party successfully navigated 350 miles of the Rio Grande, including the three great canyons that are now within Big Bend National Park.

The Camel Corps

Lumbering across the Chihuahuan Desert in the summers of 1859 and 1860 were two of the oddest expeditions to venture into the heart of the Big Bend. The army, seeking the most efficient means of transportation on the western frontier, chose the Big Bend area as one place to test camel power. In the first expedition, led by Second Lieutenant William H. Echols of the Topographical Engineers, two dozen camels carrying 400 pounds each marched

Preceding overleaf: The Rio Grande flows for 118 miles along the southern boundary of the park.

south from Fort Davis. The caravan probably passed through Dog Canyon and down Tornillo Creek to the Rio Grande and returned by a similar route. The following summer the Camel Corps explored the area west of the Chisos Mountains. The camels had proved themselves under scorching skies and over rugged terrain, leaving horses and mules in their dust.

The promise of camel transportation across the western United States was to be unfulfilled, however. The Civil War halted the experiment, and after the war the railroad made camels obsolete.

Ranching

Relatively lush grasslands around the Chisos Mountains attracted ranchers to the Big Bend in the late 1800s. Cattle, horses, sheep, and goats grazed the region until the park was established in 1944. Overgrazing was especially devastating between 1942 and 1944, when the state of Texas granted free grazing privileges to the ranchers whose land it had purchased. Recovery of the grasses has been slow, but revegetation appears to have accelerated in recent years. Because of erosion of topsoils, however, some areas, such as Tornillo Flat and along Terlingua Creek, may never recover.

Settlers, Miners, Waxmakers, and Revolutionaries

The Big Bend is not a land to support a large human population. But as the Indians faded into legend and the ranchers made inroads, other groups filtered into the area around the turn of the century. Mexicans migrated northward to farm the flood plain of the Rio Grande. Working for themselves or for American landlords, they raised cotton as well as food crops to help supply the nearby mines.

In 1909, an ore tramway began carrying loads of silver, lead, and zinc ore from the Corte Madera mine above Boquillas to the ore terminal in Ernst Valley. Mariscal Mine on Mariscal Mountain near the very tip of the Big Bend yielded 894 flasks of mercury between 1917 and 1919. Candelilla, or waxplant, was commercially harvested from Big Bend's limestone soils, and factories to extract the high-quality wax from the plant sprang up at McKinney and Glenn Springs in 1911.

When the Mexican Revolution broke out in 1911, it spilled across the Rio Grande to involve Big Bend's early settlers. Bands of revolutionaries roamed the border, and fearful settlers on both sides of the river left their homes to seek security farther north in the United States. After revolutionaries attacked the villages of Glenn Springs and Boquillas on the night of May 5, 1916, President

Woodrow Wilson called up the National Guard. By the end of July, more than 100,000 men had gathered in Texas and Arizona to guard the border. Other raids occurred in the surrounding country, but not within the area of the present-day park. After a decade of tension and border unrest, peace finally returned to the Big Bend.

Establishment of the Park

The National Guardsmen who had been stationed in the Big Bend spread the word about its rugged beauty and supported efforts to create a national park there. The man who really got the ball rolling was Everett Ewing Townsend, a former Big Bend lawman turned Texas state legislator. Through Townsend's efforts and influence, Santa Elena, Mariscal, and Boquillas canyons were included in Texas Canyons State Park, which was established in May 1933. Later that year the Chisos Basin was added as a site for a Civilian Conservation Corps camp, and the name of the park was changed to Big Bend State Park. National-park proponents were still not satisfied with this piecemeal approach and continued to push for a larger, more complete park. With private donations and state funds, more land was purchased until the state of Texas donated 1,100 square miles of land to the people of the United States. On June 12, 1944, Big Bend National Park was established.

GEOLOGY

So jumbled, mixed, inverted, extruded, and intruded are the rocks of Big Bend National Park that some geologists wryly refer to this conglomeration as the "eggbeater formation." Yet it *is* decipherable, and the rocks are usually well exposed. Geology classes from throughout the United States travel to Big Bend to study the earth's history in stone.

Some Paleozoic era rocks are exposed at Persimmon Gap, but most of the rocks in the park are from the Cretaceous period or later. Lower Cretaceous seas covered the Big Bend area, and as sea creatures died over millions of years, their shells and skeletons piled up to form massive layers of limestone that are thousands of feet thick. Close examination of the huge cliffs of the Sierra del Carmen and Mesa de Anguila reveals sea-shell fragments embedded in the solid limestone. As the sea grew shallower, lime mud deposits formed layers that are now exposed in the flagstone formations that are easily seen at Hot Springs.

Opposite: Fascinating colors and textures are evident on numerous Big Bend rocks.

The Age of Dinosaurs

Plesiosaurs and other marine reptiles swam in the increasingly shallow waters. As the land rose and the sea receded, the succession of plant and animal life changed with the environment. Dinosaurs, flying reptiles, a huge crocodilelike creature, and other reptiles of all sizes slogged, splashed, and swam through or soared over lush forests and swamps. Their fossilized bones are still being found in the park's badlands formations, such as those near the Maverick entrance and on Tornillo Flat. Perhaps the most famous park fossil is from this period: the Big Bend pterosaur. This flying reptile, which had a wingspan of about 40 feet, was the largest animal ever to fly over the surface of the earth. At the end of the Mesozoic era, the giant reptiles vanished from the Big Bend country (as they did worldwide) for reasons that are still unclear. At about the same time—give or take a few million years—a 40-mile-wide trough, known as the Sunken Block, formed between Mesa de Anguila and the Sierra del Carmen.

Mammals and Mountains

Now began the Age of Mammals, the Cenozoic era. The land rose higher, and a milder climate produced lush grasslands and forests. A wide variety of now-extinct mammals flourished. Some were similar to today's rhinoceros, horse, camel, deer, dog, and cat.

This was a time of mountain building, erosion, deposition, and igneous activity that deposited molten rock underground and left layers of lava and volcanic ash across the earth's surface. In the center of the Sunken Block, the Chisos Mountains were born. The rounded peaks of the Chisos began as molten underground masses that have since been exposed by erosion. The blocklike peaks and the South Rim were formed by successive lava flows that also have eroded into their characteristic shapes. Two collapsed volcanoes, or calderas, have been found in the foothills of the Chisos. From these spewed the volcanic ash that settled and hardened in various sections of the park.

Geology Today

In this place of little water, its influence is nonetheless scrawled across the land. Canyons that have cut through solid rock, patterns of erosion on the flats, arroyos that lead into mountain canyons— water plays a role. Visitors can watch it work as summer thunderstorms create flash floods that move tons of rock closer to the river. Pieces of Emory Peak, the highest point in the park, can be found along the Rio Grande. The face of Big Bend is always changing.

Climate and Precipitation

Big Bend National Park is near the northern end of the Chihuahuan Desert, four-fifths of which is in Mexico. The Big Bend climate is gradually becoming more arid. Ten thousand years ago, trees and other vegetation covered what today is desert. Reduced precipitation forced this vegetation and associated animals to retreat to higher, moister elevations in the Chisos Mountains, where they now exist on mountain islands surrounded by a sea of aridity.

Annual precipitation varies from less than 4 inches near Castolon to 25 inches in the High Chisos, where two or three light snowfalls may occur each winter. (True desert conditions exist in areas that receive less than 10 inches of rainfall annually.) Summer temperatures in the river canyons can exceed 115° F.

With park elevations ranging from 1,800 feet to more than 7,800 feet, the stage is set for a wide variety of plant and animal habitats in relatively close association. If they are so inclined, del Carmen white-tailed deer meandering through pinyon pines and junipers on Emory Peak can graze at desert flats 6,000 feet below where kangaroo rats hop among cactus and creosote bush. The diversity of environments enables Big Bend to support more than 1,000 kinds of plants.

Trees and Shrubs

The warm, moist river flood plain encourages the growth of many plants that are not usually found in the desert. Several are not native to the area. Among these are tree tobacco and the bamboo-like giant reed. Perhaps the most significant of these newcomers is the salt cedar, which grows not only on the flood plain but also at desert springs; it often dries up the springs with its spendthrift use of water. Native plants and animals suffer as a result. Species of cottonwood not native to the area have been planted at Rio Grande Village and Castolon Campground, but the native lance-leaf cottonwoods can be seen in a grove between Castolon and the river. Trees in the legume (pea) family are abundant along the river, and some species such at catclaw acacia and honey mesquite follow the washes and arroyos into the foothills. The desert willow, with its lovely orchidlike flowers, is often a companion of these trees in the arroyos.

While the vegetation may look sparse and sometimes monotonous across the desert, a surprising variety of plants reveal

Left: A family of collared peccaries.
Top: Buttonbush flower.
Above: Desert millipede.

themselves to those who walk among them. One must use some care, though, as emphasized by an old cowboy who said, "Everything out there either sticks, stings, or stinks." One of the "stickers" is lechuguilla, the indicator plant of the Chihuahuan Desert. A small agave related to the century plant, lechuguilla blooms and dies after about fifteen years of growth.

Plants here exhibit interesting strategies for desert survival. The ocotillo sheds its leaves during dry periods and grows them again after rains. Flowers cover the ceniza, or barometer bush, soon after a rainstorm; they then wither, die, and fall to the ground a few days later. Four yuccas grow in the park. The Torrey yucca is the most common, but the diant dagger yucca is the most spectacular. Every three or four years, the display of flowering stalks at Dagger Flat is breath-taking. Flowering shrubs that color the desert and grasslands include feather dalea, skeleton-leaf goldeneye, damianita, and yellow trumpet flower.

Two familiar desert plants that thrive in Big Bend are the creosote bush and the century plant. The creosote bush is common throughout the desert, and its yellow blossoms can be seen somewhere in the park at almost any time of year. To the true desert lover, the aroma of creosote bush after a summer thunderstorm is heaven-scent. Growing for perhaps fifty years with little or no fanfare, the century plant suddenly one spring begins to shoot up a huge stalk that is tipped with platters of nectar-fich flowers. Insects and birds flock to the banquet and feast on the nectar, or on one another. Then, having used up fifty years' worth of stored energy, the plant dies and gradually decomposes.

The Chisos Mountains are a north-meets-south environment for trees. The flaccid-foliaged drooping juniper is primarily a tree of Mexico, while ponderosa pine and quaking aspen are more common to the north. Within the United States, some plants grow only in the Chisos Mountains. One, the mountain sage, with its dark green leaves and brilliant brick-red flowers, is a hummingbird's delight. The Chisos also are host to at least nine kinds of oaks, two of which are thought to be endemic to the Chisos.

Wildflowers and Cacti

March and April are the best months for viewing both wildflowers and blooming cacti, but some spectacular wildflower displays also may occur after summer thunderstorms. Seeds that have lain dormant for years may germinate if moisture and temperature are just right. A profusion of thyme-leaf dogwood can turn sun-baked Tornillo Flat into a golden plain. Every year brings splashes of color from the ubiquitous Big Bend bluebonnet (lupine to non-Texans).

Narrow-leaf globemallow brightens the river flood plain, while yellow rocknettle drapes nearby limestone cliffs. Both are common at Hot Springs. Prickly poppy, with its huge white flowers, and bicolor mustard occur from the river to the foothills. The wildflowers are more scattered in the mountains than in the desert, but they are no less beautiful. Longspur columbine, Mexican campion, and cedar sage decorate mountain slopes and secluded springs.

Big Bend is home to more than sixty kinds of cacti, several of which are rare and threatened by illegal collecting. Cacti range in size from the button cactus, which can be shaded by a silver dollar, to massive prickly pears, which cover many square feet of desert. Near Rio Grande Village, the brownspine prickly pear glows as sunlight is diffused by its translucent spines. Purple-tinged prickly pear is both abundant and striking, as is the tasajillo, or Christmas cactus, which retains its red fruits throughout the winter holiday season. On limestone hillsides the livingrock cactus grows flush with the soil surface until a pink flower dares new heights of an inch or so above the ground.

The hedgehog cactus flowers vary from yellow to red with many colors in between. And the fruit of the strawberry cactus tastes as good as it looks. Ripening in summer, the fruit is luscious, but protected within the park. Even the High Chisos supports a cactus population. Growing out of rocky outcrops on the highest peaks, the claret-cup cacti, with their brilliant red flowers, are fitting jewels to adorn the crown of mountaintops on the skyline.

Wildlife

When watching for wildlife in the desert, it is important to scan the nearby ground surface as well as the horizon. While a desert mule deer is bounding over a hilltop, a snake or a scorpion may be sneaking by at your feet.

The "creepy crawlies," or arthropods, of the desert take fascinating forms and are fun to watch. Sunspiders, tarantulas, and vinegarroons are predators that may be seen capturing beetles and moths. During the day, cicadas buzz; at night, crickets and katydids chirp and trill. Big Bend has more than 100 kinds of grasshoppers!

Catfish are common in the Rio Grande, and a variety of smaller fish live in the waters near the mouths of Terlingua and Tornillo creeks. The Big Bend gambusia is an endangered species. The bulk of the population is now protected in a constructed pond near Rio Grande Village, though individuals may be seen under the boardwalk on the Rio Grande Village nature trail.

Spadefoot toads often bide their time underground for months before a summer thunderstorm brings them popping from the ground in a spontaneous celebration of life. They feed on termites and other insects, lay eggs in temporary ponds, and then dig back into the earth with the spadelike growths on their hind feet. The eggs hatch, and the tadpoles quickly mature into toads before the ponds dry up (if they are lucky). Thirty kinds of snakes and twenty-one kinds of lizards live in Big Bend. Some snakes, such as the Trans-Pecos rat snake and the gray-banded kingsnake, are west Texas specialties. Four kinds of rattlesnakes and one kind of copperhead are here, but if you watch where you put your feet and hands and use a flashlight after dark, they will not be a problem. Able to withstand higher temperatures than most snakes, the western coachwhip is a large but harmless pink snake that often slithers across the path of surprised park visitors.

Big Bend is a birdwatcher's paradise. The Colima warbler nests in the Chisos Mountains and nowhere else in the United States. Foothill canyons are nest sites for the Lucifer hummingbird, which, although fairly common in the park, can be observed in few other places in the United States. The endangered peregrine falcon has been successful in the river canyons and in the Chisos Mountains in recent years. And, of course, the roadrunner, symbol of the desert, may be seen nearly any day of the year chasing lizards or snapping up grasshoppers.

Two kinds of deer make their home in the park. In the Chisos Mountains, the diminutive del Carmen white-tailed deer lives as a subspecies confined to these and other island mountaintops of west Texas and adjacent Mexico. The larger desert mule deer occupies the lower, drier elevations, where it is often seen browsing on roadside plants. Both of these deer are a major part of the diet of Big Bend's top predator, the mountain lion. The park is an island of safety for the lions. They are not protected in Texas, and can be killed without a license in any season—outside the park. Lions that leave the park are often killed. Big Bend's population remains stable only because all niches in the park are filled. In the mid-1990s, there were about twenty-four adult lions in the park.

The coyote, another symbol of the Southwest, is occasionally seen, but more often heard as a howl across the desert nights. Its prey species—black-tailed jack rabbits, eastern and desert cottontails, kangaroo rats and other rodents—are common.

One mammal that draws a great deal of attention, perhaps because it is relatively large and yet unfamiliar to many park visitors, is the collared peccary, or javelina. These piglike animals live throughout the park and travel in herds of from ten to twenty individuals. They are tough critters that eat cactus and lechuguilla, but they are not dangerous to humans.

The rainbow grasshopper spits "tobacco" to drive away enemies.

The Mexican black bear, a subspecies more common south of the border, had nearly disappeared from the Big Bend area by the 1930s. Bears had been targets of hunters and of ranchers protecting livestock. With the park's creation in 1944, the livestock left and the grasslands and other plant communities began to recover and to attract more animals. Bear sightings were reported regularly from 1988. In 1993, biologists put Big Bend's bear population at about twelve. By then, bears were paying nightly visits to primitive campsites in the Chisos Mountains, attracted to improperly stored food, trash, and aromatic cosmetics. They tore into tents and pulled backpacks from trees.

The Park Service closed many campsites in the Chisos and installed storage boxes. In "problem" areas, visitors are now required to store food, beverages, and toiletries in the boxes or in a vehicle trunk or a hard-topped passenger compartment with windows closed. Campers and hikers must keep sites clean, carry out trash, and empty liquids in utility sinks.

Keep a safe distance from a bear; do not feed it. If it approaches, try to scare it away by shouting or throwing objects. However, if cubs are present, back away slowly.

The Rio Grande at Santa Elena Canyon.

Visitors to Big Bend have several ways to travel through the park and discover its diversity. Paved roads lead to major developed areas and to sites of interest along the way; backcountry roads go to lesser-used park areas; trails and primitive routes range from short self-guided walks to mere lines on a map that show a general route through some of the park's most remote wilderness; float trips can take boaters on quiet, open stretches of river and into the depths of the three great canyons of the park.

Paved Roads

Persimmon Gap to Panther Junction (26 miles). Driving south from Marathon, Texas, on U.S. 385, you will enter the park at Persimmon Gap, the same point at which the Comanche War Trail passed through the Santiago Mountains. Continuing south, the road passes Dog Canyon, Devil's Den, Dagger Mountain, and the improved dirt road that leads to Dagger Flat, with its concentration of giant dagger yuccas. For several miles the road stretches across Tornillo Flat, one of the areas in the park with the least vegetation. At the Fossil Bone exhibit are displayed fossil skulls and other bones of early mammals that roamed this country 50 million years ago. Just south of this exhibit a bridge spans Tornillo Creek, which drains most of the north and east sides of the park. (If you have ever seen a desert flash flood, you will understand why the bridge has a wide span.) The road finally climbs up a long, gentle slope past Hannold Grave and pioneer homesite to park headquarters and the Visitor Center at Panther Junction.

Maverick to Panther Junction (22 miles). Entering the park from the west at Maverick, this road immediately passes through Big Bend's painted desert, a beautiful badlands area that was a lush environment 70 million years ago when dinosaurs roamed the land and pterosaurs flew above. Just past the top of a steep hill, the north end of the Old Maverick Road turns off. Farther on, the Christmas Mountains can be seen just outside the park to the north, and Tule Mountain is to the south. The road swings around the northern end of Burro Mesa, a huge fault block that was once at the same elevation as Emory Peak, the highest point in the park, but that is now 3,500 feet below. Beyond Santa Elena Junction, the road passes three backcountry roads that lead to the north: Croton Spring, Paint Gap, and Grapevine Hills. Between Basin Junction and Panther Junction, the road crosses a series of washes in a good wildlife-viewing area. Watch for javelina, mule deer, and coyotes along this stretch.

Panther Junction to Rio Grande Village (20 miles) *and Boquillas Canyon* (23 miles). This road is downhill most of the way from foothill grasslands through typical Chihuahuan Desert to the banks of the Rio Grande. The majestic Sierra del Carmen are visible to the southeast throughout the journey. A few miles below Panther Junction, the rough dirt Glenn Springs Road angles off; about 1 mile beyond along the paved road, a short improved gravel road leads to Dugout Wells, where an active community thrived in the early 1900s. As the road continues its gradual descent, Chilicotal Mountain can be seen to the southwest. The road levels out, and just beyond the turnoff of the east end of the River Road, it crosses the Lower Tornillo Creek Bridge and climbs into rolling hills. After passing the Hot Springs Road and the south end of the Old Ore Road, the main road passes through a tunnel and drops down onto the Rio Grande flood plain.

Straight ahead is Rio Grande Village, which includes a visitor center, campground, picnic area, store, service station, and trailer facilities. The Boquillas Canyon Road leads off to the east. About 1 mile down the road, a dirt road goes to the International Crossing, where a villager from Boquillas, Mexico, ferries visitors across the river in a rowboat for a fee. One may then walk or ride a burro (again, for a fee) .75 mile into the village. Beyond Boquillas Crossing, the road leads to Boquillas Canyon parking area, where the Boquillas Canyon Trail begins.

Basin Junction to the Chisos Basin (7 miles). This road goes into the heart of the Chisos Mountains. Because of the steep grades and switchbacks, trailers longer than 20 feet are not recommended on this road.

The road begins at the Basin Junction, 3 miles west of Panther Junction. As the road climbs through Green Gulch, the rounded intrusive igneous rocks of Pulliam Ridge are to the right, and the blocklike extrusive igneous rocks of Panther and Lost Mine peaks are to the left. Desert plants give way to woodland species such as oaks, juniper, and pinyon pine as the land rises. The road crests at 5,800 feet at Panther Pass, where there is a parking area at the

TRAILS OF BIG BEND NATIONAL PARK

CHIHUAHUAN DESERT NATURE TRAIL: Starts at Dugout Wells; ends at parking area; .5 mile round trip; .5 hour; introduction to Chihuahuan Desert ecology; fine point for photographs of Chisos Mountains and Sierra del Carmen; evidence of historic human occupation of desert; self-guiding. See map on pages 38-39.

HOT SPRINGS HISTORIC WALK: Starts at Hot Springs parking area; ends at Hot Springs; 2 miles round trip; 1 hour; must for history buffs; excellent view of Rio Grande; good photographic opportunities for old rock and adobe buildings; hot springs flow out of limestone at ruins of bath house. See map on pages 38-39.

TUFF CANYON TRAIL: Starts at Tuff Canyon parking area; ends at canyon bottom; .8 mile round trip; .5 hour; water-carved route between walls of tuff; harder lava flows farther into the canyon often contain pools of water; interesting contrast between views from overlook and from canyon bottom.

BURRO SPRING TRAIL: Starts along Burro Mesa Pour-off spur road; ends at Burro Spring; 2.2 miles round trip; 2 hours; overlook above Burro Spring provides good opportunities for viewing and photographing wildlife. See map on pages 38-39.

BURRO MESA POUR-OFF TRAIL: Starts at end of Burro Mesa Pour-off spur road; ends at Burro Mesa Pour-off; 1 mile round trip; .75 hour; cross sections of ancient lava flows form canyon walls; desert blooms in spring. See map on pages 38-39.

BOQUILLAS CANYON TRAIL: Starts at end of Boquillas Canyon spur road; ends at Rio Grande; 1 mile round trip; 1.5 hours; 30-foot ascent; first 50 yards steep, then easy walking; Indian-made bedrock mortar holes in limestone shelf at river edge; huge sandslide formed by down-canyon winds; excellent view of canyon entrance. See map on pages 38-39.

GRAPEVINE HILLS TRAIL: Starts at Grapevine road; ends at a "window" of balanced boulders; 2.2 miles round trip; 50-foot ascent at the end of trail; probably prettiest desert hike in park; fascinating rock formations; good trail for children. See map on pages 38-39.

SANTA ELENA CANYON TRAIL: Starts at end of Santa Elena Canyon road; ends inside canyon; 1.7 miles round trip; 2 hours; dramatic walk into mouth of Santa Elena Canyon; fossil sea shells and 1,500-foot-high canyon walls; excellent photographic point looking out of canyon at Chisos Mountains. See map on pages 38-39.

LOST MINE TRAIL: Starts at Panther Pass; ends at Lost Mine Overlook; 4.8 miles round trip; 3 hours; 1,250-foot ascent; excellent introduction to plants and animals of the Chisos Mountains; views of Pine Canyon, Juniper Canyon, and East Rim; colorful rock formations at end of trail; self-guiding leaflet.

WINDOW VIEW TRAIL: Starts and ends at Basin trail head; .3 mile round trip; .5 hour; excellent stroll in evening; view of sun setting through the Window is a unique photographic opportunity; benches along trail. Wheelchair accessible.

WINDOW TRAIL: Starts at Basin trail head; ends at pour-off; 5.3 miles round trip; 4 hours; 800-foot ascent; wide variety of plants and birds; one of the best photographic points for Casa Grande in the late afternoon; pools of water near pour-off contain aquatic insects and may attract large wildlife.

THE BASIN TRAIL MAP

Ranger Station	🚓
Campground	🏕
Amphitheater	🎦
Horse Stable	🐎

ROAD
TRAIL ●●●●●●●●●●●●●●●

HIGH CHISOS COMPLEX: Starts at Basin trail head; ends at various points; up to 14.5 miles round trips; 1 hour to overnight; 1,800-foot ascent; extensive complex of trails in Chisos Mountains between 5,400 and 7,200 feet; passes Laguna Meadow and moist woodland in Boot Springs Canyon; dramatic panorama of Sierra del Carmen, Sierra Quemada, and the mouth of Santa Elena Canyon from the South Rim; check map at trail head.

BLUE CREEK TRAIL: Starts .2 mile south of Laguna Meadow; ends at Blue Creek Ranch overlook; 5.5 miles one way; 2 hours one way; 2,400-foot ascent; several plant zones; fine photographic opportunity for colorful geologic formations in Red Rocks Canyon; buildings from ranch at lower end.

JUNIPER CANYON TRAIL: Starts .2 mile above springs; ends at Juniper Canyon road; 4 miles one way; 2 hours one way; 300-foot ascent; ascends to a high pass and then drops into Juniper Canyon; Upper Juniper Springs has old concrete water trough, but spring is undependable in dry years.

EMORY PEAK TRAIL: Starts at Pinnacles Pass; ends at Emory Peak; 2 miles round trip; 2 hours; 600-foot ascent; ascends to highest point in park (7,835 feet); 360° panorama with views deep into Mexico and Texas; last few yards require a steep scramble over rock.

head of the self-guiding Lost Mine Trail.

Dropping into the Chisos Basin, the road winds through a series of switchbacks with massive Casa Grande Peak looming above. About 1 mile from Panther Pass, a paved road leads right to the lower Basin, where a campground and an outdoor amphitheater are situated. Straight ahead in the upper Basin are the Chisos Mountains Lodge, a store, and a ranger station. This is also the trail head for the High Chisos.

Santa Elena Junction to Santa Elena Canyon (30 miles). Beginning at the Santa Elena Junction, 13 miles west of Panther Junction, this road (the newest in the park) comes close to some of the park's geological formations, historic sites, and spectacular views.

The road stretches south along the east side of Burro Mesa; a few cottonwood trees are visible along Cottonwood Creek. The Chisos Mountains are to the left, and soon Casa Grande Peak comes into view through the Window. A short trail leads from the Old Sam Nail Ranch parking area to the adobe ruins of a ranch house surrounded by an oasis of vegetation. A windmill still pumps water that attracts birds and other wildlife. Beyond the ranch, volcanic dikes run across the hillsides like random rock walls. The road climbs a hill and arrives at the Homer Wilson Ranch parking area, from which a trail leads into the Blue Creek drainage to a stone building that was a line camp on the Homer Wilson Ranch.

Just past Homer Wilson Ranch, a short road goes to Sotol Vista, perhaps the finest view accessible by paved road in the park. The road now drops out of the Sotol grasslands back into the true desert at the southern base of Burro Mesa. Soon a paved road turns right and curves 3.5 miles back to a dead end near an arroyo that comes out of Burro Mesa. Along this road is the head of the Burro Spring Trail, and at the end of the road begins the Burro Mesa Pour-off Trail, which leads 1 mile to a huge dry waterfall, or pour-off.

The road now winds through one of the most geologically spectacular areas of the park, passing such volcanic and igneous features as Goat Mountain, Mule Ears Peaks, Tuff Canyon, and Castellan Peak.

About 1 mile past Cerro Castellan (Castellan Peak) is the Castolon Historic District, which retains the flavor of a turn-of-the-century border trading post. Built and used briefly as an army post, Castolon has been a frontier trading post since the early 1900s. A store and ranger station are here. Immediately past Castolon, on the left, is the Alvino House, the oldest adobe structure in the park. Next comes a dirt road leading to the International Crossing to the Mexican village of Santa Elena. The road is now in the flood plain, where cotton and other crops were grown until 1959. Notice Old

Castolon on the right, part of the early settlement.

The road is not on the Rio Grande flood plain, where cotton and other crops were grown until 1959. Along the road is the oldest building in the park, an adobe structure in an area called Old Castolon. The road now parallels the Rio Grande, and the 1,500-foot cliffs of the Sierra Ponce across the river in Mexico dominate the scene. Several historic buildings are scattered between here and Santa Elena Canyon. Near the canyon, at a parking area, is an impressive view of the canyon mouth.

Just past the parking area, the south end of the Old Maverick Road turns right, and the road (now paved) continues to the canyon. At the end of the road begins the .5-mile Santa Elena Canyon Trail, which leads into the awesome canyon mouth.

Backcountry Roads

None of these roads is paved, but some are improved so that normal passenger cars can be driven on them. The primitive roads should be driven only in a high-clearance vehicle. Visitors should check at park headquarters or with a park ranger for road conditions before driving any backcountry road.

Improved Dirt Roads

Old Maverick Road (13 miles). The Old Maverick Road, which connects Santa Elena Canyon with Maverick, may be taken to avoid retracing the route over the paved road to Santa Elena Canyon. Starting at the canyon, the road follows Terlingua Creek for a few miles; an unimproved side road leads down to the creek at Terlingua Abaja, the site of a small farming village in the early 1900s.

The road then crosses normally dry Alamo Creek. To the right is Peña Mountain, and just beyond is Luna's Jacal, former house of Gilberto Luna, who raised a family in what may appear to be an inhospitable environment. The road skirts around the right side of the Rattlesnake Mountains and overlooks an eroded badlands area that is especially colorful in morning or evening light. The junction with the paved road at Maverick is just beyond the badlands.

Croton Spring Road (1 mile). The short Croton Spring Road starts about 3 miles east of the Santa Elena Junction. The area around the spring at the end of the road shows evidence of use by Indians, and the spring itself was developed to some extent by ranchers. Look for mortar holes in the rocks where Indians ground mesquite seedpods and for patches of dark gray earth where their campfires may have burned.

Overleaf: The Chisos Mountains tower 6,000 feet above the Rio Grande.

Grapevine Hills Road (8 miles). Beginning just west of Basin Junction, the Grapevine Hills Road turns north and immediately passes Government Spring, a good place to watch for wildlife at twilight. In a few miles the road curves around the Grapevine Hills and arrives at a parking area, which is the trail head for the Grapevine Hills Trail. The road continues around the hills and eventually ends at the Grapevine Hills Ranch Site. Some large trees, a spring, a rock water tank, and other remains of the ranch make this an interesting area for exploration.

Dagger Flat Road (7.5 miles). The Dagger Flat Road turns off the road to Panther Junction about 13 miles south of Persimmon Gap. Pick up a road guide from a box at the beginning of the Dagger Flat Road; it identifies Chihuahuan Desert plants visible from a car. The road ends at Dagger Flat, a small valley filled with giant dagger yuccas. These 10- to 15-foot-tall yuccas are impressive even unadorned, but they provide a majestic floral display during a good blooming year, when hundreds of plants are crowned with flowering stalks.

Hot Springs Road (2 miles). About 1 mile below the Lower Tornillo Creek Bridge, the Hot Springs Road turns south and travels through rolling limestone hills until it squeezes through a narrow canyon and ends near the confluence of Tornillo Creek and the Rio Grande. J. O. Langford homesteaded at Hot Springs in 1909 and built a health resort. The store and motor court buildings remain standing, and the foundation of the bathhouse still collects 105° F water that flows out of the rocks on the banks of the Rio Grande. Trailers and recreational vehicles should avoid this road.

Primitive Roads

The *Paint Gap Road* is 5 miles long, passes through the Paint Gap Hills, and ends at an old ranch site at Dripping Spring. The *Old Ore Road* follows part of the route of the ore wagons that hauled their loads from the ore terminal in Ernst Valley to Marathon, Texas. This 25-mile road winds along the west side of the Deadhorse Mountains. The 15.5-mile *Glenn Springs Road* has an elevation range of about 1,100 feet and travels through both grassland and lowland desert. It passes the site of the tragic 1916 Glenn Springs raid. The *Pine Canyon Road* and *Juniper Canyon Road* are spurs into these canyons off the Glenn Springs Road. The longest backcountry road in the park is the 51-mile *River Road*, which extends across the southern end of the park. Several side roads lead south off this road to fishing camps on the Rio Grande and to historic sites, including Mariscal Mine. Check with a ranger before attempting any of these roads.

Self-Guiding Trails and Walks

These seven trails provide a good introduction to the varied environments and historical features of Big Bend National Park. Most trails are described in an interpretive leaflet or on signs along the way. Except for the Lost Mine Trail, which is somewhat strenuous, all are easy walking.

Rio Grande Village Nature Trail (leaflet) winds through lush flood-plain vegetation and then climbs onto a desert hill with excellent views of the Rio Grande and Mexico. *Santa Elena Canyon Trail* enters the mouth of Santa Elena Canyon and dead ends at a dramatically claustrophobic point where the river is squeezed wall-to-wall between sheer 1,500-foot cliffs. *Panther Pass* (leaflet), a short walk through a desert garden at park headquarters, and *Chihuahuan Desert Nature Trail* (signs), at Dugout Wells, provides a close-up look at some common desert plants and their remarkable adaptations to this arid environment. *Lost Mine Trail* (leaflet) begins at Panther Pass and climbs to 6,850 feet to reveal superb views of Green Gulch, Pine Canyon, Juniper Canyon, and the East Rim. This is the quickest access to the plants and animals of the High Chisos Mountains. *Hot Springs Historic Walk* (leaflet) and *Castolon Historic Compound* (leaflet) let you follow in the footsteps of Big Bend's pioneers as you learn about their lives and visit the structures they left behind.

Developed Trails

Boquillas Canyon Trail. The Boquillas Canyon Trail climbs over fossil-shell-encrusted limestone rock that is 100 million years old and then drops down to the Rio Grande near a group of Indian bedrock mortar holes. Along the river in the canyon, displacement of the limestone layers along faults in the canyon wall can be seen on the Mexican side. Near the entrance to the canyon, a large sand slide appears to have poured out of a shallow cave high up on the Texas side, but it is actually formed by down-canyon winds. The sand slide is a wonderful renewable resource for children of all ages to play on.

The trail begins at the Boquillas Canyon parking area, and is 1.4 miles round trip.

Grapevine Hills Trail. The magical and mysterious qualities of this park are nowhere more apparent than among the weirdly shaped rocks along the Grapevine Hills Trail. Formed from a dome-shaped underground volcanic intrusion that has since been exposed and shaped by erosion, the Grapevine Hills offer hikers the opportunity to walk through an enchanted jumble of rocks. The trail follows an arroyo through boulder-covered hillsides to a small pass. A series of metal stakes to the right of the pass leads to a large "window" formed by boulders.

The trail begins 1 mile from the end of the Grapevine Hills Road, and is 2.2 miles round trip.

Burro Spring Trail. In the desert, where there is water there is wildlife. Burro Spring is a good place to see signs of wildlife activity. The Burro Spring Trail curves around a small mountain to an overlook above the spring. Sit quietly, and javelina, mule deer, or coyote may come to drink. Drop down to the spring and look for tracks and droppings. Aquatic insects and sometimes tadpoles can be found in the small pools. Here the contrast of aquatic life juxtaposed with cacti and ocotillo is dramatic. To avoid retracing your steps, follow the wash below the spring, turn left around the end of the mountain, and turn left again at the next wash to return to the starting point.

The trail begins at the parking area along the Burro Mesa Pour-off spur road, and is 2.2 miles round trip.

Burro Mesa Pour-off Trail. The Burro Mesa Pour-off Trail leads around a small hill and up the right fork of an arroyo. Sand and gravel are underfoot as the trail continues past graceful desert willow and Mexican buckeye trees, which are covered with pinkish-purple blossoms in the spring. A box canyon is formed at the end of the trail, with the pour-off standing as a huge dry waterfall. The power of erosion is evident on the polished black rock on the upper part of the pour-off.

The trail begins at the parking area at the end of the Burro Mesa Pour-off spur road, and is 1 mile round trip.

The 3,000-foot-high volcanic cores of Mule Ears Peaks are aptly named.

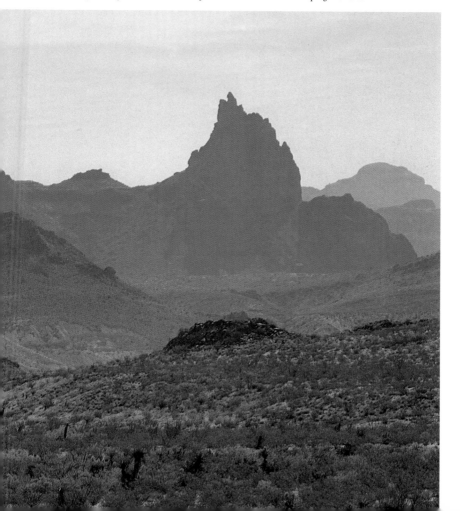

Tuff Canyon Trail. At Tuff Canyon, water has carved through relatively soft layers of hardened volcanic ash, or tuff. Before taking the trail into the canyon, stop at the overlooks on the canyon rim to get a different perspective on the gray-white canyon walls. The trail goes south down the hillside to the canyon mouth. From there the route is through the canyon until the harder rocks and terraces formed by lava flows are reached. The semicircle of the upper terrace resembles a miniature, dry Niagara Falls. The soft tuff and loose rock on the canyon walls are dangerous to climb, so the safest return trip is along the same route. The trail begins at the Tuff Canyon parking area, and is .75 mile round trip.

Window View Trail. The short paved Window View Trail can provide a leisurely walk in the heart of the Chisos Basin. It circles a small hill and has benches along the way that encourage relaxation and contemplation. The trail is a good place to watch for del Carmen white-tailed deer in the evening as the sun sets through the Window.

The .3-mile trail, wheelchair accessible, begins at the Basin trail head.

Chisos Basin Loop Trail. The two trails that lead out of the Chisos Basin into the High Chisos are linked in the Basin to form this short loop trail. Most of the mountain peaks that encircle the Basin are visible from points along the way. Grasses, oaks, juniper, pinyon pine, century plant, and other typical mountain plants grow here. Since summer temperatures in the upper Basin rarely climb higher than 80° F to 90° F, this is a pleasant hike most of the year.

The trail begins at the Basin trail head, and is 1.6 miles round trip.

The Window Trail. All surface water that may occasionally flow out of the Chisos Basin must exit through a V-shaped notch in the west side known as the Window. The Window Trail descends through an open area of grasses and chaparral into shaded Oak Creek Canyon. A variety of birds may be seen and heard in these different habitats. The canyon narrows, and the trees eventually give way to polished bedrock. Usually a few pools of water are present and populated by aquatic insects such as water boatmen, backswimmers, and water striders. On the return hike, Casa Grande forms an impressive backdrop, especially when it seems to glow in the warm afternoon light.

The trail begins at the Basin trail head or at the Basin Campground, and is 5.2 miles round trip from the trail head and 4 miles round trip from the campground.

High Chisos Trails Complex

South Rim Trail. A long loop hike with many interesting highlights, the South Rim Trail is one of the finest in the park. In a counterclockwise direction, the trail ascends, via the Laguna Meadows Trail, out of the Chisos Basin through woodland until it reaches a chaparral area near the Basin rim that is covered with Coahuila scrub oak. The trail then levels out, and just beyond is Laguna Meadow, an open area covered with stipa grass, and a favorite haunt of the uncommon yellow-nosed cottonrat. Watch for the Colima warbler in the woodlands around the meadow. Mescalero Apaches probably baked the hearts of sotol and agave in the pit at the north end of the meadow.

As the trail leaves the meadow, look uphill to the left for a grove of about 100 quaking aspens growing on the talus slope below Emory Peak. Soon Blue Creek Trail turns off to the right, and beyond that the Colima Trail leads off to the left and reaches Boot Spring in about 1 mile. Continuing toward the South Rim, hikers will see new vistas open up to the southwest. Finally, the trail abruptly reaches the cliffs of the South Rim, with the desert spread 2,500 feet below and a classic panorama of mountains—some nearly 100 miles away in Mexico.

The trail continues along the edge of the South Rim past the Boot Canyon "short-cut" trail. Either turn left on this trail to reach Boot Spring or proceed to the East Rim, which provides more lovely vistas and is a marvelous place to watch a sunrise. From the East Rim, the trail drops down past the junction with the Juniper Canyon Trail to Boot Spring, a moist woodland environment that harbors an interesting assemblage of plants and animals. Another good spot to look for the Colima warbler or hear the flammulated owl, Boot Canyon contains tall Arizona cypress and Douglas-fir. After leaving Boot Spring the trail, now called the Pinnacles Trail, passes the area's namesake, the "Boot," a spire of volcanic rock shaped like an inverted cowboy boot. Past the junction with the Emory Peak Trail, the Pinnacles Trail descends back into the Basin; steep and rocky, it has many switchbacks. Nonetheless, it is beautiful; cliffs, spires, woodland, and meadows can be seen along the way.

The trail begins at the Basin trail head, and is 13 miles round trip or 14.5 miles if the East Rim is included.

Other High Chisos Trails. Just south of Laguna Meadow, the *Blue Creek Trail* descends steeply through Blue Creek Canyon to Blue Creek Ranch and parking area on the road to Castolon. The trail passes through several plant zones and among some colorful rock formations in Red Rocks Canyon. The *Juniper Canyon Trail* begins above Boot Spring, ascends to a high pass, and then drops down to the end of the Juniper Canyon primitive road. The *Emory Peak Trail* begins near Pinnacles Pass and in 1 mile attains the 7,835-foot summit of Emory Peak, the highest point in the park. The 360° view of the Big Bend country is breath-taking.

Primitive Routes

Sometimes little more than an imaginary line between two geographic features, a primitive route is not for the novice desert hiker. About twenty of these routes exist in the park, and other unnamed cross-country routes offer similar opportunities to explore the wildest parts of Big Bend. Consult with a park ranger before attempting any hikes of this type.

Float Trips

Float trips on the Rio Grande offer visitors a means of exploring the park at a leisurely pace in a canoe, a kayak, or an inflatable raft. The river flows for 118 miles along the southern boundary of the park, but the most popular float trips are through the river-carved canyons. Outfitters outside the park conduct guided trips, or you may obtain a permit from the National Park Service and go on your own.

Remote river campsites and unattended vehicles parked near the river in remote areas are often targets of thieves. Rafters and campers should check with park rangers for advice on safe parking areas and on other precautions.

Hot Springs Canyon. A good place to get your feet wet and to whet your appetite for longer Rio Grande float trips is the 2.5-mile Hot Springs Canyon trip. Put-in is at the site of the historic Hot Springs resort, where Tornillo Creek joins the Rio Grande. No difficult sections are encountered, and the canyon walls provide a feeling of remoteness even on this short trip. Watch for cliff swallow nests stuck to the canyon walls overhanging the water and for turkey vultures soaring high above near the canyon rim. Several take-out points are available in the Rio Grande Village area. Check with a ranger for details and free permits.

Santa Elena Canyon. The 17-mile river segment provides a challenging and inspiring 1- or 2-day trip. Put-in is near Lajitas on the west side of the park. The first 11 miles are through rugged desert mesa country with colorful interfaces of limestone and igneous rocks. Just past Arroyo San Antonio, which enters from the

Mexican side, the river makes a right turn and slips into a deep, narrow slot in the Mesa de Anguila: Santa Elena Canyon. Not far inside the entrance, Mirror Canyons face each other from either side of the river. Soon the roar of the Rockslide can be heard echoing off the canyon walls. At the Rockslide a huge piece of limestone cliff on the Mexican side crashed down into the canyon, creating a slope of boulders that extends into and across the river. These house-size chunks form a maze that is decipherable only from above. River runners must stop on the Mexican shore above the Rockslide, climb up the slope, memorize a route, and then hope their memory does not fail as they paddle through the labyrinth. The Rockslide can be portaged with difficulty, or rafts and canoes can be guided through with ropes at certain water levels. All but the most experienced boatmen should follow these procedures, and even experienced boatmen should scout it before running it.

Past the Rockslide the river is gentle, but the blue-gray vertical canyon walls that rise 1,500 feet to a slit of sky make floating

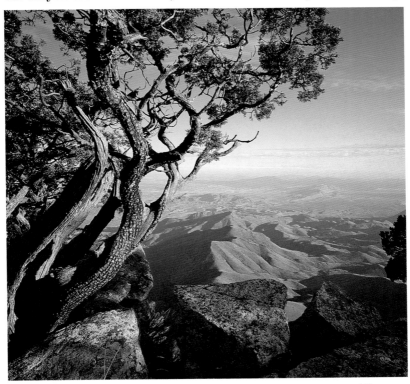

The South Rim Trail through the Chisos Mountains is one of the park's finest hikes.

this section an awesome and humbling experience. Arch Canyon and Fern Canyon on the Mexican side are fragile jewels that may be carefully explored, perhaps accompanied by the downward spiraling song of the canyon wren. The canyon mouth eventually appears, revealing the Chisos Mountains far in the distance. The take-out is 1 mile below the mouth, where a boat ramp leads from the river's edge to a paved parking area.

Mariscal Canyon. This 7-mile trip can be done in one day, but because of the amount of driving time involved, boaters may want to spend the night at the put-in or take-out or within the canyon itself. The usual put-in is at Talley, and the usual take-out is at Solis, both of which are accessible only via the River Road using a high-clearance vehicle.

The open country around Talley quickly becomes more confining until the river is squeezed into the crack of the canyon entrance. There the river extends across the width of the canyon, and not far ahead a small rockslide requires scouting and maneuvering to get through without upsetting. About .5 mile beyond, a large flat-topped block of limestone sits in the middle of the river forming the Tight Squeeze. At normal water levels, the 10-foot-wide gap between this boulder and the Mexican shore can be run with care. Stay near the Mexican side, and turn sharply left after clearing the slot to avoid being pushed into a rock dead ahead. The Tight Squeeze is easily portaged.

About 1.5 miles downriver a large arroyo enters from the Mexican side. A wax camp is sometimes in operation here, extracting wax from the candelilla plant, which has been gathered nearby. Also look for Indian petroglyphs and mortar holes on rocks on the right side of the arroyo. The canyon is more open through this stretch and then becomes confined again briefly before breaking out into desert again. The take-out at Solis is about 2 miles below the canyon mouth.

Boquillas Canyon. Floating through Boquillas Canyon offers different opportunities from those on the Santa Elena and the Mariscal trips. There are no difficult spots, the canyon is more eroded and open, and several side canyons await exploration. With a put-in at Rio Grande Village and a take-out at La Linda, this trip is about 30 miles long, so 2 to 3 days should be planned to enjoy it fully. This is an excellent trip for canoeing and for photographing the eroded geological formations along the river and in the side canyons.

Opposite: Mescalero Apaches roasted and ate the tender heart of the agave.

BRYCE
CANYON
NATIONAL PARK

BRYCE CANYON NATIONAL PARK
BRYCE CANYON, UTAH 84717
TEL.: (801) 834-5322

HIGHLIGHTS: Fairyland Point • Rainbow Point • Sunrise Point • Sunset Point • Inspiration Point • Yovimpa Point • Natural Bridge • Agua Canyon • Navajo Loop Trail • Queen's Garden Trail

ACCESS: From west, take U.S. 89 to junction with Utah 12, south of Panguitch. Turn east at this junction and follow Utah 12 and 63 to entrance.

HOURS: Daily, 24 hours, year-round.

FEES: At entrance and for camping, per vehicle. Free entry to senior citizens and disabled visitors.

PARKING: At Visitor Center and each viewpoint. Limited in summer.

GAS: Outside park only.

FOOD: In park, April to October. Rest of year, surrounding area (within 7 miles).

LODGING: In park at Bryce Canyon Lodge, April to October.

VISITOR CENTER: On main road, 1 mile from park boundary, by entrance station. Publications; 10-minute slide program. Closed Thanksgiving, Christmas, New Year's Day.

MUSEUM: Exhibits in Visitor Center.

GIFT SHOP: In Bryce Canyon Lodge, April to October.

PETS: Permitted on leash, but not within the canyons or in public buildings. Horseback riding from spring through fall; rentals available in park and at motels in area.

HIKING: Permitted only on designated trails because of crumbly rock. Water must be carried. Maps available at Visitor Center.

BACKPACKING: Permitted in southern portion with a free permit. Water availability varies; carry it. Camping at designated sites only. No fires.

CAMPGROUND: 210 campsites in North and Sunset campgrounds. From April to October, showers available in park. Some sites year-round. First-come basis. Reservations taken only for group site. Senior citizen discount. Some sites for trailers; no hookups.

TOURS: National Park Service tours in summer; concession van tours, April to October.

OTHER ACTIVITIES: Cross-country skiing; snowshoeing; sightseeing flights outside park.

FACILITIES FOR DISABLED: Most park buildings, rim trail, restrooms, and viewpoints accessible.

For additional information, see also Sites, Trails, and Trips on pages 89–96 and maps on pages 76–77 and 91.

EIGHTEEN MILES LONG, UP TO 5 MILES WIDE, and, in places, 800 feet deep, Bryce Canyon National Park is an example of unique erosional patterns. More properly called an amphitheater because of its configuration, Bryce Canyon itself is the largest of the many horseshoe-shaped canyons that radiate from the eastern rim of the high Paunsaugunt Plateau. The canyons and the tableland make the park a 35,835-acre wonderland of forests, mountain meadows, and bizarre rock formations that have been sculptured primarily from limestone.

Bryce Canyon National Park ranges in altitude from 6,600 to 9,100 feet. Between these elevations are situated three distinctly different plant communities that strongly influence where the park's approximately 50 species of mammals and more than 450 species of plants are most apt to be seen. The 164 recorded bird species of Bryce Canyon are also dependent to a large extent on these plant communities, but they, of course, can fly to other areas where food may be more abundant.

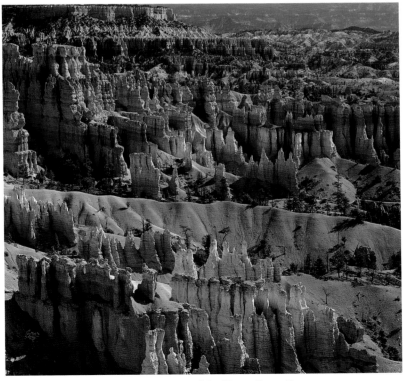

The thirty-mile-long Pink Cliffs are part of the Claron Formation.

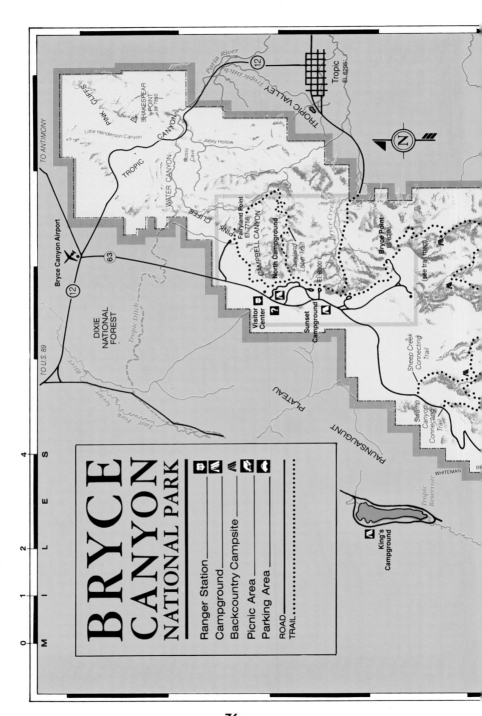

BRYCE CANYON
NATIONAL PARK

Ranger Station
Campground
Backcountry Campsite
Picnic Area
Parking Area

ROAD
TRAIL

MILES
0 1 2 4

TO ANTIMONY

PINK CLIFFS

SHAKESPEAR POINT
El 7850

Little Henderson Canyon

TROPIC

WATER CANYON

CANYON

PINK CLIFFS

Mossy Cave

Jolley Hollow

Paria River

TROPIC VALLEY Tropic Ditch

12

Tropic
El 6295

N

Bryce Canyon Airport

63

12

TO U.S. 89

DIXIE
NATIONAL
FOREST

Tropic Ditch

East Fork Sevier River

Fairyland Point
El 7758

CAMPBELL CANYON

North Campground

Fairyland
Loop Trail

El 8000

Bryce Creek

Bryce Point
El 8296

(see trail map)

Visitor
Center

Sunset
Campground

PLATEAU

PAUNSAUGUNT

Sheep Creek
Connecting
Trail

Swamp
Canyon
Connecting
Trail

WHITEMAN

Tropic
Reservoir

King's
Campground

VICINITY MAP

12

Cannonville

12

89

Hatch

BRYCE
CANYON
N. P.

INSET SCALE

0   5   10
M I L E S

MUD
CANYON
BUTTE

NOON
CANYON
BUTTE

NOON CANYON

Wash

Creek

Trail

Piracy
Point

Farview
Point
El. 8823

PINK CLIFFS

PONDEROSA CANYON

Under the Rim
Trail

Natural
Bridge

Agua
Canyon

Agua Canyon
Connecting
Trail

View Point

PINK CLIFFS

Iron
Spring

Black
Birch
Spring

The Pinnacles

Corral Hollow

Yovimpa
Point

Yovimpa
Pass
El. 8360

Mutton Hollow

Riggs Spring Loop Trail

Riggs
Spring

PINK CLIFFS

East Fork Sevier River

HISTORY

Early Inhabitants

The Basket Makers may have been the first Native Americans to inhabit the Bryce region. They may have been succeeded, sometime after A.D. 1000, by Puebloans, who lived along some tributaries of the Paria and Sevier rivers. Members of the Desert Culture may also have entered and remained in the vicinity.

As the last of the earlier occupants departed from the Bryce area by around A.D. 1200, the nomadic Paiutes began moving in. Visitors occasionally may see arrowheads that attest to the presence of the Paiutes, who left no remains of permanent structures. (Do not remove any artifacts; report them to park personnel.) Bryce apparently was used only as a hunting ground during the summer months, when the Paiutes migrated into the park looking for deer, elk, and small game such as rabbits. They also gathered edible foods such as pinyon nuts and the bulb of the sego lily. The Paiutes were a peaceful though superstitious people. The somewhat familiar shapes that they found among the weathered Bryce Canyon rocks gave rise to several legends that were passed down through the years. For example, Paiutes described the rock forms with a phrase that, according to one interpretation, means "red rocks standing like men in a bowl-shaped recess." According to one legend, birds, animals, and lizards that once had lived in the canyon had the power to make themselves look like people. For some reason, their conduct did not please Shin-Owav—a Paiute demigod of great power—and he turned them into rocks. Imaginative visitors to the park will be able to see these human forms. Look for them, and try to discern individuals standing erect, groups gathering in a row, or hunters stalking game.

Explorers

The first recorded travel near Bryce Canyon occurred in 1866, when a militia of the Church of Jesus Christ of Latter-Day Saints (the Mormons) pursued marauding Indians south of the park area. Scouts were undoubtedly sent out by the Mormons between 1851 and 1860 in search of agricultural lands, but there is no written record of such exploration. It is believed that these explorers entered the Paria Valley, which lies to the east of Bryce.

In 1872, a one-armed explorer, Major John Wesley Powell, climbed the Pink Cliffs. Accompanying Powell on this and on several other explorations was Captain C. E. Dutton. Dutton, a man of eloquence, wrote in *Geology of the High Plateaus of Utah* that "the

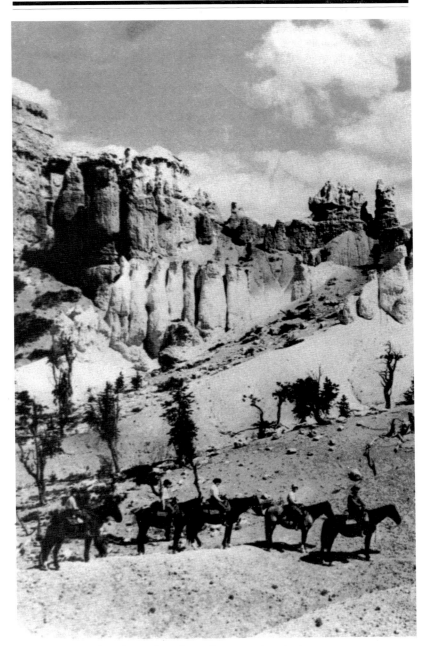

An early party of tourists explores Bryce Canyon on horseback.

upper tier of the vast amphitheater [the Bryce Amphitheater] is one mighty ruined colonnade. Standing obelisks, prostrate columns, shattered capitals . . . all bring vividly before the mind suggestions of the work of giant hands, a race of genii now chained up in a spell of enchantment, while their structures are falling in ruins through centuries of decay." Prose such as this was later used to excite the imagination of visitors, but it did little to lure the hard-working Mormon ranchers and farmers who were intent on earning a living from the "badland" of Bryce.

Around 1875, Ebenezer and Mary Bryce homesteaded on land that penetrated the main canyon of the present-day park. They raised sheep and cattle, built a road for hauling timber, and dug an irrigation ditch from Pine Creek. Soon the canyon became known as Bryce's Canyon. But in 1880, Ebenezer and Mary departed the arid lands for Arizona, summarizing their feelings for the canyon in far less laudatory terms than those of Dutton. Bryce reportedly exclaimed, "It's a hell of a place to lose a cow."

In 1892, the last of the early settlers established a community near the site of the Bryces' former cabin. Because of the mild climate, the town was called Tropic. The town still exists essentially because water was diverted to it from the East Fork of the Sevier River, whose headwaters originate in Bryce.

Establishment of the Park

The earliest reports of this extraordinary region to reach the general public were penned in the early 1900s. Of these authors, J.W. Humphrey may have been the most instrumental in attracting visitors to the area. In 1915, Humphrey, a forest supervisor in the old Sevier National Forest, was coerced into accompanying a friend to the rim of the Paunsaugunt Plateau, from which Bryce Canyon National Park has been carved. Later, Humphrey wrote, "You can imagine my surprise at the indescribable beauty that greeted us, and it was sundown before I could be dragged from the Canyon view." Humphrey then began to promote Bryce through articles that glorified the beauties of the area. He even offered to pay one skeptic ten dollars if he was disappointed with Bryce.

Enthusiasm grew, and national recognition followed. Bryce Canyon National Monument was created on June 8, 1923. One year later, Congress approved legislation that authorized changing the monument to Utah National Park. Eventually, in 1928, the area was doubled in size and given the name by which it is known today.

Opposite: Fantastic rock shapes, known as hoodoos, form an eerie landscape below Inspiration Point.

Bryce Canyon National Park is an exemplary result of three major geological forces—deposition, uplift, and erosion.

Deposition

The foundations of the park were laid down by a shallow sea that existed about 150 million years ago. Although these sedimentary layers are quite apparent in the lower-elevation Zion National Park, they are largely covered up by younger deposits at the higher-elevation Bryce Canyon.

The depositions that form the most colorful exposures at Bryce began to be laid down about 60 million years ago. Helping to delineate these sediments were a series of mountains. One group, the north-south ranging Rockies, began rising to the east. They eventually were joined by unnamed east-west ranging mountains that existed close to the present location of the Grand Canyon of the Colorado. Simultaneously, yet another mountain range began to rise along what is now the Idaho border. These three chains merged to form a bowl-shaped series of mountains; into this bowl, rivers and streams carried sediments that settled at the bottom of shallow lakes. These sediments contained the various components that constitute the Claron Formation, from which—millions of years later—the beautiful pinnacles and spires of the modern-day Bryce Canyon have been carved.

The rivers and streams brought to these ancient lakes the compound calcium carbonate, a limy substance that acts as a binding agent and helps add strength and rigidity to the rocks with which it becomes associated. Alternating layers of hard and soft rock, which geologists call differential hardness, contribute directly to some of the unique formations in Bryce Canyon National Park. Coloring these structures are minute amounts of iron and manganese. Iron creates the reds; manganese, the blues and lavenders.

Uplift

In some areas of the world, similar sediments undoubtedly were deposited, and they have lain undisturbed through the eons. But 10 million years ago, deep within the earth beneath southern Utah and northern Arizona, powerful forces were at work. Gradually, over millions of years, the Colorado Plateau was uplifted until parts of it were 2 miles above sea level. The ancient lakes disappeared at about the same time that the land was uplifted, but their legacy, of course, is that sequence of sediments now known as the Claron Formation. Because of its vivid coloration, this 30-mile-long formation is also called the Pink Cliffs.

The pressures exerted on the Colorado Plateau were so great that the uplifted land broke into huge chunks along fault lines— breaks in the continuity of a body of rock. Southwestern Utah is dominated by seven of these masses. Bryce Canyon has eroded from one of them, the Paunsaugunt Plateau, while Zion National Park has been formed from another, the Markagunt Plateau.

Concurrent with the pressures that created the Colorado Plateau and its subsequent fault lines was the creation of joints, or weak areas of fracture within an individual rock or group of rocks. The existence of many such areas has contributed substantially to some of the park's major geological formations.

Erosion

Bryce Canyon is the result of deterioration on a grand scale. While deposition and uplift occurred many millions of years ago, erosion maintains its relentless onslaught against the Colorado Plateau.

In Bryce, it is water—"time and raindrops, time and snow, time and ice," as naturalists frequently say—that creates the spires and pinnacles. Wind plays an insignificant part in forming these imposing hoodoos. A study of the weather records has indicated that a cycle of freeze and thaw occurs in Bryce more than 200 times a year on south-facing slopes. During the day, snowmelt drips into the cracks in rocks and is held fast. Then during the night, the water cools, freezes, and expands. The expanding ice exerts such a strong force that it widens the cracks and joints in the rocks. Over a period of a few years, massive rocks are pushed, shoved, and broken down by the action of ice; indeed, freeze-thaw action is probably the most important way bedrock is broken down into successively finer fragments. Eventually, whole sections of wall may fall, windows may collapse, and the rim of the canyon is pushed back.

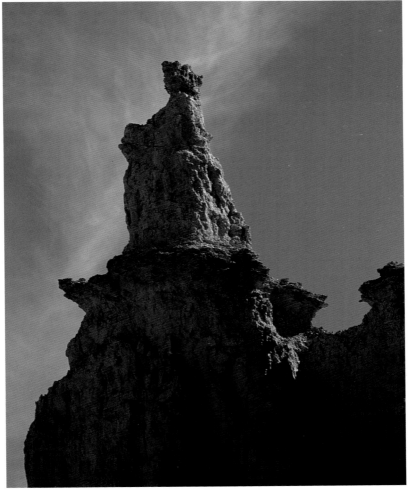

This hoodoo, near Bryce Creek, has been christened Queen Victoria

Vegetation

The vegetation of Bryce is arranged in tiers, or zones. Because of variations such as rainfall, temperature, and the stability of slopes, different plant communities are found in each zone.

The lowest tier is the Pinyon–Juniper zone, which occurs at elevations below 7,000 feet—areas usually found below the canyon rim. This zone receives about 12 inches of precipitation a year. One of the most common species growing in this zone is the Utah juniper, which is more a shrub than a tree. Two other common trees in the pinyon and juniper forest are the Gambel oak and the pinyon pine. Both produce floral parts that provide deer and birds with an abundance of food. In the autumn, when its leaves turn a rich golden-brown, the Gambel oak gives additional color to the already brilliant canyon.

At about 8,000 feet, the forest complex changes into the Ponderosa Pine zone. (The changes between zones are gradual; nature does not tend to make sharp distinctions.) Increased precipitation, which averages about 16 inches a year, supports a more luxuriant growth of trees. Because of the greater variety of vegetation, wildlife is attracted to this zone.

One of the most abundant shrubs that is associated with trees characteristic of the 8,000-foot elevation is the green-leaf manzanita. Growing in profusion along the canyon rim, it often carpets the slopes beneath the towering ponderosa pine. Leaves of this shrub tend to be vertically oriented with respect to the ground. Furthermore, they often face in a north–south direction. These features permit the stronger rays of the sun to strike only a small surface of the leaf, which thus conserves water. Winter snows also protect the leaves from freezing; as a result, the manzanita has evolved to grow no higher than the snows that usually surround it in winter.

The highest tier is the Spruce–Fir–Aspen zone, which is above 9,000 feet. One tree often found in the more exposed portions of this zone, the bristlecone pine, is named for the long, slender, bristlelike prickles that grow on the end of each cone scale. Unlike most trees, the bristlecone pine can eke out a living under extremely adverse climatic conditions because small sections of the tree remain alive, although the greater part dies off. With the return of clement weather, growth resumes in the surviving portions of the tree. Because of its unique ability, the bristlecone pine is the longest-lived organism on earth; the oldest pine in Bryce Canyon is estimated to be 1,700 years old.

Interspersed between bush and trees in the Spruce–Fir–Aspen

Opposite: A limber pine at canyon rim. The buttressed roots indicate heavy erosion.

zone is a profusion of wildflowers whose brief existence comple-
ments the beauty of the understory. These species add vivid coloration to the drab brush, which is predominantly green or brown.

One of the first flowers to herald the approach of spring is the
star lily, which dots the high forest floor. The tufted, grasslike
leaves of this flower surround one or more small, fragrant white
flowers. Blossoms begin to open while patches of snow remain in
the May forest.

Other flowers common to the park are the Indian paintbrush,
penstemon, wild iris, and columbine. Rabbitbrush is another abundant plant; when cool air turns its green leaves a radiant yellow,
residents know that autumn cannot be far away.

Wildlife

Prairie dogs have long been controversial animals. Ranchers and
farmers detest them because they dig holes into which horses occasionally step and because they consume vast amounts of vegeta-

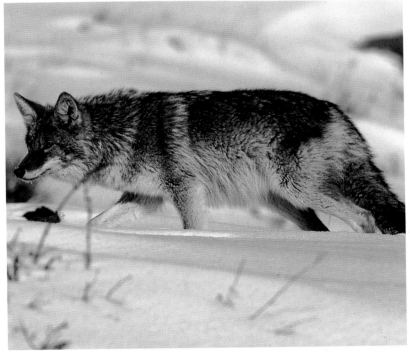

Opposite: The shy bobcat spends its days hidden among rocks or perched in trees.
Above: The wily coyote prowls for food through deep snow.

tion, including alfalfa. But they are vital contributors to the ecology of their natural habitats. Their presence is a key to the existence of other species of wildlife. For instance, some of their communities attract burrowing owls and snakes.

Although prairie dogs are native to Bryce Canyon, they had been eliminated by the early 1950s. In 1974, the National Park Service, in conjunction with the U.S. Fish and Wildlife Service and the Utah Department of Wildlife Conservation, began to reestablish this rodent in sites near the Visitor Center and Sunset Campground. By 1978, a few successful breeding colonies had been established. These colonies have flourished, and prairie dogs again inhabit the park in relatively stable numbers.

Three chipmunk species live in Bryce. The most prevalent is the Uinta chipmunk, which abounds on the plateau and along the rim. In the canyon, the least and cliff chipmunks may sometimes be seen. The only animal with which chipmunks may be confused is the golden-mantled ground squirrel, which is particularly abundant along the rim and at automobile turnouts along the road. It can be differentiated from chipmunks by its markings: its body stripes do not extend along the face, but stop near the base of the neck.

Mule deer are common on the plateau and are frequently seen in summer in meadows at dawn or dusk. During the winter, should heavy snows blanket their food supplies, these animals may drift down from the plateau to lower elevations outside the park.

Many mammals that make their homes in Bryce are secretive and seldom seen. Examples include the bobcat, the skunk, and the gray fox.

Many resident birds soar among the park's hoodoos or flit from branch to branch. Among these are the Steller's jay, the golden eagle, the raven, the red-tailed hawk, the Clark's nutcracker, the pygmy nuthatch, a variety of woodpeckers, and the engaging blue grouse. Blue grouse, which are common in the spruce–fir–aspen community, conduct courtship displays in the spring that add interest to them as a species.

Another resident is the white-throated swift, which may dive at speeds of up to 200 miles per hour when foraging for insects. The vividly colored western tanager is a frequent visitor.

Most reptiles find Bryce too cold. However, the skink, a small-scaled lizard, is seen occasionally, and the short-horned lizard is found in abundance. The skink darts among the rocks for protection, while the short-horned lizard, unusual among reptiles in that it gives birth to live young, relies on changing coloration to evade its predators, which are legion. These reptiles are active during the day, and sharp-eyed visitors may see one basking in the sun on a rock or against a fallen tree.

Park Road

"Window" rocks.

Bryce Canyon National Park can be entered only from the north. The dead-end park road terminates in 18 miles and one could easily drive to its southern end in an hour were it not for the numerous enticing viewpoints. Each offers a different perspective of the varied domes, temples, spires, pinnacles, and arches of the park. The highway passes along a slightly canted plateau that ascends to the south through the Ponderosa Pine Zone to the Spruce–Fir–Aspen Zone. The Pinyon–Juniper Zone lies below the rim and is best appreciated by hiking one of the trails.

Overlooks

Fairyland Point. The first view of the Canyon is from Fairyland Point, which is accessible by a 1-mile spur road. Nothing has prepared visitors for the array of colors and for the bizarre shapes that erosion has wrought. This viewpoint brings onlookers close to the spires and pinnacles.

Sunrise and Sunset Points. Spur roads that lead to the next pulloffs go to the canyon that is specifically referred to as Bryce Canyon. These spurs terminate at Sunrise and Sunset points and provide expansive views of this canyon. Of the two viewpoints, only one has been appropriately named. Sunrises can be seen from Sunrise Point, but for a view of a sunset, go to Inspiration Point, which is higher than the Paunsaugunt Plateau.

From these points, areas more than 100 air miles away can be seen. Off in the distance and outside the park is the Aquarius Plateau, the highest plateau in North America. It rises to elevations of more than 10,000 feet. Sunset Point also offers views of Boat Mesa, an area described by naturalists as an ellipse. Approximately 320° of the mesa is exposed, and cliff faces plummet 800 feet. During the summer, the park is frequently assaulted by lightning strikes, and Boat Mesa is not a safe place during a summer thunderstorm.

TRAILS OF BRYCE CANYON NATIONAL PARK*

RIM TRAIL: Starts at Fairyland Point; ends at Bryce Point; 11 miles round trip; 3.5 hours; 550-foot ascent; easiest trail in park skirts Bryce Amphitheater; numerous access points; unmaintained side trails to Boat Mesa; spectacular panorama of amphitheater.

QUEEN'S GARDEN TRAIL: Starts and ends at Sunrise Point; 1.5 miles round trip; 1–2 hours; 320-foot ascent; one of the most colorful trails into Bryce Canyon; "natural stucco" coats and colors rocks; views of Queen Victoria and Gulliver's Castle.

NAVAJO TRAIL: Starts at Sunset Point and ends in Wall Street where the 1984 rock slide is visible; 2.2 miles round trip; 1–2 hours; 521-foot ascent; moderately strenuous.

QUEEN'S GARDEN AND NAVAJO TRAIL: Starts and ends at Sunrise or Sunset Point; 3 miles round trip; 2–3 hours; 521-foot ascent; strenuous hike with some of park's most diverse scenery; climb more gradual from Sunset Point; luxuriant plant life.

PEEKABOO LOOP TRAIL: Starts and ends at Bryce, Sunset, or Sunrise Point; 5-6.5 miles round trip; 3–4 hours; 500–800-foot ascent; strenuous foot and horse trail; abrupt switchbacks and unexpected tunnels; view of the Wall of Windows and other examples of erosion.

FAIRYLAND LOOP TRAIL: Starts and ends at Sunrise Point or Fairyland View; 8 miles round trip; 5 hours; 900-foot ascent; strenuous; views of the Chinese Wall, Tower Bridge, the remains of Oastler's Castle, and Boat Mesa; passes bristlecone pine and pinyon–juniper forest; shuttle to Fairyland View eliminates 2.5-mile hike along Rim Trail.

HAT SHOP TRAIL: Starts and ends at Bryce Point; 3.8 miles round trip; 4 hours; 900-foot ascent; little-used, strenuous trail to area of many pillars, each capped by a "hat," or caprock; very steep climb back.

UNDER THE RIM TRAIL: Starts at Bryce Point; ends at Yovimpa Point; 22.5 miles round trip; 2 days (minimum); 1,500-foot ascent; remote hike through older sections of Bryce; numerous elevation changes with marked transition in vegetation and abundant wildlife; panoramic views; registration required for primitive camping on trail; no fires; shuttling a vehicle recommended.

RIGGS SPRING LOOP TRAIL: Starts and ends at Yovimpa Point; 8.8 miles round trip; 4–5 hours; 1,675-foot ascent; drops below rim through ponderosa pine forest; easy hike if follow sign to Yovimpa Pass; backcountry camping. See map on pages 76–77.

BRISTLECONE LOOP TRAIL: Starts at Rainbow Point; 1 mile round trip; 1 hour; 100-foot ascent; dramatic views of canyons and cliffs.

*All trails negotiate areas high above sea level. With exception of the Rim Trail, trails in Bryce commence with an abrupt descent. The return ascent can tax the most physically fit.

TO UTAH 12

FAIRYLAND POINT
El. 7758'

Trail

PINK

CLIFFS

FAIRYLAND

Visitor Center and Ranger Station

ENTRANCE

Rim

CAMPBELL

Fairyland

Loop

Trail

BOAT MESA
El. 8076

North Campground

Campfire Programs

CHINESE WALL

Store
Showers
Laundry

Nature Center

SUNRISE POINT
El. 8015'

CANYON

Campbell

Creek

TOWER BRIDGE

Horse Trail
(Horses Only)

Corral

Lodge

Queen's

QUEEN'S GARDEN

Sunset Campground

SUNSET POINT
El. 8000'

Garden Trail

Bryce Creek

Campfire Programs

SILENT CITY

Navajo Loop Trail

FAIRY CASTLE

**B R Y C E
AMPHITHEATER
TRAIL MAP**

THE CATHEDRAL
El. 7660

INSPIRATION POINT
El. 8143'

Rim

WALL OF WINDOWS

Peekaboo Loop Trail

Ranger Station	⬛
Campground	⬛
Picnic Area	⬛
Amphitheater	⬛
Information	⬛

ROAD
TRAIL ••••••••••••••

Trail

N

BRYCE POINT
El. 8269'

Under-the-Rim Trail

M I L E S
0   ½   1

PARIA VIEW

Natural Bridge. One of the pulloffs, about three-fourths of the way along the drive, offers a view of Natural Bridge. This structure is not really a bridge, but rather an arch that is 95 feet high and 54 feet wide. Geologically speaking, a bridge spans a streambed, while an arch is created when a hole is worn through rock by the erosive action of weathering.

Running water played only a minor part in the formation of Natural Bridge. The arch is the direct result of a recess that developed thousands of years ago in the soft underlying layers of the cliff area; the strong, weather-resistant top layer remains as the bridge. Initially, particles were pried away from the softer portion of the wall by mechanical weathering. Gradually, the indentation worked backward and upward, aided by underground water, until the arch isolated itself from the main rim of the plateau. Enlargement of the recess continues as surface water widens and deepens the channel by moving material away from beneath the arch. The structure is becoming less secure, and someday it will fall.

Agua Canyon. Another interesting point along the highway is Agua Canyon, at an elevation of 8,800 feet. *Agua* is the Spanish word for "water," and Agua Canyon is therefore a good place to consider the runoff of precipitation. The water from any snowflake or raindrop falling below the rim drains eastward and joins the Paria River, then flows to meet the Colorado River, and eventually enters the Gulf of California (assuming it isn't diverted for irrigation purposes). Water from a raindrop falling on the rim, perhaps just an inch from the drop that fell just below the rim, drains westward into a tributary of the East Fork of the Sevier River, and eventually flows northward via the Sevier River into the Great Basin.

From the Agua Canyon Viewpoint can be seen two prominent monoliths that have been given familiar names, The Hunter and The Rabbit. Recognizing them may require a little imagination, but none is required to appreciate the brilliantly colored walls of orange and gold. Following a rain shower, or when the sun is at an appropriate angle, this is one of the most vividly colored areas in the park.

Yovimpa and Rainbow Points. The last highway overlooks are Yovimpa Point and Rainbow Point, which are separated by only a few hundred yards. At 9,015 feet, these pulloffs are at the park's highest elevation. From either point, visitors may embark on a hike of less than 1 mile and reach an area where bristlecone pines may be seen. At Yovimpa Point is found the oldest (1,700 years) specimen of these long-lived trees within the park.

The view from Yovimpa appears endless. From the relatively

The erosion of shale and sandstone sculptured the pinnacles in Fairyland.

young rocks on which Yovimpa Point now reposes, the eye can journey back 136 million years to the Jurassic period, when dinosaurs roamed over some of the upper sediments near Zion National Park. The land continues to fall away to the Kaibab Plateau, into which the Grand Canyon of the Colorado River has been carved.

Hikes

Bryce Canyon is worthy of a more intimate acquaintance than can be gained from standing on the plateau rim. There is a rare fascination in threading one's way through a bewildering multitude of marvelously carved figures.

More than 50 miles of trails wander through the park; although not impressive in total miles, even short hikes can sap your energy. Remember that virtually all hikes start from the rim and descend distances that sometimes total 1,700 vertical feet. Also keep in mind that hikes are made at altitudes ranging between 7,000 and 9,000 feet. Climbing back up in the heat of the day can be an excruciating experience. Water is generally scarce and when found may not be potable, so hikers should carry canteens. One gallon per person per day is recommended.

Backpack stoves are required equipment if any cooking is contemplated. For several reasons, it is illegal to build fires. One, of course, is to prevent forest fires. Another is to prevent the burning of downed logs, which, as they rot, recycle essential organic compounds into the particularly thin topsoil of the park. Finally, stoves do not leave the land scarred with unattractive fire rings.

Moist trips into the depths of Bryce are best made as day excursions. A number of loop trails that can be hiked in a few hours to a single day offer the intrigue of continuously changing views. It is difficult to provide an estimate of the time involved for any of these trips, because that depends entirely on the individual's physical condition.

Fairyland Loop. The loop begins at the Fairyland Point overlook. The loop is 8 miles long and drops 850 feet. Many of the prominent features of the park can be seen by the hiker along this path. Look for the Chinese Wall, Tower Bridge, and views of Boat Mesa. A few ancient bristlecone pines dot the trail, and occasionally a hiker's shadow may send a skink scurrying among the rocks. In dry sites, hikers may also find the short-horned lizard. In August, the 1- to 2-inch newborn lizards may be found clinging to limbs and twigs. The Rim Trail continues on to Bryce Point.

Peekaboo Loop. This loop, which begins at Bryce Point or Sunrise Point (via the Queen's Garden Trail), wanders for 5 miles through the Bryce Amphitheater. This is also the park's horse trail. The amphitheater is the main showpiece of the park. It contains the headwaters of several branches of Bryce Creek, and in some areas manzanita grows in profusion. Rock formations in the amphitheater resemble minarets, camels, turtles, and humans. In the early morning, elongated shadows play tricks with your imagination, and you may find that curiosity will lure you almost unknowingly down into the recesses of the amphitheater.

Take a topographical map and see if you can pinpoint The Cathedral, the Wall of Windows, and the Silent City. At the Silent City, standing on the trail overlooking the "city," you may be reminded of the onion-domed churches of medieval Russia. In early morning, you may hear sounds from a few of the "city's" residents. But as you climb back up to the rim, you will be jolted back to reality and realize that the hum of the "city" may actually have been the shriek of a hawk.

Navajo Trail. Another fascinating day hike is that along the Navajo Trail, which begins at Sunset Point. This trail drops 520 feet in .75 mile. Along the way are examples of the various types of erosion that have made Bryce what it is today.

Wall Street is a prime example of a geological oddity that exists because of the park's system of joints. When the land began to be pushed upward millions of years ago, areas of stress were created that weakened the rock along vertical lines, or joints. The forces of erosion went to work, and gradually separated the rock into towering segments. An eastern traveler probably looked up and, remembering a familiar sight, christened the area "Wall Street." At several points along the base the walls of the "street" are a mere 25 feet apart and several hundred feet high.

Thor's Hammer, another feature along the Navajo Trail, illustrates differential erosion. Sediments laid down in those ancient

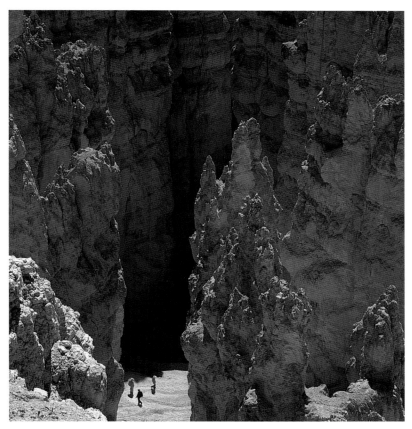

Below-the-rim hiking trails are steep, and the return ascent will require much energy.

lakes varied in their degree of hardness. Thor's Hammer is one of those structures that has a layer of hard rock overlying a layer of soft rock. Because of the resistance of the harder cap rock to erosion, the structure has assumed the appearance of a mushroom. The Twin Bridges, which also are seen along this trail, are other examples of differential hardness. If it were not for the presence of a hard layer of rock on top of each of these structures, the canyon that houses these bridges would be an uninterrupted pair of walls.

Queen's Garden Trail. Not all structures that exhibit differential deposition retain their original forms. A path that joins the Navajo Trail is called the Queen's Garden Trail. Hikers on this trail see a formation that many believe looks like Queen Victoria. Older photographs reveal that the queen's "crown" has eroded dramatically.

Rim Trail. In addition to the park's loop trails, others offer a further variety of experiences. Of these, the Rim Trail is the easiest to negotiate. Beginning at Fairyland Point, this trail progresses along the rim for 5.5 miles. After passing both Sunrise and Sunset points, it terminates at Bryce Point. Chipmunks and golden-mantled ground squirrels are constant companions. Occasionally hikers see a nuthatch.

Along this trail, hikers will notice trees that appear to be raised on buttressed roots. Such trees show that the rim of the canyon is gradually receding. By one calculation, the canyon rim is eroding westward at an average rate of 1 foot every 50 years. Geologically, that is a rather rapid rate, although by human standards it is virtually imperceptible. Bryce Canyon Lodge, which is about 200 feet from the rim, will be with us for another 10,000 years. Bryce Canyon National Park will last a little longer. The process of erosion, which both creates and destroys, will continue for many more millions of years. There is creation in destruction, and as old spires and pinnacles crumble, new ones will appear.

Under-the-Rim Trail and Riggs Spring Loop. For those who wish to undertake hikes longer than day trips, overnight camping is available. The 22.9-mile Under-the-Rim Trail and the 9-mile Riggs Spring Loop are recommended for backpacking. Both trails pass through the park's three plant communities and offer skyline views of the Pink Cliffs. Prior to embarking on such outings, a backcountry permit must be obtained. (Hikers using any of these trails are advised to watch where they place hands and feet, as the Great Basin rattlesnake is occasionally sighted.)

Opposite: Thor's Hammer at sunrise as seen from the Navajo Trail.

CANYONLANDS NATIONAL PARK

A sure-footed mule deer follows a narrow path across a steep cliff face.

CANYONLANDS NATIONAL PARK
125 W. 200 SOUTH
MOAB, UTAH 84532
TEL.: (801) 259-7164

HIGHLIGHTS: The Needles • The Maze • The Grabens • Tower and Keyhole Ruins • Salt Creek Ruins • Doll House • White Rim • Island in the Sky • Grand View Point • Land of Standing Rocks • Cataract Canyon • Upheaval Dome • Angel Arch

ACCESS: From Moab, 35 miles on U.S. 191 and Utah 313 to Island in the Sky; 76 miles on U.S. 191 and Utah 211 to The Needles.

HOURS: Daily, 24 hours. Visitor Centers, 8 A.M.–4:30 P.M.; extended hours in summer. Hans Flat Ranger Station closed in winter.

FEES: At entrance, per vehicle and per person; and for camping, backpacking, and float trips.

PARKING: At major points.

GAS, FOOD: In Moab, Monticello, Green River, and Hanksville. Gas stations relatively rare. Gas and limited supplies at Needles Outpost (March to October) near entrance to Needles District.

LODGING: In Moab, Monticello, Green River, and Hanksville.

VISITOR CENTER: Information Center in downtown Moab. Year-round, 8 A.M.–4:30 P.M. daily except winter holidays. Visitor Centers in each district of the park, year-round 8 A.M.–4:30 P.M., with extended summer hours.

PETS: Permitted on leash, except on trails; do not leave unattended; not permitted in backcountry. Horseback riding; bring own weed-free feed and water.

PICNICKING: Facilities available at several points in park.

HIKING: Permitted; many trails available. See ranger for information.

BACKPACKING: Permitted with permit. Carry extra water. Reservations recommended, (801) 259-4351. Walk-in permits may be available.

CAMPGROUND: In Needles and Island in the Sky: fee only at Needles from March to October. First-come basis. No hookups. Groups, 3 sites in Needles district; reservations accepted, (801) 259-4351. No wood gathering. Primitive backcountry campgrounds on 4-wheel drive routes.

TOURS: Commercial river trips, four-wheel drive trips, and mountain-bike trips.

OTHER ACTIVITIES: Sightseeing flights, river trips (with permit), commercial bus tours.

FACILITIES FOR DISABLED: Restrooms, surface pathways (limited).

For additional information, see also map on pages 102–103 and Sites, Trails, and Trips on pages 116–128.

OR DIVERSITY, CANYONLANDS NATIONAL PARK
gives even the Grand Canyon a run for its money. Its 337,570
acres range in elevation from 3,700 feet at the head of Lake
Powell to more than 7,000 feet at the highest point on the
south boundary above Salt Creek. Like the Grand Canyon,
Canyonlands protects a great inner gorge carved by the Colorado
River, with a rim high above that offers awesome views. But here,
too, are flats studded with slickrock needles and spires, an intricate
system of side canyons decorated with massive stone arches, and
rich archeological resources famous for fine rock art.

Two rivers slice Canyonlands into three districts. Between the
Green and Colorado rivers lies the Island in the Sky mesa, with
expansive vistas from its rims, and midway down toward the rivers
the 100-mile White Rim Road encircling it. On the east bank of
Cataract Canyon lies The Needles, spires and canyons that include
Salt Creek's arches, ruins, and rock art. To the west of the rivers
lies The Maze, the most isolated and least visited area of the park.
The rivers themselves form a fourth district—lovely flat water on
the upper Colorado and Green, and the twenty-four of Cataract
Canyon's fifty-two rapids that remain undrowned by Lake Powell.

Canyonlands vista, with the Green River in the distance.

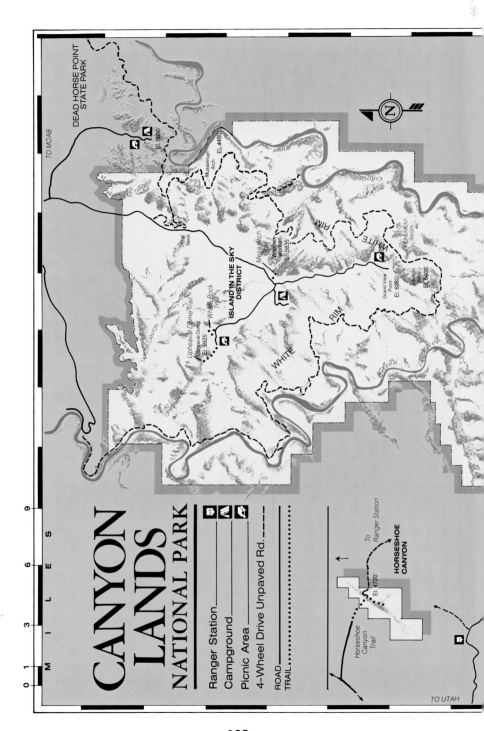

CANYON LANDS
NATIONAL PARK

Ranger Station
Campground
Picnic Area
4-Wheel Drive Unpaved Rd.

ROAD
TRAIL

MILES

0 1 3 6 9

TO MOAB

DEAD HORSE POINT
STATE PARK

El. 5600

Musselman
Arch
El. 4480

The
Neck

Mesa Arch
Trail

Washer
woman
El. 5835

WHITE RIM

Whale Rock
Trail

ISLAND IN THE SKY
DISTRICT

Upheaval Dome Trail

Upheaval
Dome
El. 5925

Upheaval Canyon

Taylor Canyon

WHITE RIM

Grand View
Point
El. 6080

Junction
Butte
El. 6400

MONUMENT
BASIN

Colorado River

Green River

HORSESHOE
CANYON

El. 4720

To
Ranger Station

Horseshoe
Canyon
Trail

TO UTAH

TO MONTICELLO AND U.S. 163

NEEDLES OUTPOST

Salt Creek

Tower Ruin
El. 5280'

HORSE CANYON

Peekaboo Spring

Squaw Flat
El. 5200'

Peekaboo Spring Trail

Squaw and Lost Canyons Trail

Angel Arch Trail

Angel Arch
El. 6160'

Cedar Mesa
El. 6987'

Wedding Ring Arch
El. 6560'

BIG SPRING CANYON

ELEPHANT HILL

Squaw and Big Spring Canyons Trail

Druid Arch Trail

LOST CANYON

Druid Arch
El. 6080'

NEEDLES DISTRICT

Confluence Overlook

El. 4800' Overlook

THE GRABENS

Chesler Park Trail

RED LAKE CANYON

El. 5563 Chimney Rock

Spanish Bottom

Colorado River Trail

Doll House

CATARACT CANYON

Pete's Mesa

FRASER CANYON

MAZE DISTRICT

ERNIE'S COUNTRY

Colorado River

Tea Pot Rock
El. 6221'

GLEN CANYON NATIONAL RECREATION AREA

TO HITE

VICINITY MAP

MOAB
191
45
La Sal

191
Monticello

CANYONLANDS N. P.

NATURAL BRIDGES MON.

84

Hanksville

8

Fry Canyon

GLEN CANYON NAT'L REC. AREA

INSET SCALE
0   15   30
M I L E S

Canyonlands has living things—high desert shrubland, pinyon and juniper woodland, and the animals that are tied to such plant communities. Desert bighorn sheep roam its cliffs; rodents scale its sheer mesas. Wildflowers bloom after rains. But this is mostly a landscape of rock. The sheer immensity, the sweep, of the stone impresses as much as anything. From the Island, The Needles, The Maze, or the rivers, Canyonlands puts life in perspective against a background both reassuring and suggestive, an immense reach of silence and wilderness, endless time and unfathomable rock.

HISTORY

The earliest Canyonland peoples hunted and gathered for thousands of years in the land that would become the park, but left few marks of their passage. Not until just after A.D. 1000 did the two village-dwelling prehistoric peoples of Utah, the Fremont and the Anasazi, come to Canyonlands.

Prehistoric Peoples: Canyon Frontier

The Anasazi moved north into Canyonlands when the San Juan–Mesa Verde country to the south began to get crowded. Here on the skimpy outer limits of essential resources, perhaps 1,000 people lived in stone pueblos. Not many canyons had enough bottom land for corn fields and for bean and squash patches to support more than a few families. The people supplemented crops with every imaginable local food—from tiny rice-grass seeds to nutritious pinyon nuts, from pocket gophers and frogs to bighorn sheep.

The Fremont people migrated to Canyonlands from the north and west. They relied more on hunting than on sedentary farming. One aspect of their culture remains strong and communicative, however. Fremont pictographs and petroglyphs are truly art— huge, hollow-eyed human figures wearing great shields, head-dresses, and necklaces. Perhaps the best rock art in North America covers the walls of Horseshoe Canyon at Canyonlands; "The Great Gallery" is believed by some archeologists to be the work of a separate culture—the Archaic people—even older than the Fremont or Anasazi.

The Salt Creek area has the densest concentration of Anasazi ruins at Canyonlands—pueblos perched in alcoves, and granaries. Right next to Anasazi ruins, enigmatic Fremont faces guard the silent side canyons. Scholars have not yet untangled the relationship of the two cultures.

Even this central core of Anasazi activity in Canyonlands seems to have been abandoned by 1250. Perhaps a drought or a change in weather patterns that brought arroyo-cutting flash floods destroyed the capability of the land to support even marginal agriculture. The fragile success of the farmers was ended by something in the unforgiving cycle of nature.

When the Anglo-Americans arrived, Ute and Navajo peoples were using the future park as hunting grounds. These peoples, too, allowed the obstacle of the barren canyons to form the frontier of their territories, a buffer between mounted Ute raiders of the north and Navajo sheepherders of the south.

Trappers, Surveyors, and the Man with One Arm

As in so many places in the West, the beaver men were the first Americans to explore this country. One trapper, Denis Julien, left his signature, accompanied by dates in 1836, on cliffs throughout the canyons of the Green and Colorado rivers. We know little more of him, but with Julien began not only the history of Canyonlands, but also the evident onset of Colorado River running.

In 1859, Captain John Macomb tried to reach the confluence, and became the first white explorer overland into the future park. His journal keeper, geologist John Strong Newberry, gives us our first glimpse of The Needles. He was impressed with the "battlemented towers of colossal but often beautiful proportions, closely resembling elaborate structures of art," but he judged the land "worthless and impracticable."

Next came John Wesley Powell. Newberry's report remained unpublished when Major Powell began his historic river trip in 1869. His work on the Colorado Plateau in the next few years, with that of his brilliant colleagues and rivals, filled in the last great blank on the United States map. Powell's river trips in 1869 and 1871 took him down the Green and through Cataract Canyon, and the canyons owe most of their place-names to the one-armed major and his men.

Near the confluence, Powell looked out at the heart of the future park and declared: "Wherever we look there is but a wilderness of rocks—deep gorges where the rivers are lost below cliffs and towers and pinnacles, and ten thousand strangely carved forms in every direction, and beyond them mountains blending with the clouds."

Nothing has changed.

Powell was followed by other river runners, including the disastrous Brown–Stanton party of 1889, which surveyed the canyon for a water-level railroad from Colorado to the sea. Stanton spent a month in Cataract Canyon, enduring near-starvation for his dream, but the railroad was never built.

Cattle Raising and Rustling

Large cattle herds worked down toward the rims as early as 1874, and in the next two decades tens of thousands of cattle grazed The Needles. By 1940, the Scorup and Somerville brothers' Indian Creek Cattle Company was the largest cattle outfit in Utah and one of the largest in the West.

With the cattle came rustlers, and the canyons were the perfect place to fatten up stolen herds in secrecy, or to hide out after a bank robbery. Robber's Roost, just west of the park, was headquarters in the 1880s and 1890s for Butch Cassidy and his Wild Bunch, and their Outlaw Trail crossed the Green River near Mineral Bottom. Few lawmen would risk following Butch and his boys into the Canyonlands. The outlaws knew the canyons and trails by heart, and the lawmen were greenhorns.

In the 1950s, uranium prospectors searched the length of every outcrop in Canyonlands for hot spots; nearly all the area's four-wheel-drive roads began as prospector's tracks. Charlie Steen's incredible Mi Vida strike east of the park touched off a boom that changed the local economy forever.

Left: Cattle herds grazed in the Canyonlands area until the park was established in 1964. Above: Major John Wesley Powell with a Paiute Indian guide.

Establishment of the Park

Canyonlands was included in the proposed Escalante National Monument, which conservationists sought in the 1930s. It would have preserved 7,000 square miles of southeastern Utah, including Glen Canyon, which has since been lost under Lake Powell. But this effort never made it to fruition, and only the isolation and limited resources of Canyonlands saved it from exploitation in the following decades.

Finally, in the early 1960s two men combined their efforts to create Canyonlands National Park. Stewart Udall, Secretary of the Interior under President John F. Kennedy, took a flight along the Colorado River to examine a proposed dam site at the confluence, looked out at the spectacle of The Needles and the Doll House, and said to himself, "My God, that's a national park down there!" Arches National Monument Superintendent Bates Wilson also recognized Canyonlands' potential. Wilson proceeded to feed Udall the information he needed in Washington, and, with the help in Congress of Utah Senator Frank Moss, they propelled Canyonlands National Park into existence in 1964.

GEOLOGY

Angel Arch.

Canyonlands National Park surrounds the confluence of the Green and Colorado rivers, the isolated focal point of the Canyonlands section of the Colorado Plateau. The park takes its name from this official geography: it is a dazzling sample of the best of the canyon country.

Deep canyons slice through high mesas; isolated buttes tower over mazes of needles and fins; natural stone arches grace side canyons; and island mountains stud the cardinal points of the horizon. Canyonlands is a bedrock landscape; rock defines the place, with only a few spare touches of soft, gentling plants.

The River and the Rocks

As at the Grand Canyon, the Colorado River reigns in this world. The river has rasped down through 300 million years' worth of rocks, and as its tributaries eat back into surrounding mesas to keep pace, the grand rock stair-steps of the canyonlands evolve.

The Colorado and Green rivers divide Canyonlands in a great Y. In the center lies Island in the Sky Mesa, isolated 2,000 feet above the two rivers with its wide ledge of White Rim Sandstone halfway between the mesa top and the rivers. East of the Colorado, The Needles and the twisting canyons of Salt Creek lie below Hatch Point Mesa and the Abajo Mountains. The Orange Cliffs rim the western Canyonlands basin—The Maze and Land of Standing Rocks.

Underneath Canyonlands lies the Paradox Formation, 300 million years old, which is exposed only in the deepest reaches of Cataract Canyon. With this oldest rock begins the stack of formations that reads like a sorcerer's chant: Paradox, Honaker Trail, Halgaito, Cutler, Cedar Mesa, Organ Rock, White Rim, Moenkopi, Chinle, Wingate, Kayenta, Navajo.

The rocks of Canyonlands span just 125 million years of the earth's history. Those of the most recent 175 million years already have been eroded off the top, and the early rocks—the first 4 billion years of earth records—still lie hidden below the Paradox. Thirty-five hundred feet of sandstones, siltstones, mudstones, shales, limestones, salt, gypsum, and jasper spread beneath the viewpoints at the tips of the high mesas in an extravaganza of sedimentary variety. A whit more diversity, and comprehension of this place might pass beyond reach.

A Few Characters in the Stratigraphic Drama

Each layer reads in several ways—cause and effect, color and texture, age and strength. At the top of the stack, the Navajo Sandstone—monarch of the plateau's cross-bedded dune-deposited sandstones—remains in a few buttes and domes on mesa tops. The mesas themselves stand on walls of Wingate Sandstone—the orange-brown "Great Wall" of Canyonlands, instantly recognizable columnar cliffs tapestried with lustrous desert varnish.

Midway through the walls of Canyonlands is a complex of rocks from the Permian period, which began about 270 million years ago and lasted for 45 million years. In the higher walls of Cataract Canyon, The Needles, The Maze, and on up to the White Rim, confusing evidence remains of the swiftly changing environments of this period. Most of these Permian rocks belong to the Cutler Formation, whose complicated interfingerings (described by one geologist as a "stratigraphic nightmare") record the sweeps of the Permian ocean across Canyonlands.

Conspicuous red and white bands layer The Needles. The red beds were deposited by Permian rivers flowing from the northeast, interfingering with near-shore sand bars of the Permian ocean and wind-blown dunes along its coast—the origins of the white Cedar Mesa Sandstone layers.

Salt: The Director

The old underlying Paradox beds have a firm grip on all that happens above them. These beds contain thousands of feet of salt, which was deposited by a deep but evaporating ocean in Pennsylvanian time. As the ocean shrank, salts—vast amounts of gypsum, "table" salt, and other "evaporites"—crystallized from its briny waters.

Under pressure, salt flows like plastic, and because it is less dense than other rocks, it tends to rise. The thousands of feet of rock above the Paradox Formation have weighed down on the salt beds for 300 million years, giving the salt ample time to push upward. The salt seeks the easiest path—where cover is thinnest—doming up the overlying rocks, usually without breaking the surface.

Such salt domes mark Canyonlands with landforms that are enigmatic to those who do not know about the Paradox salt oozing about deep underground. The Colorado River follows one such salt dome. The river's path evidently is controlled by the long crest of the fold. And salt flowing from under the Needles region toward the river has dragged with it ("rafted") the overlying layers, which have broken under this stress along faults in The Grabens and in parallel cracks (joints) in The Needles themselves.

Water: The Stage Changer

The creation of such joints is the beginning of an erosional process that often leads to the formation of natural stone works of art. Over a long period of time, the original solid block of stone—now jointed—will eventually separate into individual slabs that water can further erode into fins, spires, and needles.

And it is water that has created the Canyonlands landscape. The river carves no wider than its course; it sets the gradient—the tempo—for its tributaries, which each year cut farther back into mesas and benches. Undercut cliffs collapse in crashes of dust and stone. Flash floods tumble the debris downstream, scouring clean the canyons and widening the Canyonlands basin by a boulder's width each time a slab ruptures.

The fine details of erosion create everyone's favorite small-scale wonders. Arches emerge from sandstone as alcoves retreat; potholes scattered across mesa rims grind downward; ice expands inside a crack and wedges off a chunk of sandstone to transform a spire.

The rock landscape of Canyonlands continues to crack, crumble, and roll away down the river, toward the sea.

Opposite: View from Island in the Sky, toward Behind-the-Rocks and the distant La Sals.

At the first sweeping look from the Island in the Sky, Canyonlands seems barren of life. The weather, too, runs to extremes; San Juan Country boasts a 144° F annual temperature range—from -29° F to 115° F—one of the widest in the world. A temperature range of 50° F may occur in a single day. Grassy green is not a color that comes to mind when you picture the Canyonlands; rather, the colors are those of the rocks—red, cream, brown, orange, black.

Down in the canyons, however, there is plenty of greenery. Not the smug, profligate greens of endless mountains and meadows, but the careful, wise, singular greens of desert plants that have adapted to both severe summer heat and dryness and winter cold.

The Sometimes-Green Desert: Plant Communities

In cracks and joints on exposed slickrock grow Colorado pinyon pine and Utah juniper. Unable to survive on the 7–9 inches of precipitation that reaches the park yearly, these canny trees have gotten around the problem by growing in fissures that concentrate runoff and provide much greater effective moisture.

Other shrubs also take advantage of such cracks, with their pockets of silt and moisture, forming a rich plant community. Here small mammals reach their greatest diversity: Colorado chipmunk, rock squirrel, and several species of mice and wood rats. This woodland-shrubland also provides important resting cover for deer.

Under these trees and in open patches among the shrubs grows a unique complex of lichens, algae, moss, and fungi, which covers the ground surface like a skin disease or a carpet of lumpy black crud. This unflattering description may suit its appearance, but the importance of this "cryptobiotic" soil crust cannot be overestimated. It soaks up water, ponding runoff to encourage absorption and slow erosion. Its cyanobacteria (formerly known as blue-green algae) convert atmospheric nitrogen into a form that can be used by higher plants. But it is so fragile that light grazing or even a single footstep can destroy tens of years of growth.

Rocks in Canyonlands will not hold still long enough for soils to develop; flash floods are too busy sweeping erosional debris away to the rivers. Sandy debris does accumulate in places, and if it is uniformly shallow, blackbrush grows in vast stands. Blackbrush "perches" its roots just above the bedrock, where ground water also perches, ready for slow uptake. This humble shrub covers 1 million acres in southeastern Utah. But its small leaves, which drop in drought, and tiny yellow blossoms have not inspired poets in search of symbols or even many botanical researchers.

Where soils deeper than 18 inches cover bedrock, blackbrush scrub gives way to grassland. Galleta, needle-and-thread, Indian ricegrass, and blue grama sway in spring green and summer golds in meadows in The Needles and on top of the Island. Here flourish seed-eating animals and birds, typified by Ord's kangaroo rats and horned larks and black-throated sparrows.

These three communities cover 80 percent of the park area. Lesser plant communities include saltbush and shadscale on Chinle shales; sagebrush and four-wing saltbush on thick alluvial deposits on benches above arroyos with seasonal access to the water table; cottonwood-, willow-, and tamarisk-banked river bottoms; and hanging gardens at seeps.

During the last century, The Needles area has been heavily grazed; inaccessibility luckily softened the impact on The Maze and the Island. Overgrazing tramples the cryptobiotic soil cover, and allows exotic plants such as cheatgrass, halogeton, and Russian thistle to replace native grasses in disturbed areas. In the 1880s and 1890s, in particular, tens of thousands of cattle grazed southeastern Utah. Uranium exploration has taken its toll, too, particularly on the White Rim.

Canyons and Mesas: Challenge to Dispersal

The rivers dictate to the living world of Canyonlands, just as they rule the rockscape. They harbor unusual fish in their turbid waters: the endangered Colorado squawfish, razorback sucker, and the humpback and bonytailchubs. Their drainage system maps out the mosaic of park ecosystems. Their powerful currents and deep canyons form monumental barriers to dispersal for most terrestrial vertebrates.

Rodents account for more than one-third of all the different mammals found in Canyonlands National Park. Many of the rodents have crossed the rivers from district to district. Once across, however, their populations often remain so isolated from each other that they eventually evolve into distinct subspecies.

The environments of the canyon country appear harsh. Nonetheless, the infinite array of cracks, crannies, and ledges forms a home for a diverse group of mammals. Bats flourish. Four species of white-footed mice live within the park; three species of wood rats live in The Needles alone. Indeed, that part of the Four Corners canyon country has been called "wood-rat heaven" by one mammalogist.

Slickrock can form a significant barrier, too, when it stands vertically in Wingate walls. Recent research on isolated buttes in Canyonlands has answered some tantalizing questions about the kinds of animals that live on top of these sheer-walled mesas. A number of small mammals are capable of climbing the 400-foot cliffs to colonize these buttes. But habitat preferences make many species unlikely colonizers; they simply do not live near enough to the cliffs. Others climb well, but require moist vegetation and cover, which are absent on the ascent route. Still other mammals might be capable of climbing the cliffs, but could not succeed in the habitat on top.

The canyon mouse is the slickrock-dweller *par excellence* of Canyonlands, and it is this beautiful little animal that turns up on every isolated butte so far examined. On The Jug—a mesa in Holeman Spring Basin off the "mainland" of the much larger Island in the Sky—the canyon mouse is the only mammal on the 20-acre mesa top. Other buttes have bushy-tailed wood rats, chipmunks, and other mice species. Isolated mesa tops seem to resemble true islands; they support fewer species of both small mammals and reptiles than do mainland areas like the Island in the Sky, but they allow for more individuals of each kind.

Bighorn Sheep: Life at the Edge

Cliffs also are crucial to Canyonlands' most romantic mammal, the desert bighorn sheep. The park has the largest native desert bighorn population in the West. Sheep clamber about in broken bench lands of the White Rim, in The Needles, and (since 1982) in The Maze, where they have been reintroduced. Rams wander right up to the rim of the Island. And in dry periods, when potholes are empty, the sheep come down to the rivers for water.

Cliffs form more than mere background for the sheep—more than shelter for lambing, or range for feeding on their preferred blackbrush and galleta grass. In a park where mountain lions and bobcats roam, the cliffs are absolutely essential escape cover; in one long-term study on the White Rim, 99 percent of all bighorn spotted were within .6 km (just over .37 mile) of rough escape terrain. They carefully avoid venturing farther into open country and thus never waste their incredible cliff-climbing ability when danger threatens.

Some threats to the sheep—and the park—will not be so easily avoided. Development proposals bordering the park and destructive to its wilderness character come up over and over again. Some are outrageous enough to be killed, like the national high-level nuclear waste repository proposed on the edge of The Needles in the early 1980s. Other activities, such as aircraft overflights and oil and gas development northeast of the park, remain constant threats. One enormous potential danger sits on the banks of the Colorado just upriver from the park: a radioactive tailings pond left by the uranium mill long a mainstay of the Moab economy.

Clockwise, from top:
Fishhook cactus. Whiptail lizard. Cottonwood with catkins. Horned lark.

The ecology of Canyonlands seems simple—it is "only a desert," after all. But connections—real, if invisible —lead outward from the park to the entire lower Colorado River basin and beyond. They can snap without our knowing, even when treated with respect.

SITES, TRAILS, AND TRIPS

There are many ways of being in a canyon landscape. Drivers can travel through it—at 55 miles per hour on pavement; at 30 miles per hour on smooth dirt roads; or at a grinding, bone-jolting 5 miles per hour on barely drivable four-wheel tracks. Loiterers can perch on a high mesa and look down, or lie in a shaded crack and look up. The more adventurous can ride horseback, walk marked trails, or navigate wilderness cross-country. And boaters can travel by raft or kayak through thrilling rapids and along peaceful flat water on rivers.

Canyonlands National Park offers all these ways of seeing canyon landscapes. Sample several; each has its own rewards. And each of the three sections of the park protects unique resources; Canyonlands, in a way, is three separate parks.

Island in the Sky District

Between the Green and the Colorado rivers lies an enormous mesa that is accessible by car only across The Neck, which is not much wider than the road itself. The entrance road to the Island leaves U.S. 191 about 10 miles north of Moab. Seventeen miles in, a road to the left (east) leads to Dead Horse Point State Park, a developed viewpoint that overlooks a stunningly beautiful vista of the Colorado and its canyons, including a bend in the river called the Goose Neck.

Retrace the Dead Horse Point road to rejoin the road leading south to the Island in the Sky. Beyond The Neck, the Island road continues for 12 more miles to the tip of the mesa at Grand View Point. The flat top of the Island makes a great natural corral, with its easily fenced Neck. Native vegetation still shows the changes brought about by grazing, which ended on the Island in 1975. From the main stem, branch roads go to Green River Overlook (and campground) and Upheaval Dome. Wander anywhere on the rims of the Island to find spectacular views. But Grand View Point is the climactic overlook.

From Grand View the park falls away below, canyons and spires and rims leading to a horizon dominated at middle distance by the

Opposite: Backpack trips of up to two weeks are allowed by park permit.

TRAILS OF CANYONLANDS NATIONAL PARK*

ISLAND IN THE SKY DISTRICT

MESA ARCH TRAIL: Starts at east side of Island in the Sky; ends at Mesa Arch; .5 mile round trip; .5 hour; 80-foot ascent; through pinyon–juniper woodland to arch in sandstone; magnificent views of La Sal Mountains and below to fin known as The Washerwoman.

WHALE ROCK TRAIL: Starts at Upheaval Dome road; ends at Whale Rock; 1 mile round trip; .5 hour; 120-foot ascent; climb to top of sandstone butte with spectacular view of Upheaval Dome.

UPHEAVAL DOME TRAIL: Starts at Upheaval Dome picnic area; ends at Upheaval Dome Rim; 1 mile round trip; .5 hour; 40-foot ascent; easy walk along sandstone rim of Upheaval Dome, with views into the center of the "crater."

NEEDLES DISTRICT

CHESLER PARK TRAIL: Starts at Elephant Hill or Squaw Flat Campground; ends at Chesler Park; 5 or 9 miles round trip; 4 hours; 500-foot ascent; Chesler Park is a great meadow dotted with islands of spires and enclosed by a circular wall formed by The Needles; Joint Trail, which starts at Chesler Canyon on the far side of Elephant Hill, passes through a deep slot between two fins.

DRUID ARCH TRAIL: Starts at Elephant Hill; ends at Druid Arch; 10 miles round trip; 8 hours; 640-foot ascent; winds through the buttes of The Needles and then follows the wash of Elephant Canyon to the 200-foot arch; fine views.

CONFLUENCE OVERLOOK TRAIL: Starts at Big Spring Canyon Overlook; ends at Confluence Overlook; 10.2 miles round trip; 8 hours; 320-foot ascent; along jeep road into Big Spring Canyon, across fields and meadows, crossing Devil's Lane and Cyclone Canyon; .5 mile from end of road to rim of Colorado River's Cataract Canyon above confluence of Green and Colorado rivers; hot; carry water.

COLORADO RIVER TRAIL: Starts at Elephant Hill; ends at Colorado River at Lower Red Lake Canyon; 16 miles round trip; 2–4 days; 1,200-foot ascent; rough, difficult hike, partly on jeep roads; riverbank routes lead upriver to Confluence and down-river to rapids in Cataract Canyon, but this is not an established trail and depends on the water level; carry food and water.

PEEKABOO SPRING TRAIL: Starts at Squaw Flat Campground; ends at Peekaboo Spring; 10.8 miles round trip; 7 hours; 500-foot ascent; leads up Squaw Canyon, then crosses a pass and drops into Lost Canyon, crosses another pass and drops into Salt Creek at Peekaboo Spring; two ladders; very rough with much strenuous up-and-down hiking; carry water.

SQUAW AND LOST CANYONS TRAILS: Starts at Squaw Flat Campground; ends at Lost Canyon; 5.2 miles round trip; 4 hours; 500-foot ascent; loop variation on the Peekaboo Spring Trail; leads into upper Squaw Canyon, crosses a pass into Lost Canyon, leads down Lost Canyon, and crosses back into Squaw Canyon; one ladder; fine taste of canyon floors and slickrock cliffs; extensive views.

SQUAW AND BIG SPRING CANYONS TRAIL: Starts at Squaw Flat; ends at Big Spring Canyon; 7.5 miles round trip; 6 hours; 400-foot ascent; another loop, up most of Squaw Canyon, across a strenuous pass into Big Spring Canyon; difficult slopes on both sides of the pass, but fine views; watch for potholes.

ANGEL ARCH TRAIL: Starts at end of Salt Creek jeep road; ends at Angel Arch viewpoint; 1 mile round trip; .5 hour; 240-foot ascent; leads to the classic view of Angel Arch, with Molar Rock in foreground.

MAZE DISTRICT§

HORSESHOE CANYON TRAIL (from east): Starts at end of Horseshoe Canyon jeep road; ends at Great Gallery; 3.5 miles round trip; 3 hours; 20-foot ascent; easy walk in canyon bottom with cottonwoods, to several panels of magnificent rock art; please do not touch fragile pictographs. It is also possible to reach trail from the west on a two-wheel drive road. Information available at park.

NORTH TRAIL CANYON TRAIL: Starts at North Canyon Point turnoff on jeep road; ends at Maze Overlook; 28 miles round trip; 2 days; 1,450-foot ascent; hiker's access to The Maze; 6 miles in North Trail Canyon, then on jeep road; check with rangers for up-to-date information.

THE MAZE TRAIL: Starts at Maze Overlook; ends at Harvest Scene; 6 miles round trip; 5 hours; 640-foot ascent; drops off past the sandstone Nuts and Bolts balanced rocks, and down to the floor of The Maze; the Harvest Scene pictograph panel lies up the easternmost major canyon to the south (*not* south fork of Horse Canyon).

GOLDEN STAIRS TRAIL: Starts 1.5 miles from ranger station on Flint Trail jeep road; ends at Doll House; 22 miles round trip; 2 days; 800-foot ascent; along jeep road from mesa above The Fins, past the Standing Rocks to the rim of Cataract Canyon; hot.

PETE'S MESA TRAIL: Starts at Chimney Rock; ends at Pete's Mesa; 6 miles round trip; 5 hours; 100-foot ascent; follows narrow plateau between The Maze and Jasper Canyon; spectacular views.

CONFLUENCE OVERLOOK TRAIL: Starts at Doll House; ends at Confluence Overlook; 13 miles round trip; 10 hours; 500-foot ascent; primitive trail on slickrock behind rim of Cataract Canyon to precipitous ledge immediately above confluence of Green and Colorado rivers.

SPANISH BOTTOM TRAIL: Starts at Doll House; ends at Colorado River at Spanish Bottom; 2 miles round trip; 3.5 hours; 1,200-foot ascent; steep descent to river, with sweeping views to The Needles and along Cataract Canyon.

*An infinite variety of off-trail hiking routes exist. Some are well known, used by several parties each year, and may even be marked with rock cairns. Others have been hiked once or twice. Still others remain to be discovered. If you are interested in hiking unmarked routes off established trails, talk with park rangers and be certain that your party has the equipment and experience necessary to handle problems associated with "bushwacking," as well as potential emergencies.

§It is 65 miles from the turnoff on Utah 24 to the Maze District ranger station, and perhaps a few hours' hiking farther to the chosen trail head. It is a major commitment to hike in the Maze District, and you should not attempt it without plenty of water and a good topographical map. Dogs should not be taken into the Maze District.

SEE MAP ON PAGES **102–103.**

island mountains of the canyon country—the Abajos, the La Sals, and the Henrys. Directly below lies Monument Basin, sliced through the White Rim into the red Organ Rock Tongue of the Cutler, and packed with monoliths as high as 300 feet. Beyond, sunk deep in the labyrinth of rock, the Green and the Colorado join.

From the road, the trailless rim leads south for 1 mile to the final tip of Grand View Point, just across the gulf that separates the Island from its outlier, Junction Butte. Nowhere else can you so quickly grasp the park's formidable topography.

Mesa Arch Trail. On the east side of the Island a short trail (.5 mile round trip) leads to Mesa Arch. The trail winds through pinyon and juniper woodland, blackbrush scrub, cryptobiotic soil, and slickrock to an arch in the Navajo Sandstone that clings to the edge of the cliff. This "cliff-hanging" arch frames magnificent views eastward to the La Sal Mountains and below to the arch known as The Washerwoman.

This trail is a good place to learn to avoid the soil that the locals call "cryptos". Vibram soles—or even the gentle footfalls of sandals—crush the black soil crusts of lichen, moss, cyanobacteria, and fungi. They take decades to recover. Whenever you walk off trails in the Canyonlands, follow slickrock or sandy washes and small drainages.

Upheaval Dome Trails. Upheaval Dome is unique. It may be a sharply folded circular salt dome that has been breached by erosion, right down to its roots. Other geologists believe that a meteorite about one-third of a mile in diameter slammed into the earth about 60 million years ago to create the impact crater now eroded into Upheaval Dome. The dome is best seen from the air, but the .5-mile trail up Whale Rock gives a fair approximation of an aerial view. The central dome (or anticline) is surrounded by a ringlike recurved syncline. Eroded strata turned on end have left a Wingate cliff standing over the "crater" of soft, easily washed-away Chinle and Moenkopi. Great chunks of White Rim Sandstone lie jumbled in the center of the structure. A second short trail leads to the crater rim, on top of the Wingate.

The Needles District is filled with spires and arches about 400 feet high.

Longer hikes are possible in the Upheaval area. Circle the dome in Syncline Valley and enter the crater through Upheaval Canyon—a 4-mile walk that leads 1,200 feet below the Wingate rim overlook. From here, head down Upheaval Canyon 3 miles to the Green River—the only water available on the hike—for a glimpse of Stillwater Canyon.

The White Rim. Midway between the top of the Island and the rivers lies the broad, arid ledge of the White Rim. A moderate four-wheel-drive road circles below the Island for 100 miles through prime bighorn sheep habitat. The White Crack provides a lively hiking route below the rim, and, at Lathrop Canyon, vehicles can reach the Colorado. The White Rim road winds around Monument Basin on a creamy ledge with fine potholes and stunning views.

The Needles District

The Needles District is as rich in spires, arches, ruins, and side canyons as any place on the Colorado Plateau. Four-wheel-drive roads lead beyond the pavement, but considerable country still is reachable only on foot.

The entrance to the Needles area lies 14 miles north of Monticello on U.S. 191, and thence 38 miles on paved road down Indian Creek Canyon to Squaw Flat.

Squaw Flat is a broad grassy park surrounding Squaw Butte, in the center of the drainages that lead from Salt Creek to the Colorado. The paved road continues to Big Spring Canyon Overlook, passing by the Pothole Point Trail, a few minutes' walk on a Cedar Mesa Sandstone surface pocked with natural tanks of rain water, with superb views to The Needles and north to the Island.

The main dirt road reaches 3 miles from Squaw Flat Campground to the foot of Elephant Hill, where four-wheel-drive roads pass over the 40 percent grade on into The Grabens and foot trails start to The Needles. A rough dirt (four-wheel-drive) road heads north to Colorado River Overlook. It crosses Salt Creek at Lower Jump—a high sandstone ledge that turns into a frothy red waterfall when the creek floods—and ends just above the deeply carved confluence of Salt Creek and the Colorado. Lastly, the road into upper Salt Creek starts near Cave Spring.

Salt Creek. Salt Creek and Horse Canyon, its largest tributary, drain the eastern half of The Needles district—in an intricate, extensive canyon system that has many arches and ruins. Four-wheel-drive vehicles can maneuver far up both canyons, mostly in the sandy washes. Salt Creek does not feel much like a road. At its undrivable extremes, the sandy track can be deep and dry, or wet

The Fremont pictographs called Thirteen Faces are in Horse Canyon.

enough to be saturated—quicksand.

Without a four-wheel-drive, you must walk even the lower canyon. Either way, Angel Arch is 13 miles up Salt Creek from Cave Spring at the edge of Squaw Flat; Fortress Arch is 8.5 miles up Horse Canyon. Cowboys used Cave Spring for years; the spring and cowboy line camp, under sheltering Cedar Mesa ledges, make a short historic walk. Watch for lazuli buntings and blue grosbeaks in tamarisk along the wash.

In Horse Canyon, fine Anasazi masonry survives at Tower and Keyhole ruins. The canyon contains three impressive arches—Gothic, Castle, and Fortress—and the powerful Thirteen Faces, unusual Fremont pictographs that line a cliff in somber dignity—perhaps a single shaman's painted "audience" for his chants.

Salt Creek itself passes Peekaboo Spring, where more pictographs speak in cryptic symbols. From Peekaboo Spring, trails lead through Lost and Squaw canyons back to Squaw Flat. Cottonwoods shelter the creek; they ease from green to gold in autumn, highlighting yellow hues in the banded Cedar Mesa cliffs. Side canyons hide rock art, ruins, blooming datura, wary lizards. And at the road's end is Angel Arch!

Angel Arch is the symbol of Canyonlands, as Delicate Arch is that of Arches National Park. A .5-mile trail leads to its classic view with "Molar Rock" in the foreground. A scramble up to the base of the arch itself is crucial to comprehending its size.

Beyond Angel Arch Campground, the upper Salt Creek hiking

An autumn storm over the Colorado River from Dead Horse Point.

route reaches 13.5 miles from the end of the four-wheel-drive road past the park boundary to the mesa that rims its headwall. This walk—longest established hike in the district—leads through miles of empty, eventful wilderness, to arches, the remarkable pictograph of the All-American Man (a unique red, white, and blue Fremont shield figure), and the abandoned cabin of unsociable Claude Kirk, who lived for years in one of the canyon country's most isolated spots.

Lavender and Davis Canyons. The park protects the headwaters of Lavender and Davis canyons, which drain northeastward to Indian Creek. The canyons can be reached on foot along their washes from the paved road east of the park. (The park also issues limited numbers of four-wheel-drive permits for Lavender Canyon.) Both resemble Salt Creek in intricacy and rich resources, including many arches and ruins. Lavender Canyon is named for author David Lavender's Colorado ranching family. Lavender's *One Man's West* tells of his experiences as a cowboy in the days of Al Scorup's cattle empire in this place he describes as "wild, weird sandrock."

The Needles. To the west of Salt Creek are The Needles proper. Salt flowing in the Paradox created tensions that cracked this section of the Cedar Mesa in a checkerboard of joints. Water worked on the cracks to make The Needles a city of spires, with round bristling barricades surrounding grassy parks and tortuous canyons.

A network of trails extends into The Needles, with connections to Salt Creek, Squaw Flat, and The Grabens. Most popular are routes from Elephant Hill to Chesler Park (3 miles) and Druid Arch (5.4 miles one way), and the 1-mile slot of the Joint Trail, which provides access to Chesler Park from four-wheel-drive roads in The Grabens. Needles ring the meadows of Chesler Park.

The trail to Druid Arch runs for several miles in Elephant Canyon, where the creek has cut a narrow channel beneath the Cedar Mesa into the Elephant Canyon Formation. This walk feels like a secret passage running beneath a great city; it remains soothingly shaded in early morning, while glare from scorching slickrock hovers just above the inner channel. Druid Arch is monumental—a towering dolmen.

The Grabens. Salt solution and flowage toward the Colorado has created its most dramatic effects just west of The Needles. The brittle sandstone, yanked along by moving salt, released stress along a series of very recent faults (starting perhaps 500,000 years ago). Blocks of the earth's crust that have dropped down between faults are called grabens, and The Grabens complex includes canyons 300 feet deep that vary in width from 7 feet to nearly 2,000 feet.

The dry valleys of The Grabens contain well-developed four-wheel-drive roads, and one important hiking route extends 5 miles down Lower Red Lake Canyon to the Colorado River across from Spanish Bottom.

The Maze District

The journey to The Maze is still adventurous, and it will remain so; the National Park Service plans to manage this district to preserve its remote, primitive character. The Green and Colorado canyons isolate The Maze from other districts, and the roundabout approach is long. From Utah 24, 40 miles south of Green River, take a sandy track for 46 miles to Hans Flat Ranger Station on the summit of the Orange Cliffs.

The land gradually rises as you drive in across the treeless San Rafael Desert, past the dunes and pastures of Robber's Roost—little changed since Butch Cassidy made himself comfortable there. Kit foxes may loom up in headlights at night. Drifting sand and blowing snow in winter may stop passenger cars. But traffic will not be a problem.

Three branch roads lead from the ranger station—one to the head of the Flint Trail (definitely the end of two-wheel drive), the second out to Cleopatra's Chair and Panorama Point (four-wheel drive), and the third (four-wheel-drive) north along The Spur, rounding the head of big, dry Millard Canyon, to Horseshoe Canyon's 2-mile trail.

Horseshoe Canyon. At Horseshoe, Barrier Creek has cut a beautiful curving Cedar Mesa canyon with smooth desert-varnished walls. Pictographs decorate these faces. Included among them is the 100-foot Great Gallery of ghost figures, which is unsurpassed by any other North American rock art. Archeologists as well as park visitors fall under the spell of these hollow-eyed, life-size figures. Scholars believe that the painters of these Barrier Canyon-style figures were archaic people, and they may be 2,000 or more years old.

Under the Ledge. Fourteen miles past Hans Flat, switchbacks of the Flint Trail four-wheel-drive road plunge over the rim of the Orange Cliffs. After 3 slow miles, it meets the road that comes up 40 miles from Hite along the base of the Orange Cliffs. A back track along this road goes to the branch leading out past Ernie's Country and the Land of Standing Rocks toward the Doll House. The Standing Rocks rise as a series of remnant monuments of red Organ Rock; some are capped with White Rim Sandstone, and others are uncapped and doomed soon to disintegration: The Wall, Lizard Rock, The Plug, Standing Rock. From Chimney Rock, a 3-mile trail leads north to Pete's Mesa, in the center of the Maze canyon system.

Turn left at the foot of the Flint Trail, and you are headed for Maze Overlook. The road crosses Elaterite Basin—named for the petroleum resin that seeps from the White Rim—winds around the high, spiky Wingate tower of Elaterite Butte and along the rim of Horse Canyon, and finally ends at the brink of The Maze—some 80 miles from pavement and 170 miles by road from park headquarters in Moab, though just 34 linear miles for a raven or an eagle.

The Maze. The view down into The Maze makes the long, tantalizing drive worthwhile. Even for those who arrive by foot, walking the 14-mile North Trail Canyon, The Maze is the climax of the journey. Its canyons are a labyrinth in large scale. A 2.5-mile trail starts at the overlook, passes through the White Rim pillars known as the Nuts and Bolts, and reaches into The Maze as far as the Harvest Scene, a phenomenal Barrier Canyon-style pictograph panel.

In this painting, an eyeless being gracefully offers up puffs of Indian rice grass. Rabbits run down its arms, while birds fly around its crowned head. Hunchbacked attendants carry seedbeaters and sickles; their humpbacked profile may be an abstraction of conical burden baskets. Ricegrass was a major resource for the Anasazi and Fremont. In small hunting parties, they made seasonal trips to the canyons and uplands from home bases on farmable river bottom to search for wild game, wild grass to harvest, and jasper for spear points.

The Doll House Area. The Cedar Mesa Sandstone forms the walls of all the inner canyons of The Maze—Jasper, Shot, Water, The Fins, and The Maze itself. In *Desert Solitarie,* Edward Abbey likens its banded spires to "melted . . . Neapolitan ice cream." The same formation stands in pinnacles above Cataract Canyon at the Doll House, and shelters little Surprise Valley perched on the brink of the river gorge.

Semideveloped trails circle through the mischievous spires of the Doll House. And a primitive route leads to a spectacular overlook of the confluence. Unmarked hiking routes traverse all these Cedar Mesa canyons; hikers must pay attention to detail to avoid losing their way. Park rangers can suggest possible backpacking trips.

Lastly, a good trail leads from the Doll House down to Spanish Bottom on the Colorado, forming a link between bench lands and rivers.

The park's canyons are composed of sandstone, shale, siltstones, mudstones, limestones, salt, gypsum, and jasper.

The Rivers

Anyone who rides the white water of Cataract Canyon will understand the experience recorded by Fred Dellenbaugh, a member of Powell's 1871 expedition. When the party rowed out onto the Colorado at the Confluence, Dellenbaugh wrote of feeling "at last on the back of the Dragon" itself.

The run down the Green from the town of Green River takes boaters through 120 miles of gliding canyon walls, through Labyrinth and Stillwater canyons, to the Confluence. The Colorado runs for 47 miles from Potash to the Confluence; starting at Moab adds 17 river miles. Some prefer these quiet reaches to the rapids of Cataract.

Nothing so merges one's being with the slowness and silence of the Canyonlands as floating with the lazy current, basking in the sun, surprising deer, beaver, and fox on the banks, and spotting Anasazi granaries mortared in cracks like wasp nests. Great blue herons flap heavily downstream from sand bar to sand bar, keeping a precise distance ahead until they tire of the disturbance and fly up to the rim of the inner canyon to let boaters pass—settling gracefully into stillness, a pose like a shrine or a lookout, waiting.

Both the Green and the Colorado rivers above the Confluence meander in gentle grades—flat waters that are navigable by rafts, canoes, and power boats captained by amateurs. But below the Confluence, the Colorado runs in formations whose gradient dips southward. The river steepens as it flows *with* the dip of the rocks, and bears almost straight through Cataract Canyon. Its average drop of 8 feet per mile exceeds that of the Grand Canyon.

To run Cataract requires skilled boaters, professional equipment, and a permit from the park. At high water, the rapids above Lake Powell remain awesome. The biggest are The Big Drops, where the river drops 30 feet in 1 mile. When side creeks are flooding, the river turns to chocolate and red, roiling with debris and extra power. The red dust gives the water a unique smell that is not instantly recognizable. Even immersion in water cannot take away its character.

This flooding Canyonlands river has an aroma like its paradoxical nature. It smells like the land it creates and destroys, like red rock baking in the sun. Its red waters smell like dryness.

Opposite: Gnarled, shaggy bark of Utah juniper. In the distance, the Green River.

CAPITOL REEF
NATIONAL PARK

Sulphur Creek has several small waterfalls and the oldest exposed rock in the park.

CAPITOL REEF NATIONAL PARK
TORREY, UTAH 84775
TEL.: (801) 425-3791

HIGHLIGHTS: Capitol Gorge • Cathedral Valley • Fruita • Waterpocket Fold • Muley Twist Canyon • Wingate Cliff • Navajo Domes • South Desert • Thousand Lake Mountain • Strike Valley Overlook • Hartnet Desert • Grand Wash

ACCESS: From east or west, take Utah 24. From south and Bryce Canyon, take Utah 12.

HOURS: Daily, year-round; Visitor Center, 8 A.M.–4:30 P.M.; from May to October to 7 p.m. Closed Christmas day.

FEES: At entrance and for camping.

PARKING: At Visitor Center, picnic areas, scenic pullouts.

GAS, FOOD: At Hanksville, Torrey, Bicknell, Loa.

LODGING: At Hanksville, Torrey, Bicknell, Loa.

VISITOR CENTER: Off Utah 24; slide show and book sales.

MUSEUM: Exhibits in Visitor Center.

PETS: Permitted on leash, except on trails and in backcountry.

PICNICKING: At 5 sites.

HIKING: Designated trails in headquarters area; routes in backcountry. Carry water.

BACKPACKING: With permit. Carry water.

CAMPGROUNDS: 3 locations; first-come basis; Fruita Campground, 70 sites; Cedar Mesa primitive, 5 sites; Cathedral Valley primitive, 5 sites. No showers.

TOURS: In summer. In English only.

OTHER ACTIVITIES: Evening programs daily, April to October.

FACILITIES FOR DISABLED: For mobility impaired, access to Visitor Center, restrooms, part of Fremont River Trail. For hearing impaired, printed texts available. For visually impaired, some exhibits have touch access; cassettes available.

For additional information, see map on pages 134–135 and Sites, Trails, and Trips on pages 148–160.

THERE IS NO MISTAKING CAPITOL REEF. ON any approach to the park, its great cliffs loom in a line 100 miles long, cleaving south-central Utah in two. The pencil-shaped park outlines these cliffs in a long, narrow 270,000-acre strip that runs from Thousand Lake Mountain almost to the Colorado River; the cliffs, in turn, outline a major feature of the earth's surface: the Waterpocket Fold. Here, the flat rock layers of the Colorado Plateau were uplifted unevenly, creating a giant stair-step. Overlying formations did not break, but drooped over the step in a great S-curved bend. Erosion has exposed the upswept layers in a barrier line of sandstone cliffs that pioneer travelers likened to an ocean "reef."

A single paved road crosses the Reef along the Fremont River canyon; paved and gravel/dirt roads parallel either side of the Fold; and trails and hiking routes lead to potholes, natural arches and bridges, overlooks, and tortuous narrows. At the north end of the park, Cathedral Valley spreads below the Fold, its isolated temples rising above harsh desert flats. Irrigated orchards, the remnant of the old Mormon village of Fruita, surround park headquarters. This green oasis—in a vast sea of aridity—is as much a symbol of the park as are the domes atop the Fold.

Away from the Fremont River and the few perennial creeks, pinyon and juniper woodland and desert shrubs scatter across slick-

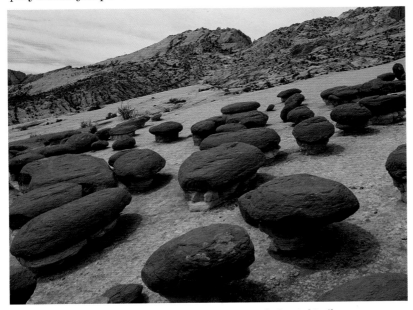

The Hamburger Rocks, in a a remote area, are not on a designated trail.

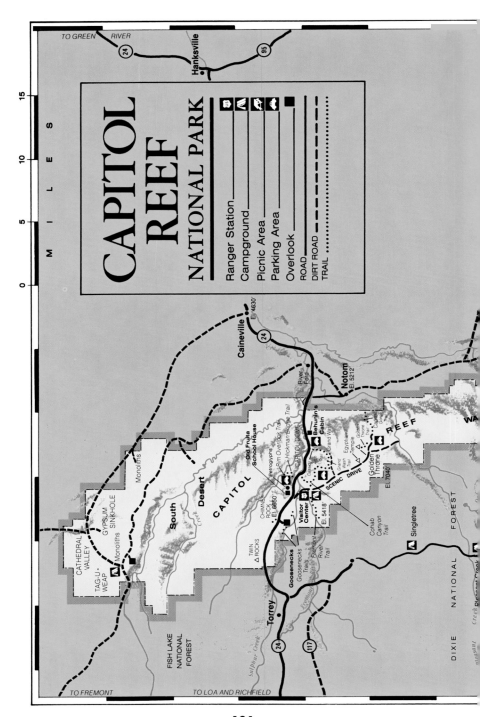

CAPITOL
REEF
NATIONAL PARK

Ranger Station
Campground
Picnic Area
Parking Area
Overlook
ROAD
DIRT ROAD
TRAIL

M I L E S
0   5   10   15

TO GREEN RIVER
24
Hanksville
95

Caineville
24
El. 4630'
Notom
El. 5212'
River Ford
CAPITOL REEF
Old Fruita School House
Petroglyphs
Behunin's Cabin
Hickman Bridge Trail
Rim Overlook Trail
CAPITOL DOME
Grand Wash
Egyptian Temple
Grand Wash Trail
Golden Throne Trail
Golden Throne
El. 7040'
SCENIC DRIVE
CHIMNEY ROCK El. 6050'
Visitor Center El. 5418'
Cohab Canyon Trail
WA
REEF
South Desert
CAPITOL
Sulphur Creek
Oak Creek
Monoliths
CATHEDRAL VALLEY
GYPSUM SINKHOLE
Monoliths
TAG-U-WEAP
TWIN ROCKS
Goosenecks
Goosenecks Trails
Fremont River Trail
Torrey
24
117
Singletree
DIXIE   NATIONAL   FOREST
FISH LAKE NATIONAL FOREST
Sailpaw Creek
Pleasant Creek
TO FREMONT
TO LOA AND RICHFIELD

VICINITY MAP

UTAH TO 276

TO BULLFROG MARINA

Hanksville
95
276

Caineville
24
CAPITOL
REEF
NAT'L PARK

Fremont
Torrey
Grover
Boulder
12

Greenwich
62
DIXIE
NATIONAL
FOREST
Escalante

INSET SCALE

0   10   20
M I L E S

BIG THOMSON MESA

Hall
Divide
El. 4201'

TARANTULA
MESA

SWAP MESA

The Post

Red Slide

Brimhall
Natural
Bridge

El. 4635'
Muley Tanks

MULEY   TWIST   CANYON

Halls   Creek

Arches   El. 5163'

WAGON
BOX
MESA

BITTER
CREEK
DIVIDE
El. 5680'

El. 7270'

FOLD

ROAD

...KET

BENCH

CEDAR
MESA
El. 6132'

CIRCLE
CLIFFS

BURR   TRAIL

Steep   Creek

Deer   Creek

Anasazi State Park
Boulder

Boulder   Creek

Wash

Harris

Calf Creek
Recreation
Area

12

TO BRYCE CANYON NAT'L PARK

rock and sand. Animals of the high desert live here in abundance, although the only vertebrates that risk the heat of daytime are ground squirrels, lizards, and birds. The rest of the life of Capitol Reef waits for cool nighttime, secreted by day in shade or burrows. It is this sense of hiding—of latent possibility—that gives Capitol Reef much of its appeal: the rocks hide the real life of the park; the blank wall of the Fold opens into side canyons lush with hanging gardens; the fiercely barren badlands give rise to delicate wildflowers; a sandy wash transforms into a raging river in flood. With a delight in surprise, Capitol Reef yields up endless wonders.

HISTORY

The Waterpocket Fold is a paradox; it stands as an implacable barricade to travel, yet the few canyons that do pierce it funnel travelers across south-central Utah right into its heart. On either side of the passageways, the Fold runs on for miles, an inhospitable humpback of golden sandstone. The history of Capitol Reef, then, is the history of its canyons.

The Fremont: A River and a Culture

First to follow these drainages through the cliffs were members of a simple Desert Culture, the earliest people in the Southwest. Ten thousand years later, the Fremont people came to the rivers and creeks of Capitol Reef and dominated Utah for 600 years. They first were recognized and named as a result of research along the Fremont River at Capitol Reef in 1931.

Fremont farmers lived in pit-houses on hills above their fields, and they hunted and gathered intensively to supplement their crops. Their strain of maize was unique—extremely resistant to drought and climatic extremes, and able to flourish in a short growing season. The Fremont made no elegant stone houses, as did their Anasazi neighbors. But they left behind other evidence of their sophisticated culture: ornately decorated figurines, and on canyon walls remarkable paintings (pictographs) and carvings (petroglyphs) of magnetic spiritual power.

Human figures dominate the Fremont galleries—broad-shouldered beings resplendent in headdresses, necklaces, earrings, sashes, and shields. Animals, particularly bighorn sheep, surround them. It will never be known for certain just what the Fremont artists meant to communicate, but their messages are more than an undeciphered code—they are art.

The Fremont abandoned their farmsteads by A.D. 1300, when climatic changes destroyed their crops, thus pushing them past the

The members of the Wild Bunch who hid out in the park in the 1890s are identified by number in this photograph: 1. Robert LeRoy Parker (Butch Cassidy); 2. Harvey Logan; 3. Ben Kilpatrick; 4. Bill Carver; 5. Harry Longabaugh (Sundance Kid).

boundary of possibility in a land given to the impossible. Their destination remains a mystery, but Southern Paiutes newly arrived on the Colorado Plateau may have begun to compete with the Fremont for native plant harvests. Only the Southern Paiutes were living in the area when the first whites arrived several centuries later—a few families hunting through Capitol Reef in winter, summering at Fish Lake, and demonstrating an incredible ability to survive on slim resources.

Explorers Off the Beaten Track

Capitol Reef lay off the trappers' and traders' beaten trails, so there is no definite evidence of explorers having passed through the Fold before 1866. In that year, a troop of Mormon militia chased cattle-rustling Paiutes down the Fremont River. Five years later, two prospectors left the first signatures in the "pioneer register" on the walls of Capitol Gorge, a corridor within the Fold.

The first real exploration began when John Wesley Powell's men turned their attention this way in their great survey of the Colorado Plateau. In 1872, Almon H. Thompson, Powell's chief topographer, worked down from the Aquarius Plateau and crossed the Fold by way of Pleasant Creek. The Powell Survey also named the Fremont River for John Charles Fremont, who had struggled across its headwaters, which lie west of the park, in the winter of 1853.

The Mormon Frontier

As the Latter-Day Saints population burgeoned, Brigham Young sent his people in search of new land. By 1880, the Mormon frontier reached down the Fremont River to Capitol Reef. In the 1880s, pioneers moving into southeastern Utah left Escalante and navigated the Waterpocket Fold via the "road" through Muley Twist Canyon, which had been pioneered by Charles Hall, who operated a ferry at Hall's Crossing. In 1884, Elijah Cutler Behunin took the first wagon through Capitol Gorge; this spectacular narrows served as the main road across south-central Utah until 1962, when the paved Fremont River Highway was completed.

Fremont bottom land provided good grazing land and irrigable farmland, and the protected valleys at the base of the Fold were as mild at hothouses. At the junction of the Fremont River and Sulphur Creek, a few families established the village of Fruita. For the next eighty years, they sold peaches, cherries, apples, and apricots to settlers upriver and to travelers headed east from the High Plateaus. Besides selling produce, the little town supplied prospectors dashing for the San Juan River in the gold rush of the 1890s, cowboys trailing cattle down from the plateaus to winter range in the canyons, and Butch Cassidy and his Wild Bunch riding for their hideout at Robber's Roost. Later came moonshiners, anthropologists, tourists, and uranium prospectors. The last combed the Fold in the 1950s, widening many old trails to jeep roads, including the Burr Trail—the only road across the southern Fold.

Establishment of the Park

In the 1920s, local people led by Joseph Hickman and Ephraim Pectol began to press for the establishment of a national monument to promote tourism and to preserve the spectacular country. In 1937, their efforts were rewarded. The last residents of Fruita moved away in the 1960s, although their orchards remain. In 1971, the whole length of the Waterpocket Fold was added to the small original monument to create Capitol Reef National Park.

Aerial view of Hall's Creek Narrows.

More than those of any other national park in the region except Grand Canyon, the boundaries of Capitol Reef follow the outline of its major geographic feature. A look at a relief map of the Colorado Plateau reveals a striking line of cliffs in south-central Utah. Running for about 100 miles, these cliffs trace the structure of the earth that Capitol Reef National Park preserves—the Waterpocket Fold.

The Waterpocket Fold: Creation

The Fold is a great step in the rocks of the plateau: a single, sideways, S-shaped bend that links flat-lying rocks at two levels. The Fold owes its existence to tremendous pressures that were generated in the West as the Rockies were formed some 60 million years ago. Over a span of 10 million years, regional uplift associated with this mountain building also raised the Colorado Plateau, but not without side effects. A wrinkle or three developed in the surface of the rising plateau in Utah, well west of the Rockies themselves.

One such blemish in the flat rock stack took the form of a sharp upsweep in more than a dozen layers, rolling up and over from east to west in the arching stone of the Waterpocket Fold. Layers below were uplifted at different rates, and the layers above gradually "drooped" over the step between the two buried blocks.

Almost all the rock formations that were contorted by the Fold date to the Mesozoic era (230 to 65 million years ago), the Age of Dinosaurs. Later sediments buried the Fold with flat-lying formations, but this even-keeled plain could not survive when regional uplift of the Colorado Plateau really hit its stride.

Uplift and Erosion: The Great Race

In the last 10 million years, the Colorado Plateau has been lifted 1 mile above its neighboring landscapes. As it rose—ever so slowly—the unavoidable forces of erosion whittled and whirred at it: rasping out canyons, whisking rock debris down rivers, slicing away whole formations from the land.

Uplift raised some chunks of the earth's crust higher than others; just west of Capitol Reef are the 11,000-foot-high plateaus of Boulder Mountain and Thousand Lake Mountain. Lava caps these high mesas; as ice-age glaciers on their summits melted, chunks of the plateaus' lava flows tumbled down the flooding rivers to come to rest at Capitol Reef as deposits of black lava boulders.

Younger rocks that were stripped from the Fold left the great flexure in the earth exposed to winter ice and summer storms, to the persistent power of flooding streams and sandstone-loosening seeps. Because soft rocks erode more quickly than hard ones, the tough sandstones of the Fold began to stand higher and higher above rapidly eroding shale valleys on either side. On the west, the steepest face of the Fold forms a barrier "reef" between Torrey and Pleasant Creek that gives the park its name. On the east, the Fold plunges into the earth in stone humpbacks that form what the Paiutes called a "Sleeping Rainbow."

A Vocabulary of Rocks

The rocks that warped in the Waterpocket Fold already were ancient—records of Permian rivers, Triassic mud flats, Jurassic deserts, and Cretaceous seas. Sandstones of the Glen Canyon Group make up the great cliffs of the Fold: Wingate, Kayenta, and Navajo. The Wingate face of the reef is unmistakable—fluted red walls that wind from Thousand Lake Mountain southward along the park's Scenic Drive, a palette for ever-changing light and shadow. Above inconspicuous Kayenta Formation ledges lie the domes and thrones of Navajo Sandstone—massive, cross-bedded, and dune-deposited like the Wingate, but creamy and golden in hue. The Navajo erodes grain by grain, unlike the Wingate, whose undercut blocks fall free to create vertical cliffs. Navajo domes crown the reef; one that resembles the United States Capitol gives the reef its name.

Above and below these cliff-formers, every formation has its distinctions. Moenkopi shales along the Scenic Drive support precariously balanced Shinarump Conglomerate boulders from the overlying Chinle Formation. Moenkopi slabs show ripple marks that were formed in tidal shallows and the fin marks of primitive amphibians that swam in early Triassic seas. The clays of the much younger multihued Morrison and gray Mancos east of the Fold erode into the intricate mazes of drainages that make for truly "bad" badlands.

And along the north end of the park, 500-foot cathedrals of soft Entrada Sandstone grace the dry valleys of South Desert and Cathedral Valley. These monoliths stand in broad flats that are completely different from any other park landscape.

Opposite: Splintered battlements of the 650-foot Castle make it a prominent landmark.

The word *canyon* may owe its origin to a medieval Spanish word for "street." Passages that wind through the Waterpocket Fold certainly fit this meaning; their rocky pavement is used by creatures seeking water, food, and migration routes. Along such streets are alcoves and cracks, burrows and crannies—"houses" in the cliffs.

Canyon Streets and Pothole Wells

Along the Fremont River "street," a permanent stream waters lush banks of cottonwood, willow, and tamarisk, irrigates historic orchards, and creates an oasis used by such diverse creatures as mule deer, yellow warblers, leopard frogs, and beaver. Elsewhere in the park, year-round moisture nourishes living communities along Pleasant Creek, Oak Creek, and Lower Hall's Creek.

The Fold owes its name to another water source: potholes that collect rain water in natural tanks, or "waterpockets." Potholes nourish a finely tuned community of organisms that are adapted to long dry spells. Adult toads wait out the time encased in a protective "bivouac sack" of mucus and burrowed deep beneath the dried mud crust. Gnat larvae can lose 92 percent of their body weight and still swarm into activity when water comes. Fairy and tadpole shrimp eggs stay viable for twenty-five years in pothole dust, waiting for rain with a patience that approaches that of the tough seeds of desert annual wildflowers.

Mature pinyon pines, though often gnarled and twisted by age and the elements, may survive for 200 years; some trees have lived as long as 500 years.

Usually, they need not wait quite that long. Along most of its length, Capitol Reef gets a bit more than 7 inches of rain yearly. Summer thundershowers make August the wettest month. Winter brings about 30 inches of snow, which does not often take long to melt.

Plants on the Fold

At its north end, the Waterpocket Fold laps onto the flanks of Thousand Lake Mountain. There the park reaches an elevation of 8,800 feet and includes ponderosa pine forest and perhaps as many as 100 montane plant species found nowhere else in the park.

A cross section of the Fold nearly anywhere else along its length would map a standard sequence of plant communities. If one follows such a course across Upper Hall's Creek, south of Bitter Creek Divide, the real force behind the diverse life of Capitol Reef will be discovered: the variety of its rocks.

Start at the rim of Tarantula Mesa to the east. Its Mancos Shale is nutrient poor, its clays miserly about freeing water for uptake by plants. Only saltbush, shadscale, and galleta grass grow on the shales. Alluvium that once covered some of the Mancos supported an Indian rice grass and galleta grassland; but a century of grazing has weakened the native plants, and exotics such as cheatgrass and Russian thistle now flourish.

Just east of Notom Road, sage and rabbitbrush dominate on the Dakota Sandstone hogback (the Oyster Shell Reef, named for its phenomenally abundant fossil shells). To the west comes the Morrison, whose purple clays are nearly barren, but whose sandstones provide a fissure-ridden home for Colorado pinyon pine and Utah juniper, along with a number of larger shrubs such as cliffrose and buffalo berry. Here also grow astragalus and prince's plume, which tolerate—and concentrate—poisonous selenium from the uranium ores of the Morrison. Prospectors sometimes use these plants to guide them to possible bodies of ore.

Summerville sands support grassland with scattered four-wing saltbush; deeper sand eroded from the Entrada is dominated by Mormon tea, with old-man sage and grasses. A wash cut in alluvium allows plants seasonal access to the water table; Fremont cottonwood, rabbitbrush, big sagebrush, greasewood, Gambel oak, and tamarisk flourish until they are uprooted by a powerful flash flood.

As the Carmel Formation rises onto the Reef, pinyon and juniper woodland begins, and dominates through the breadth of the great slickrock bald of the Fold. Associated shrubs change with each succeeding formation: Navajo, Kayenta, Wingate. And in the center of the Fold, where Muley Twist Canyon cuts deeply into tilted rocks, shrubs that characterize open side canyons join the two conifers: single-leaf ash, squawbush, serviceberry, Apache plume, cliffrose, and Fremont barberry. The overpoweringly fragrant blossoms of the last two scent the breezes of side canyons with sweet perfume.

Beyond the Fold to the west lies another inhospitable layer of shale—the Chinle—and finally comes the ledgy Moenkopi, which at this 7,000-foot elevation supports pinyon and juniper.

At the extreme southern end of the park, where Hall's Creek Gorge drops to 3,875 feet, blackbrush forms pure stands as far north as the Burr Trail. Hall's Creek side canyons have widely diverse plant communities, particularly at seeps. Isolated from other pockets of moisture at each wet alcove, a miniature jungle grows, an elfin paradise of orchids, monkey flowers, columbines, and maidenhair fern.

Animal Voices

Through these environments wanders the wildlife of Capitol Reef. Some animals range widely, particularly predators and scavengers such as gopher snakes, bobcats, gray fox, ravens, golden eagles, and cougars.

Most Capitol Reef residents, however, prefer to remain in specific plant communities. Kangaroo rats and badgers burrow in sand under desert shrubs; pinyon jays chorus from a pinyon grove as they gather pine nuts; and canyon tree frogs stay close to potholes high on the Fold.

One mammal thoroughly tuned to the canyons is the ringtail. This slim, long-tailed relative of the raccoon hunts rodents at night from lairs in cliffs not far from water. Ringtails are agile, capable of chimneying between walls, ricocheting off cliffs, and performing handstands to reverse direction on a narrow ledge—all useful maneuvers when hunting wood rats through narrowing crevices.

The endangered Utah prairie dog has been reintroduced at the far northern end of the park. Poisoning, hunting, and habitat destruction almost wiped out this sociable mammal, but with protected colonies such as the one in the park, its prospects are improving.

As we have chosen a future for the prairie dog, we must choose a future for Capitol Reef. Coal seams in Swap Mesa, directly across from viewpoints along the Burr Trail, would, if developed, put a huge strip mine right up against the park boundary. We can listen to coal-company executives and politicians, on the one hand, or to ecologists, archeologists, and hikers, on the other. But the most vital voices are the gilt-edged call of a canyon wren, the cackle of a yellow-breasted chat, and the dry rattle of a midget faded rattlesnake. Our most trustworthy guidance lies within the enigmatic silence of flood-scoured slickrock deep in the Waterpocket Fold.

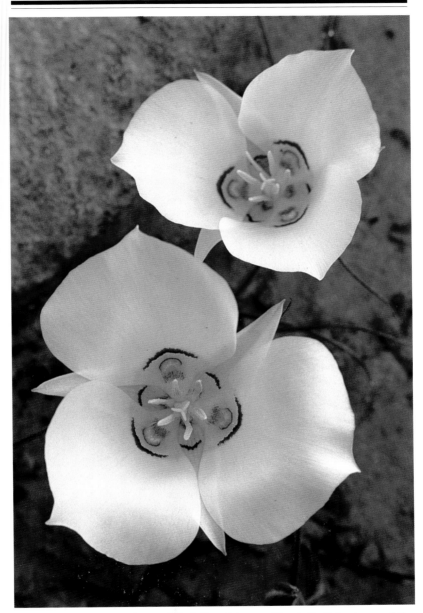

The sego lily is the state flower of Utah. Its petals resemble a butterfly's wings, and the plant has a thick underground stem that looks like a bulb. Early Mormon pioneers cooked and ate the stems.

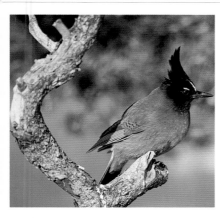

Top left: Long claws, sharp teeth, and a ferocious temper make the badger a formidable foe.

Top center: Prairie dogs' deep burrows insulate them from heat and cold.

Top right: The Steller's jay is the only jay west of the Rockies that is identifiable by its crest.

Below: The mule deer's best defense is its remarkable speed.

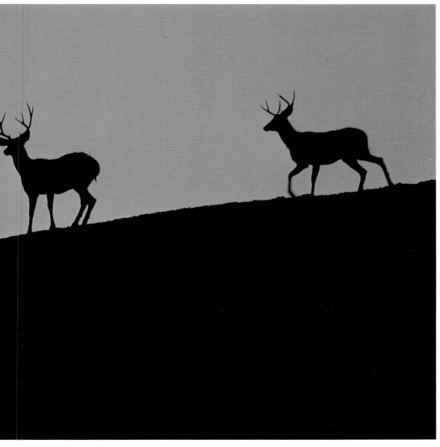

First impressions and strongest memories? For most visitors it is the orchards of Capitol Reef whose image lingers. In this land of little water, the irrigated oasis of the old town of Fruita is a green treasure not soon forgotten—especially if hand-picked tree-ripened apricots, pears, cherries, peaches, or apples sweetly cement the memory.

Little remains of the village: a house or two; lime kilns; in the campground, the old Pendleton barn built around 1905; and the Fruita schoolhouse which dates to about 1896. As late as 1924, Fruita residents used the schoolhouse for dances, town meetings, elections, celebrations, and Sunday-school classes. But the population of Fruita schoolchildren began to dwindle, and 1941 saw the last class.

Fremont River Trails

Fremont River Trail. Surrounded by orchards, the campground is situated on the bank of the Fremont River at about 5,400 feet. Wander upstream through the fruit trees, and you will find yourself on the trail to the Fremont overlook. After an easy .75 mile, the trail climbs about 800 feet in .5 mile to a point high on Miner's Mountain. Views are expansive over Fruita and along the Reef.

Cohab Canyon Trail. Just across the road from the campground, a trail leads up .25 mile of switchbacks into Cohab Canyon. This delightful little canyon cut in Wingate cliffs forms an ideal introduction to slickrock in the Reef. Slots lead off into hidden grottoes; erosion detail is infinitely various. The canyon owes its name to legends that claim its use by Mormon polygamists (cohabitationists) hiding from federal marshals. Walk 1.75 miles more through the Reef to arrive at the river across the highway from the Hickman Bridge parking area.

Hickman Bridge Trail. The 1-mile walk to Hickman Bridge provides another fine sampling of park landscapes. Small canyons lead up to a massive 133-foot natural bridge that frames Capitol Dome and the distant Henry Mountains. Black lava boulders—glacial outwash from Boulder Mountain—perch on slickrock below the great Navajo domes. Rice-grass puffs vibrate in winds that carry the scent of pinyon pitch and honeylike barberry blossoms.

Opposite: Sandstone rims, resembling reefs, tower over the Scenic Drive.

TRAILS OF CAPITOL REEF NATIONAL PARK*

FREMONT RIVER TRAIL: Starts at campground; ends at Fremont Overlook on Miner's Mountain; 2.5 miles round trip; 1.5 hours; 770-foot ascent; first .75 mile very easy through orchards along river; then steep, strenuous climb to over-look of Fremont River canyon and Fruita valley below sheer cliffs of the Reef.

GRAND WASH TRAIL: Starts at Grand Wash parking area; ends at Utah 24; 4.5 miles round trip; 3 hours; 100-foot ascent; mostly level along wash bottom; in the Narrows, walls rise 500 feet above 16-foot-wide canyon; usually hiked to Narrows.

CASSIDY ARCH TRAIL: Starts at Grand Wash parking area; ends at Cassidy Arch; 3.5 miles round trip; 3 hours; 900-foot ascent; steep climb from floor of Grand Wash to high cliffs, ending in sandstone slickrock above and behind the arch.

FRYING PAN TRAIL: Starts at 1-mile mark on Cohab Canyon Trail; ends at 1-mile mark on Cassidy Arch Trail above Grand Wash; 3 miles one way; 1.5 hours; 600-foot ascent; usually hiked as connection between Cohab and Cassidy Arch trails; many ups and downs over slickrock and canyons.

GOOSENECKS TRAIL: Starts at Goosenecks Overlook; ends at Sulphur Creek Rim; .5 mile round trip; .5 hour; 30-foot ascent; views of Goosenecks of Sulphur Creek Canyon; panoramas of Waterpocket Fold and Henry Mountains; intri-cate erosion in Moenkopi Formation beside trail.

SUNSET POINT TRAIL: Starts and ends at Goosenecks parking area; .7 mile round trip; provides panoramic views of cliffs and domes, with dramatic light-ing at day's end.

CHIMNEY ROCK TRAIL: Starts and ends at Utah 24; 3.5 miles round trip; 2.5 hours; 540-foot ascent; strenuous climb up switchbacks and moderate hike on upper loop; views of Chimney Rock from below and above and panoramas of surrounding area.

HICKMAN BRIDGE TRAIL: Starts at Utah 24; ends at Hickman Bridge; 2 miles round trip; 1.5 hours; 380-foot ascent; nature trail through small canyon and under 133-foot Hickman Natural Bridge; Indian ruins and fine views of huge sandstone domes; self-guiding.

RIM OVERLOOK TRAIL: Starts at Hickman Bridge parking area; ends at Rim Overlook; 4.5 miles round trip; 4 hours; 1,100-foot ascent; strenuous climb to top of cliffs with spectacular views over orchards of old Fruita to the face of the Waterpocket Fold. Navajo Knobs route continues from overlook.

COHAB CANYON TRAIL: Starts at Campground; ends at Utah 24; 3.5 miles; 3 hours; 400-foot ascent; steep climb for first .25 mile, then moderate; leads to hidden canyon above campground; short side trails to overlooks; details of ero-sion and small side canyons and grottoes.

OLD WAGON TRAIL: Starts and ends at Scenic Drive, 3 miles south of Grand Wash turnoff; 3.5 miles; requires strenuous climb to wagon route on Miners Mountain, with panoramic views of Waterpocket Fold.

Capitol Gorge Trail: Starts at Capitol Gorge parking area; ends at The Tanks; 2 miles round trip; 1.5 hours; 25-foot ascent; similar trail to Grand Wash plus prehistoric Indian petroglyphs. Pioneer Register, and waterpockets; hikers may continue through the Fold.

Golden Throne Trail: Starts at Capitol Gorge parking area; ends at Golden Throne; 4 miles round trip; 4 hours; 1,100-foot ascent; steep climb to top of cliffs and a lofty flat at the base of Golden Throne; panoramas.

*An infinite variety of off-trail hiking routes exist. Some are well-known, used by several parties each year, and may even be marked with rock cairns. Others have been hiked once or twice. Still others remain to be discovered. If you are interested in hiking unmarked routes off established trails, talk with park rangers and be certain that your party has the equipment and experience necessary to handle inevitable problems associated with "bushwacking," as well as potential emergencies.

SEE MAP ON PAGES 134–135.

Spring Canyon and the spring it is named for are approached by Chimney Rock Trail.

Rim Overlook Trail. A branch off the Hickman Bridge Trail at about .25 mile winds up another 2 miles to reach the point of one of the big Wingate buttresses above Fruita: Rim Overlook. A tantalizing route into the "Navajo Knobs" lies beyond.

West Entrance Trails

As you follow Utah 24 from Torrey, the Reef skirts your view on the left, growing ever higher, ever closer, until you drive down the hill from Panorama Point to the Visitor Center, headed straight for The Castle and the face of the Reef.

Goosenecks Trail. Panorama Point is a fine spot from which to view the Waterpocket Fold running both north and south, with the Henry Mountains in the background. Even better is the view from nearby Goosenecks Overlook, where the twisting course of 800-foot-deep Sulphur Creek Canyon makes a fine foreground along a short stroll. Enter the canyon of Sulphur Creek via a marked route directly across Highway 24 from the Chimney Rock parking area. Walk in the stream for 4 miles to the Visitor Center. Along the way, you will skirt three small waterfalls and get a look at the oldest exposed rock in the park, the elegant Kaibab Limestone (the layer that caps Grand Canyon) flooring the stream, with even a bit of the underlying Cutler showing through.

Chimney Rock Trail. Chimney Rock, an imposing pinnacle of Moenkopi capped by a block of Shinarump, dominates this drive from the west. A rather strenuous trail climbs for more than 500 feet to a high ridge that overlooks Chimney Rock, with views along the Reef. This loop trail runs 3.5 miles, and also provides access to the sheer Wingate cliffs in Chimney Rock Canyon, leading into the Fold to Spring Canyon.

Spring Canyon is the longest canyon in the Waterpocket Fold. It begins on Thousand Lake Mountain, at more than 8,000 feet, and runs straightforwardly to the Fremont River, some 15 miles away. The drainage receives its name from a large ponded spring 1 mile upcanyon from where Chimney Rock Canyon joins in. Below, the canyon is dry, and runs between 600-foot-high Navajo walls. The 9-mile walk from Chimney Rock to the river is a good introduction to canyon walking in the Reef.

Scenic Drive Trails

For 10 miles southward from the Visitor Center, the paved Scenic Drive parallels Capitol Reef on the west. Dirt/gravel spurs extend

Opposite: A capstone of Shinarump Conglomerate helps Chimney Rock resist erosion.

into Grand Wash and Capitol Gorge. This area encompasses the old national monument and is the most heavily visited area of the park.

Grand Wash Trail. Just 2 miles past the campground is Grand Wash, over a divide called Danish Hill, which affords one of the classic views over Fruita to the face of the Reef. The Grand Wash road reaches 1 mile into the Fold, where an easy trail continues 2.25

miles farther to the Fremont River.

Grand Wash, long a route for cattle drives through the Reef, is one of only five corridors that pierce the Reef without ending in impassable headwalls. Its Navajo Sandstone narrows rise 500 feet from the 16-foot-wide canyon floor. Wildflowers (evening primrose,

Cattle are driven through the Waterpocket Fold to winter range outside the park.

puccoon, asters, mustards) race to set seed in the floor of the wash before a flash flood sweeps through to pluck them loose. Few larger plants survive, for several times each summer the aftermath of a sudden thundershower wipes the narrows clean.

Trails and hiking routes climb from Grand Wash up side canyons and onto the summit of the Reef. Both Shinob and Bear canyons deserve exploration, and the latter leads to Fern's Nipple over a broken off-trail route. (Talk to a park ranger about hiking Bear Canyon.)

Cassidy Arch Trail. Winding up the north wall of Grand Wash, the Cassidy Arch Trail climbs 1,000 feet in 1.75 miles, through the Wingate and Kayenta to Navajo slickrock, in which the arch is cut. Pinyon and juniper grow in sandstone cracks along the trail, each striking a unique pose.

Cassidy Arch is named for Butch Cassidy, the outlaw who grew up in Circleville (west of the park). Cassidy traveled through Capitol Reef many times, and remained friendly with local ranchers throughout his daring career. The arch is difficult to see from below; only the hike shows its real character.

Frying Pan Trail. The Frying Pan Trail begins .5 mile back toward Grand Wash from the arch and leads northward for 3 miles along the crest of the Reef to Cohab Canyon. The trail is a bit strenuous, with climbs totaling 800 feet, but easy to follow. It runs mostly in the Kayenta, but hikers will be tempted to wander west to the Wingate rim overlooking the Scenic Drive and east to the great domes and fins of Navajo. Wander freely—the most magical secrets of the Reef lie in its most secluded places.

From this spot, the Scenic Drive heads southward from Grand Wash over Slickrock Divide, a good spot to check the broken slabs of red Moenkopi for ripple marks left by sun-dappled waves washing over the tidal flats of Triassic seas. The Shinarump Member of the Chinle caps Moenkopi towers in the Egyptian Temple, farther on. The scattered distribution of the Shinarump testifies to its deposition by winding river channels.

Capitol Gorge Trail. Five miles from Grand Wash, the road plunges into Capitol Gorge, Elijah Cutler Behunin's pioneer road through the Reef. It is difficult enough to picture wagons clearing this route, but even more unlikely is the vision of the gorge as the main state highway through south-central Utah, as it was for eighty years. Beyond the 2-mile scenic dirt road, Capitol Gorge again is a trail, just as it was for thousands of years.

In its first mile, the Capitol Gorge Trail leads through a bigger canyon than Grand Wash, with the extra attractions of Fremont petroglyphs, a register of pioneer signatures, and a set of waterpockets in a side canyon, whose upper tanks are frequently full in the summer rainy season.

Golden Throne Trail. Navajo towers stud the Reef in this section, and the Golden Throne is one of the most dominating. Its distinctive golden Navajo Sandstone has a thin cap of red Carmel. The trail up from Capitol Gorge climbs 1,100 feet from the parking area to a flat just below the throne; beyond lie little-visited broken heights along the Reef, which are accessible to backpackers along off-trail routes. (Talk to a park ranger before attempting these routes.)

The dirt road that goes south from the entrance to Capitol Gorge is an access route to the Sleeping Rainbow Ranch and Pleasant Creek hiking. Eph Hanks's pioneer Floral Ranch stood at Pleasant Creek. But since 1939 it has been known as the Sleeping Rainbow Ranch, long a commercial guest ranch but now part of the park. The hike down Pleasant Creek is pleasant indeed: a permanent stream, slickrock, and great Navajo domes for 3 miles in the Reef, then another 3 miles of open-country walking to Notom.

North of the Fold

Beyond the Fold to the north lie three broad, dry valleys that are protected by the park: Cathedral Valley, South Desert, and The Hartnet Desert. This is empty, little-known country. A complex of low mesas, volcanic intrusions, and great cathedrals of Entrada Sandstone is surrounded by a huge expanse of what most would judge to be wasteland: purple bentonite hills in the Morrison Formation, and the other-worldly gray badlands of the Mancos Shale. Roads reach Cathedral Valley from three directions: from the top of Thousand Lake Mountain, dropping down into the desert just north of where the Fold plunges from underneath the plateau, full-blown and headed south; along the rim of South Desert from an easy ford of the Fremont River 11.7 miles east of the Visitor Center on Utah 24; and from Caineville, through the Mancos moonscape to lower Cathedral Valley.

These huge valleys, often treeless and sometimes even shrubless, are wide open to the sun. Most visitors do little hiking, although short rambles around the temples and buttes are essential to begin to feel their size. South Desert is a good place for hikers who seek a pure desert experience; these flats offer solitude, silence, aridity, eeriness, and stark beauty. The Entrada of these valleys is soft-layered sandstone that bears little resemblance to the massive cliff-forming Entrada at Arches National Park. Its soft ledges erode easily; but hard, white Curtis caps give cathedrals an edge on survival that allows them to remain after the surrounding sandstone has washed away.

Navajo Sandstone and a crown of the Carmel formation make up the Golden Throne.

The flanks of Thousand Lake Mountain drain through the heights of the Fold to South Desert. Several drainages make rewarding walks, but isolation from trail heads and many miles without water make them challenging. Deep Creek and Water Canyon are spectacular examples of these cross-country wilderness routes.

The East Side of the Fold

The Capitol Reef Scenic Drive gives a good first look at the Waterpocket Fold. The Fremont River Highway leads through its breadth. But to grasp its incredible scale, only the drive down its east side suffices.

For 75 miles south of the Fremont, the Fold divides Utah in two. Its cliffs yawn back toward the High Plateau horizon; then, farther south, they shield the Escalante canyons. The first 5 miles of the east-side drive, the Notom Road, is paved—to the community of Notom. The good dirt road then reaches far south along the Fold, eventually veering off to Bullfrog Basin on Lake Powell. The Burr Trail road cuts up and over the Fold from Upper Hall's Creek. Lower Hall's Creek, perhaps the most exquisite place in the park, can be reached only on foot.

This long escarpment breaks naturally into sections. To the west between the Fremont River and Notom (about 4 miles) rise the already familiar high points of the Reef—dominated by the Golden Throne. From Pleasant Creek to Oak Creek (about 10 miles), four washes (Burro, Cottonwood, Fivemile, and Sheets) head in the Fold and drain outward to where the road crosses them. Hikers can enter each from the road; all have high cliffs, pockets of life, alcoves, narrows, and tantalizing glimpses of color gleaming off desert varnish. Sheets Wash actually pierces the Fold in a 1,000-foot canyon, and can be hiked through the Fold.

Oak Creek runs perennially and irrigates fields at Sandy Ranch. From there to Bitter Creek Divide (about 11 miles), the road leaves the open country and enters a gradually narrowing passage between high Tarantula Mesa on the east and the Fold on the west. A simple campground (tables, grill, toilet, no water) at Cedar Mesa forms the trail head for the 4-mile round-trip walk to Red Canyon, an enormous box canyon.

The Bitter Creek Divide area is a good one for flowers. Hood phlox makes cushions of white-blossomed green under junipers; Indian paintbrush puts out its outrageous crimsons and orange-reds; sego lilies wave delicately in white and yellow clusters. Cliffrose wafts its charms downwind: the fragrance of its nectar is the perfume of the canyons.

Hall's Creek begins at this divide, and flows southward for almost 40 miles to Lake Powell. It slices through soft formations at the base of the Fold, creating the "strike valley" that is controlled by the parallel layers, which here are tilted their steepest at 70°. Eight miles below the Divide, the Burr Trail heads west, zigzagging steeply up the only place where a road climbs *over* the Fold.

Views from the Burr Trail are phenomenal; although the Henry Mountains are not within Capitol Reef National Park, they dominate all views eastward along its entire length. Here they are close—just beyond the massive tops of the Mancos mesas, Tarantula and Swap. At the top of the Burr Trail, the road turns to pavement as it leaves Capitol Reef for the Circle Cliffs and the town of Boulder to the west. Controversy over paving the Burr Trail lasted for more than a decade; the conflict epitomizes the impasse between those who favor preservation of the primitive character of wild backcountry and those intent on development to spur tourism.

Where the Burr Trail crests the Fold, it crosses an anomalous wash. This wash, Muley Twist Canyon, runs right down the heart of the fold. Like Spring Canyon to the north, it runs *in* the Fold rather than through it. The cracked Kayenta, turned almost on end, gave the canyon its start. But now it plunges between high Wingate and Navajo cliffs as well.

North of the Burr Trail is Upper Muley Twist Canyon, with its fluted little narrows, numerous arches, and superb panorama of the Fold from an overlook 3 miles up. (The first 3 miles is the only section of the canyon that is open to vehicles—four-wheel-drive only). Beyond, the canyon leads through ledges for 5 miles, where a return route climbs to the summit of the Fold for slickrock walking and sweeping views in every direction.

Lower Muley Twist Canyon runs 12 miles southward from the Burr Trail to Hall's Creek. This is the route taken by 1880s pioneers headed from Escalante to Hall's Crossing on the Colorado. The canyon owes its name to these early travelers, who claimed that the narrows were so tight that their mules had to twist to get through. A route leads out from Lower Muley Twist about 4 miles down, up and over the Fold to The Post. Those who hike the entire canyon return to The Post through the greasewood of dry and open Upper Hall's Creek.

The Post—once a cowboy camp—lies 2.5 miles below the Burr Trail road. From The Post the road swings eastward, never to return to the Hall's Creek Gorge. The Post is hikers' last chance to enter Hall's Creek easily. Hall's lower canyon is worth weeks of their time; from The Post down to the lake, side canyons that drain the great Navajo whaleback of its flood waters turn up about every mile. Each has its own hidden potholes, springs, desert-varnished walls. Near The Post are Surprise and Headquarters canyons. Not far south are Cottonwood, Willow, and Muley tanks.

This is Capitol Reef's climax, and, fittingly, it is wild, rugged, and difficult to reach. The road toward Bullfrog swings back one last time to an overlook high above Hall's Creek Gorge, and a maintained trail heads down this cliff to Brimhall Double Bridge—an impressive span seen from the viewpoint. To the south lies Hall's Creek Narrows, where the creek has sliced back into the Fold, carving a huge canyon in the Navajo Sandstone. Seek the advice of rangers if you want to hike this most remote section of the park. Distances are great, water is sparse, and the heat in summer is intense.

But it is the intensity of the experiences that draws us. Books only whet appetites for the real thing. No matter how fine the photograph or how clever the writing, they cannot match a single juniper for vividness. The *distinctness* of scaly leaves and rough-barked limbs—as opposed to generalizations about ecology; the stubborn craziness of balanced rocks, their powerful unlikelihood—as opposed to dense geologic history: this is the *reality* of Capitol Reef.

This is why we protect the park. This is why we come here.

Opposite: The Henry Mountains, at almost 12,000 feet, flank the park's eastern boundary.

CARLSBAD CAVERNS
NATIONAL PARK

Stalagmites build upward from cave floors in spires composed of calcified water drops.

CARLSBAD CAVERNS NATIONAL PARK
3225 NATIONAL PARKS HIGHWAY
CARLSBAD, NEW MEXICO 88220
TEL.: (505) 785-2232

HIGHLIGHTS: Carlsbad Cavern • Bat Flights • Walnut Canyon • Slaughter Canyon Cave • Wild Cave Trips

ACCESS: From Carlsbad, 27 miles south on U.S. 62/180 and New Mexico 7.

HOURS: Daily, year-round, except Christmas. No overnight stopping in park.

FEES: For Carlsbad Cavern and Slaughter Canyon Cave tours; discount for Golden Age and Golden Access passes.

PARKING: At Visitor Center.

GAS, FOOD: In Whites City and Carlsbad. Food available in park.

LODGING: In Whites City and Carlsbad.

VISITOR CENTER: In summer, 8 A.M.–7 P.M.; other seasons, 8:00 A.M.–5:30 P.M. Exhibits, audio-visual program, bookstore.

MUSEUM: Exhibits in Visitor Center.

GIFT SHOP: In Visitor Center.

PETS: Permitted on leash in some areas; kennel available. Some trails suitable for horses; no rentals; bring own feed and water. Holding pen available. Register in Visitor Center.

PICNICKING: At Rattlesnake Springs and near Visitor Center.

HIKING: Permitted. Carry water.

BACKPACKING: Permitted west of Visitor Center, permit required. Must be .25 mile from road and out of sight to camp, and must carry water.

CAMPGROUND: None in park. Private campground at park entrance. Other campgrounds in Carlsbad and Guadalupe Mountains National Park.

TOURS: In Carlsbad Cavern, self-guided Natural Entrance and Big Room routes available daily; ranger-guided King's Palace tour daily, by reservation. Slaughter Canyon Cave flashlight tour daily in summer, weekends in winter; reservations required.

OTHER ACTIVITIES: Nature walks, evening bat flight program in summer.

FACILITIES FOR DISABLED: Access to Visitor Center, restaurant, part of Cavern.

For additional information, see also map on pages 166–167 and Sites, Trails, and Trips on pages 182–186.

THE BROAD DESERTS OF WESTERN TEXAS AND Southeastern New Mexico strike the car-borne visitor as an ocean that may take days to cross. The judgment is right, albeit a little late in geologic terms, for the land was formed from sediments of a great sea. Like landfall, the horizon is broken in places by mountains, each a geologic event in itself. One group, the Guadalupe Mountains and the Capitan reef formation, which stretches southward from present-day Carlsbad, New Mexico, was a huge reef complex. Today, it is one of the greatest fossil reefs on earth, and carved into it is Carlsbad Cavern, an interior window into a strange and fascinating world.

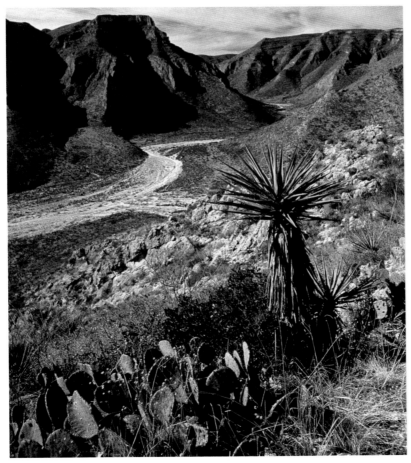

Slaughter Canyon and the rugged desert country above Carlsbad Caverns.

TO CARLSBAD

DESERT DRIVE

WALNUT CANYON

Putnam Ridge Trail

Rattlesnake Canyon Trail

RATTLESNAKE CANYON

Visitor Center
El. 4406'
(See Cavern Trail Map)

Whites City

Rattlesnake Springs

Black River

Country Road 418

Yucca Canyon Trail

Country Road 422

62 180

CAVERN TRAIL MAP

BAT CAVE

Devil's Spring

Crystal Spring Dome

Rock of Ages

Bottomless Pit

ROOM

NATURAL ENTRANCE
(Bat Flight)

(Surface) **VISITOR CENTER**

Twin Domes
Giant Dome

BIG
Temple of the Sun

Totem Pole

Lily Pads

Mirror Lake

MAIN CORRIDOR

LOWER CAVE

Baby Hippo

KEY

Tour Route
Trail to Caverns
Seating Area

BONEYARD

Iceberg   KING'S PALACE

PAPOOSE ROOM

0   200   400   600   800
SCALE IN FEET

GREEN LAKE ROOM

QUEEN'S CHAMBER

TO EL PASO AND GUADALUPE MTNS. N. P.

Discovery

There is evidence that Native Americans lived around Carlsbad Cavern. Mescal-roasting pits are nearby, one just a few feet from the cavern entrance, and pictographs are on the entrance wall; moccasins, debris, and even a skeleton reportedly were found during the early explorations of the caverns. The first Paleo-Indian people arrived in the area about 14,000 years ago. They were followed by Archaic hunters and gatherers beginning about 8,000 years ago, then the Apaches, who moved into the area before Spanish expeditions passed through. The Native Americans could not fully explore the cave, yet no doubt watched each evening as a whirlwind of millions of bats spiraled upward for hours.

It was this bat flight that led modern explorers to the cave. As with most things, the precise "first" is lost in vagueness occasionally tinged with controversy. In one story, while a father and his son were seeking a lost calf, they saw and heard the black cloud of bats swooshing from the cave entrance. In another—this one recorded rather than legend—a cowboy named Jim White discovered the caverns. In any case, by the 1890s, folks living in Carlsbad knew about the bats. And they took advantage of what the bats left behind.

Mining

What the bats left in "Bat Cave" was an enormous deposit of guano. The dry, powdery accumulation of centuries of bat dung beneath a roosting area was and still is one of the richest natural fertilizers known. California was just then developing its citrus industry, so it was not long before mining claims were filed and operations were begun. None of this was particularly startling, because other caves in the area—there are more than eighty just in Carlsbad Caverns National Park—were being mined for guano. Nor was the operation itself unusual; two shafts were punched directly into the "Bat Room," and men and equipment were lowered in buckets. In a 20-year span, more than 100,000 tons of guano were removed. The mining shafts were sealed in the 1980s to restore the bat roost to its natural condition.

Exploration

There was nothing on the surface to suggest that this one cave was any different from any other, until Jim White, cowboy turned guano miner, began to explore it during his off-hours. Today, with electric lights, paved trails, and foreknowledge, it is difficult to recapture the awe of those early explorers as they crawled and climbed and saw hints of what captivates present-day visitors. Their torches and later inefficient, smoky kerosene lanterns were Aladdin's lamps that lit up a new world. White led the way—he spent twenty years exploring, building trails, and escorting visitors—but professionals soon followed.

The guano business began to fade as transportation costs rose, but a thriving tourist industry, crude at first, became increasingly successful. Visitors rode down in the old guano mining buckets and, with some difficulty, clambered through the cave. Today's approximately 700,000 visitors must remind themselves that the easy paths are actually the result of careful engineering and construction.

Establishment of the Park

The fame of the huge cavern spread. On October 25, 1923, President Calvin Coolidge designated it a national monument. Shortly thereafter, the National Geographic Society published an extensive article in its magazine (January 1924), and the fame of the cavern spread even more. In 1930, Carlsbad Caverns became a national park.

Early tourists descend into the caverns in guano buckets.

Reconstructing an ancient landscape from clues—most of them tiny, uncoded, and constantly churned by subsequent geological events—is not easy. A few have done it for the joy of the puzzle, and some, more recently, because of oil potential. Each investigator has uncovered a small piece of the earth's history.

The entrance to the cave was once a vertical drop of more than 30 feet. Now a paved path bypasses the drop-off and descends steeply past the massive bedded rocks that loom like a large forehead over the entrance. Except for one other small, inaccessible crevice, this is the only natural entrance to the cave known today, but there may have been other openings that have since been sealed. Pleistocene animal bones have been found in areas that animals would have difficulty reaching by today's routes.

The Reef

Two hundred million years ago, the mountains out of which Carlsbad Cavern was hollowed were a reef. It was not the coral reef familiar from South Sea pictures, but a kind of reef that has no exact parallel in the world today. This reef was not at the surface, near the shore, but formed at the lip of the shelf, where the long downslope from the shore seaward broke and dropped sharply toward the depths. Here, in some places at depths as much as 600 feet, the reef formed.

Huge numbers of tiny plants and animals lived on, in, and around one another. Some contributed their shells or skeletons to the material that would eventually become the structure of the reef. Lime was precipitated from the sea water, forming limestone that in some places has much more cement than material cemented together. Sediment washing in from the land slowly piled behind this barrier and grew on itself until it reached nearly to the surface of the water.

The rock found at the cave entrance is part of the Tansill Formation. A small chip examined under a microscope would reveal the remains of tiny algae called *Dasycladaceae*. Today *Dasycladaceae* live only in very shallow, warm seas, and almost certainly they did so when this reef was formed. Other microscopic animals whose fossils are found here, the crinoids, for example, were constructed of tiny barrel-like segments attached end to end to form "stems." When the animals died, these segments easily came apart and scattered, yet here complete fossils can be found; the water must have been still. This area was the lagoon behind the reef. A line of stalactites on the cave wall marks the spot

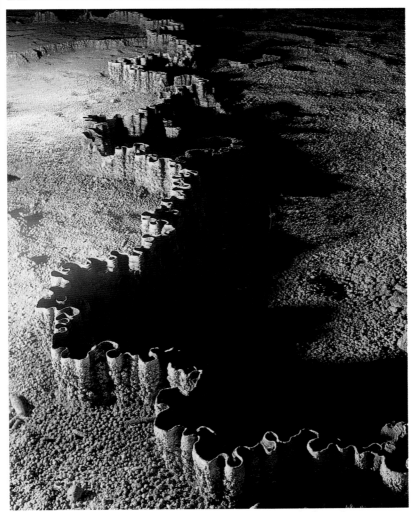

The China Wall in Slaughter Canyon Cave, one of eighty caves in the park

where the back-reef sediments meet the reef itself.

On the open side are fossils of creatures that need well-agitated, aerated water, provided by the currents and waves of the open sea meeting the reef. Typically for reefs, this outer face was steep. Pieces broke off and fell, forming a talus slope, or pile of debris against the face of the reef, which combined with sediment that was washing over as well. It appears that this consolidated debris sloped down to the depths at an angle of perhaps 30°. Today visitors walk on this talus, which is well exposed near the Bottomless

Pit in the Big Room.

The depth of the sea was considerable. (Look eastward at the desert below the reef to get the idea.) There was little deep circulation and little or no oxygen at the bottom. Organic matter that filtered down from above did not decay but began the long and still only partly understood process that leads to oil.

Cave Formation

It took eons, but as the climate changed, sediment washing down from surrounding highlands actually filled the sea as it slowly evaporated. The region became a broad plain, with the reef buried at one edge of it. Animals and plants spread across the plain; it seemed permanent.

Just a few million years ago, during the late Cretaceous period, the area was uplifted. Sometime during the process, strains cracked the great reef. Now ground water worked along the cracks. The water had absorbed carbon dioxide from the air and from organic material near the surface to become an extremely dilute carbonic acid that began to dissolve and carry away the reef rock.

Carbonic acid, however, did not explain the presence of gypsum in many of the caves. Carol Hill, in *Geology of Carlsbad Caverns*, proposed a new theory. She and other speleologists now believe that sulfuric acid dissolved much of the limestone, because gypsum is precipitated as an end product of that process. Another clue may be found in the underlying beds of oil and gas. Hydrogen sulfide from these beds could have worked its way upward through cracks, reached air or oxygen-rich water, and produced sulfuric acid. Alternatively or additionally, erosion on the surface of the land would have produced sulfuric acid as a result of the weathering of iron pyrite. It would have then trickled down into the limestone.

As with all geological processes, the excavation of caves in the manner described above moved forward at far less than a snail's pace. The very slowness of the dissolving of the limestone contributed to the multi-story structure typical at Carlsbad Caverns. The mountains rose as the caves formed. Erosion cut deeper and deeper into the mountainsides. Sulfuric acid does its dissolving best when it mixes with fresh water. Therefore, as it interacted with water as the water table fell, it excavated a room at first one level, then at a lover level. The result today are caves with rooms at several levels.

Opposite: The white-hooded Klansman, one of Slaughter Canyon Cave's features.

Cave Decoration

Once the cave was above the water, air entered and the "decoration phase" began. Indeed, it continues today. The features that visitors wander among, the fantasy-inducing stalactites and curtains and dams and flowstone, are still being formed by the action of dripping water. Drops of water, each carrying a tiny load of dissolved limestone, work slowly through the rock. When a drop reaches the air—the void in the cave—the pressure on the drop is reduced, and in a reaction that can be duplicated in the laboratory, carbon dioxide is released into the air and the tiny load of limestone is deposited at the spot. This explains why those stalactites are in a line where the back-reef sediments meet the main reef. The water was working its way along that joint, and it left the line of stalactites where it reached the void of the cave.

The process is slow; the ages involved in the geological time charts are beyond comprehension. At Carlsbad, although the cave decoration takes place during a much lesser time period, one's sense is stretched to comprehend it by the visible evidence of an eon of occasional drops slowly materializing and disappearing in the dark. One hundred million such reactions may build a small stalagmite, but some formations are huge; the Giant Dome is over 60 feet high.

The forms of decorations vary widely, depending on conditions when the limestone precipitated. A stalactite hanging from the ceiling has had an overhead supply of calcite-laden water drops. If enough drops fall and splash on the floor, a stalagmite will begin to build upward. It will be wider than the stalactite because of the water's splash. A stalactite and its stalagmite may meet to form a column.

Some forms are tiny. For reasons that are not yet fully understood, calcite sometimes precipitates in a beautiful crystalline form, aragonite. Epsonite needles are even more delicate. Perhaps most remarkable of all the forms are helictites, tiny stalks that may grow down or up or sideways. Their water passages are so tiny that the water droplets are affected by forces other than gravity, and the particular crystals involved have random ways of stacking. A helictite can look like a snake dancer or a corkscrew.

Draperies can be small or large. The Whale's Mouth and the Queen's Draperies in the Queen's Chamber are impressive. Some pools of water in the cave contain formations that look like stone water lilies. Other small pools have small, rare spheres at the bottom called "cave pearls."

Lechuguilla: A New Frontier, Underground

Astronauts may dream of walking on the moon, or even on Mars, their squinty eyes roaming over pale desertlike terrain reflecting blazing sunlight. Speleologists, on the other hand, welcome the chance to explore an unknown void of total blackness, even if they must wade in yucky water or step gingerly along a crumbly ledge above an abyss of uncertain but surely fatal depth.

The serious exploration of Lechuguilla Cave, which began in 1986, has created great excitement among underground explorers. It became more apparent with each passing year that Lechuguilla, which was named for the agave plant that is common in the vicinity of the entrance, was a very special cave in both its size and its decorations.

The entrance, consisting of a 90-foot vertical drop in a remote wilderness area near the northern border of Carlsbad Caverns National Park, had been known for a century. The 200 feet of passage beyond the entrance pit contained bat guano, once highly desirable as fertilizer. A claim to mine the guano was filed in 1914.

Otherwise, the cave drew little attention, except for one suspicious circumstance. "Lechuguilla was a small backwater cave of little interest," according to Charlie Peterson, a former cave specialist at the park, "except that the wind blew through cracks and holes in the rubble at the bottom of the pit." Peterson told *National Parks* magazine, "Park rangers and other cave researchers knew that there had to be more cave." The wind sucked first into the cave, and then blew out of it, and the volume of air movement suggested a cavity of great size.

In 1984, some Colorado cavers asked the National Park Service to allow them to undertake a limited excavation. Permission was granted, and the arduous process began, with no real breakthrough until 1986. But by the end of that summer, explorers had mapped 7,400 feet of passages, to a depth of 927 feet.

Other cavers, from all over the country, wanted to help in the exploration, and four major expeditions were launched in 1987, to be followed by nineteen more by the end of 1990. The cave "grew" rapidly, and by 1995 it ranked as the third longest known cave in the United States and the fifth longest in the world. In 1994 alone, almost 11 miles of new passages were surveyed, bringing the length to 82.6 miles. The depth now was 1,566 feet, greatest of any U.S. limestone cave. A lava-tube cave in Hawaii is 2,915 feet in depth.

Rick Bridges, a member of an early expedition, recalled that the initial dig was "miserable work." He said, "The wind howled up through the rubble, blasting us with dirt and sand. . . . We ate dirt;

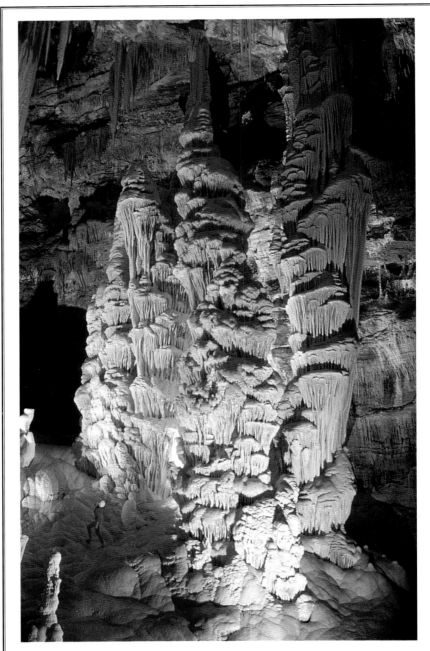

The wonders of Lechuguilla Cave were unknown until the late 1980s.

As new passages were found, Lechuguilla ranked as the world's fifth longest cave.

we breathed dirt."

Although volunteer cavers from the United States and several other countries (a British team set the depth record) have made most of the discoveries in Lechuguilla, the National Park Service has primary responsibility for overseeing the cave's management. In addition to approving explorations, the NPS must approve research projects, which range over such fields as biology, microbiology, geology, and paleontology.

And, without doubt, Lechuguilla has great scientific value. It passes through five geological formations, and contains many rare speleothems (cave formations). In reference to some underwater formations, the NPS states, "Sub-aqueous helictites of this type have never been found, or recorded, before in any other cave in the world."

Hydromagnesite balloons, 20-foot long gypsum chandeliers, and 15-foot-long soda-straw formations have been found. In the so-called Glacier Bay Room, blocks of gypsum resembling calving icebergs lie at the foot of the gypsum "glacier." White gypsum flowers are prominent in the cave.

The guano mining aside, Lechuguilla is a pristine cavern unmarked or untouched by human endeavor or pollution. In 1992, however, alarm bells went off when the Yates Energy Corporation applied for permission from the U.S. Bureau of Land Management to drill for oil and gas one-half mile from the park boundary and just 2 miles from the cave entrance. Environmentalists warned that drilling could bring oil and gas into the cave, polluting it and possibly even

Lechuguilla is open only to scientists and serious explorers, not the general public.

asphyxiating cave visitors. The following year, Congress approved the "Lechuguilla Cave Protection Act of 1993," establishing a 6,280-acre cave protection zone bordering the park near the cave. The legislation, however, did not stop drilling on existing leases.

Lechuguilla, according to the NPS, represents "an unprecedented chance to study natural cave processes and cave climate. . . ." Ron Kerbo, a cave specialist at the park, endorsed the idea of having Lechuguilla and some other caverns at Carlsbad designated as "cave wilderness"—the first in the world. The purpose would not be to put the cave off-limits altogether, but to limit its access to cavers willing and able to make a strenuous effort. Subsequently, Park Service legal staff concluded that the wilderness protection for the surface of the land also applied to the subsurface.

The cave remains closed to casual visitors, and that is unlikely to change. The Park Service does not even publicize the location of the entrance. Anyone traveling through it for any significant distance must contend with frequent long descents by rope, huge boulders, 100 percent humidity, and difficult climbs. Add dehydration as a problem for forays that could last up to five days. Entry in the mid-1990s was by permit only, and restricted to persons engaged in exploration and scientific research. Even they were admonished by the NPS to be "vertically proficient." The hardy and foolhardy may obtain a Park Service pamphlet, "Guidelines for Entering Lechuguilla Cave."

—*Donald Young*

The Landscape

The shape of the land within the park has created wide variations in temperature, sunlight, soil, and moisture, all of which, in turn, are responsible for life forms in just as wide a variety. On the flatlands near the base of the Guadalupe Mountains are creosote bush and desert shrubs. In the canyons, where there is more moisture, black walnut, oak, desert willow, and hackberry flourish. Canyon walls and ridge tops are covered with agave, yucca, sotol, ocotillo, and desert grasses. On the higher elevations are juniper, Texas madrone, and pine. More than 800 plant species have been identified.

Wildlife

Carlsbad Caverns National Park, although most famous for its tremendous cavern, has within its confines an abundance of mammals, desert reptiles, and birds. Ground squirrels, raccoons, skunks, kit foxes, jack rabbits, and gophers move through the brush, often at night (as do most desert animals). There are snakes, but visitors rarely see them, for they are both secretive and usually nocturnal. Lizards abound, fascinating small children from other parts of the country where these reptiles may not be common. More than 300 species of birds have been identified in the park; the biggest shadows are cast by the turkey vulture and the occasional golden eagle. Mule deer are plentiful; visitors should be careful when driving park roads at dawn and dusk. Appearing less often are bobcats, coyotes, badgers, even mountain lions. While each of these animals goes about seeking a living in the scrub vegetation on the surface, it is a certain small mammal that lives in the cave that visitors ask about most often.

Bats

Besides the fantasyland of the cavern, one of the chief attractions of Carlsbad Caverns National Park is the nightly bat flight. Each evening, starting at sundown and continuing for about an hour, the cave's entire population of bats (except for babies, which remain clinging to the ceiling) comes swirling out in what appears to be a black whirlwind. The population was once several million, but it declined between the 1950s and the late 1970s, perhaps to 300,000, apparently as a result of pesticides that the bats ingest with their nightly feast of insects. By the mid-1990s, the colony had rebounded somewhat to about 1 million—enough to consume several tons of

Top: A Mexican free-tailed bat, four inches long.
Above: Fossilized bat.
Right: Bats in flight.

insects nightly during the summer!

Bats use a remarkable location-finding device that is comparable to the sonar used by submarines, but much more precise. While flying, bats emit a very high sound and actually detect flying insects by their echo. The bats at Carlsbad spend the night ranging the area and, about dawn, reenter the cave, diving in from several hundred feet up. Every evening throughout the summer (the bats migrate to Mexico for the winter), visitors can enjoy a presentation by a ranger at the entrance to the bat cave.

Sites, Trails, and Trips

Carlsbad Cavern

There are two ways to enter Carlsbad Cavern. Both are equally fascinating, one for man's engineering ability, and the other for nature's eerie charm. For those who choose to take an easy, convenient trip, elevators in the Visitor Center descend to the Big Room, 750 feet below. The natural-entrance tour winds its way down for a little more than a mile to the Big Room. Both tours return to the Visitor Center by way of the elevators.

The natural entrance is the one from which the bats take their nightly flight. The tour enters there, passes the huge side chamber in which the bats congregate during the day, and then descends sharply into the cavern to the Big Room. The first .5 mile or so of the path is devoid of the familiar stalactites and stalagmites that are usually associated with caverns. Carlsbad's fantasyland becomes evident a little farther along, however, as the trail levels off at about 700 feet beneath the surface. Visitors must circumnavigate, so to speak, the great Iceberg Rock, a gigantic chunk of rock that many eons ago crashed through the network of caves then being formed; much of the descending trail follows the path of the fall of the Iceberg. On the floor of the Big Room are found the strange stone "toadstools" or "lily pads," which geologists say came from minerals in waters now long gone.

In addition to these two self-guided trips, the ranger-led King's Palace tour, available only by reservation and with a separate fee, passes through four rooms where stalactites are abundant. The tour includes the King's Palace, Papoose Room, Queen's Chamber, and Green Lake Room.

The Big Room. The Big Room cannot be seen all at once; indeed, on first entering, spectators will find this huge chamber deceptively small. Once the immensity takes hold of the imagination, however, a six-story-tall stalagmite—alongside which one may be standing—

Upper left: Aragonite crystals. Upper right: Blue stalactites. Bottom: Slaughter Canyon Cave, which was not discovered until 1937.

TRAILS OF CARLSBAD CAVERNS NATIONAL PARK

CARLSBAD CAVERN TRAIL: Starts at natural entrance; ends at Big Room; 3 miles; 3 hours; 830-foot descent; descent through three levels of cave; limestone features, including stalactites, stalagmites, and helictites; evening bat flight.

RATTLESNAKE CANYON TRAIL: Starts at Walnut Canyon loop road; ends at Putnam Cabin; 10 miles one way, 8–10 hours; 2,000-foot ascent; gradual climb to highest point in park through heart of wilderness area; most of hike is along top of ridge.

SLAUGHTER CANYON TRAIL: Starts at Putnam Ridge Trail; ends at New Cave parking area; 4.5 miles one way; 6 hours; 2,000-foot descent; rugged trail passes below the entrance to New Cave, which is 500 feet up the side of the canyon.

YUCCA CANYON TRAIL: Starts at Slaughter Canyon Trail; ends at Yucca Canyon; 2 miles one way; 3 hours; 1,000-foot ascent; climbs to the top of an escarpment.

The Backcountry trails listed above are primitive and undeveloped and should be hiked after planning and with care.

SEE MAP ON PAGES 166-167.

Above: An unusual stalactite formation in Carlsbad Cavern.
Opposite: A narrow ridge separates North Double Canyon from South Double Canyon.
Double Cave runs through this ridge and has an entrance in each canyon

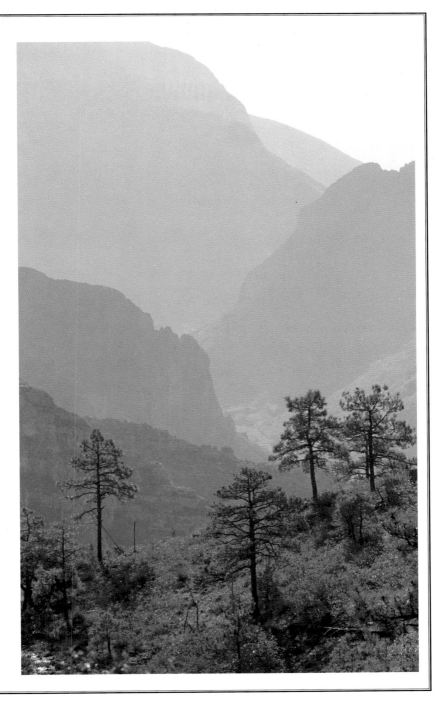

is dwarfed by its surroundings. The Big Room could house fourteen football fields; in one corner could sit the nation's Capitol, dome and all. Awesome hardly begins a description.

The cavern temperature stays at 56° F year-round. Although this temperature may seem comfortable at first, after several hours below, 56° F becomes chilly. A sweater or jacket is recommended. And for the walk from the natural entrance, shoes with good traction soles are recommended.

Slaughter Canyon Cave

The Guadalupe Mountains are laced with caves, and each, in its own way, is just as exciting as Carlsbad. All the caves that are within the national park boundaries are protected and restricted, however, and for very good reason. Many are still unexplored, still to yield their treasures, and are just as dangerous as was Carlsbad when it was first discovered. Most are closed to the public, but a few can be entered with a special permit.

Slaughter Canyon Cave, formerly called New Cave, is 23 miles from the park Visitor Center; most of the drive is outside the park; the last mile, from the park boundary to the parking area, is gravel. The hike of about .5 mile rises 500 feet, which makes it seem a lot longer. Access is only with a prearranged tour led by a park ranger.

Above Ground

Walnut Canyon Loop Drive. A 9.5-mile, one-way, gravel road leads away from the Visitor Center parking lot into Walnut Canyon and eventually loops around to the main entrance road. This is a pleasant, 45-minute drive into desert-canyon country.

Desert Nature Walk. A .5-mile nature walk that begins at the Visitor Center presents a pleasant diversion for visitors who are waiting for the evening bat-flight program. Desert plants and flowers are identified. A portion of this trail is accessible to wheelchairs.

Backcountry Hiking. Most people visit Carlsbad to see the cavern and not the general terrain. There are old ranch trails, however, and desert hiking is permitted; but these trails are not marked, as are those in other parks. This land is much like that at Guadalupe Mountains National Park, and with proper preparation, maps, and advice from park rangers, hikers can make some exciting excursions into the desert wilderness.

Opposite: Stone draperies, 60 feet high, form a false wall in the Sequoia Room.

GRAND CANYON
NATIONAL PARK

At Toroweap Point, on the North Rim, the canyon wall drops 3,000 feet straight down to the Colorado River.

GRAND CANYON NATIONAL PARK
BOX 129
GRAND CANYON, ARIZONA 86023
TEL.: (520) 638-7888

HIGHLIGHTS: South Rim • North Rim • Inner Gorge • Tusayan Ruins and Museum • Yavapai Point • Hopi Point • Yaki Point • Bright Angel Point • Walhalla Overlook • Hermits Rest • Tuweep • Cape Royal

ACCESS: For South Rim, from Tusayan (airport), 7 miles via Arizona 64. From Flagstaff, 80 miles via Arizona 64 and I-40. From Williams, 59 miles via Arizona 64. For North Rim, from Jacob Lake, 45 miles via Arizona 67. From Kanab, Utah, 81 miles via Arizona 67. See map on pages 192–193.

HOURS: South Rim, daily, 24 hours, year-round. North Rim, daily, 24 hours, May to October.

FEES: On entry, per vehicle or per person, and for commercial tours; for camping.

PARKING: Parking areas congested in developed areas and at overlooks; free shuttle operates, late May to September.

GAS, FOOD: Throughout park, and at nearby towns.

LODGING: In park: cabins, motel units, and hotels. Reserve well in advance.

VISITOR CENTER: In Grand Canyon Village. Exhibit area, auditorium, bookstore, information desk. Talks and slide program. *Park recommends that visitors write for the "Trip Planner" and/or "Backcountry Trip Planner" before traveling to the canyon.*

MUSEUM: Yavapai Observation Station and Tusayan Archeological Museum.

GIFT SHOP: General store in Mather Center and at other areas.

PETS: Permitted on leash, but not on trails. Kennel available on South Rim only. Horseback riding permitted; rentals available with guided tour on both rims; private stock needs permit.

PICNICKING: At designated areas.

HIKING: Permitted. Carry water.

BACKPACKING: Permits needed and must be obtained well in advance. Water sources intermittent; check with backcountry office near Mather campground and on North Rim.

CAMPGROUNDS: North Rim and South Rim campground reservations strongly recommended, through MISTIX, (800) 365-2267 or, from outside United States, (619) 452-0150; P.O. Box 85705, San Diego, CA 92186.

TOURS: On South Rim throughout the year; on North Rim in summer. In English. Private guides available for backcountry tours.

OTHER ACTIVITIES: Mule trips; river tours; sightseeing flights.

FACILITIES FOR DISABLED: At many public-use points. When making reservations, please specify needs. Special brochure available.

For additional information, see also Sites, Trails, and Trips on pages 209–224 and the maps on pages 192–193 and 218–219.

THE GRAND CANYON IS A LAND OF DAZZLING extremes that encompasses four life zones, ranging from arid desert to moist coniferous forest. In winter, when the North Rim is blanketed by 140 inches of snow, the weather inside the canyon is mild. Over millions of years, the great Colorado River, which bisects the canyon, has performed one of the most stupendous feats of erosion in geological history. Aided by the uplift of the land and by other geological factors, the river has cut down thousands of feet through sheer rock to form, in John Van Dyke's words, "Nature's most colossal piece of stage-setting." Many different rock strata lie exposed, varying in age and composition from the metamorphic Vishnu Schist of the Inner Gorge to the sedimentary layers of the Kaibab and Toroweap formations. Making a home along the sheer face of the canyon are almost 90 species of mammals and more than 300 species of birds, ranging in size from shrews and hummingbirds to mountain lions and turkey vultures.

The buttes and temples of the North Rim as seen from Maricopa Point.

GRAND CANYON
VICINITY MAP

S C A L E

0   10   20

M I L E S

TO U.S. 89 AND FRED[

TO FREDONIA

Marble Canyon

Jacob
Lake

89

KAIBAB
NATIONAL
FOREST

67

NEVADA
ARIZONA

Mt.
Trumbull

Tuweep

Colorado   River

Kanab   River

KANAB PLATEAU

GRAND CANYON   (locator map)
NATIONAL PARK

NORTH
RIM

LAKE MEAD
NAT. REC.
AREA

Supai

HAVASUPAI
INDIAN
RESERVATION

GRAND CANYON
VILLAGE

DESERT
VIEW

TO CAMERON

GRAND
CANYON
NATIONAL
PARK

COCONINO

PLATEAU

Tusayan

64

KAIBAB NATIONAL
FOREST

180

HUALAPAI INDIAN RESERVATION

TO FLAGSTAFF

GRANITE

Crystal Creek

TUCKUP

Rapids

Buc
Ten
El

John
Point
El. 5

TOPAZA CANYON

Tonto
Trail

Rapids

Tower of
Set

Twentyfour Mile Creek

Cheops
Pyramid

El. 2520

Phantom
Ranch

El. 2400

Bridge

Bridge

Boucher
Trail

EREMITA MESA

Hermit Trail

PIMA PT.
El. 6798'

MOHAVE
PT.

HOPI PT.

MARICOPA
POINT

Bright Angel Trail

El. 7040
YAVAPAI
PT.

MATHER
PT.

Hermit's
Rest

Rim
Trail

WEST   RIM   DRIVE

Dripping
Springs
Trail

SOUTH
RIM

GRAND
CANYON
VILLAGE
El. 6900'

N

KAIBAB
NATIONAL
FOREST

TO TUSAYAN   AND FLAGSTAFF

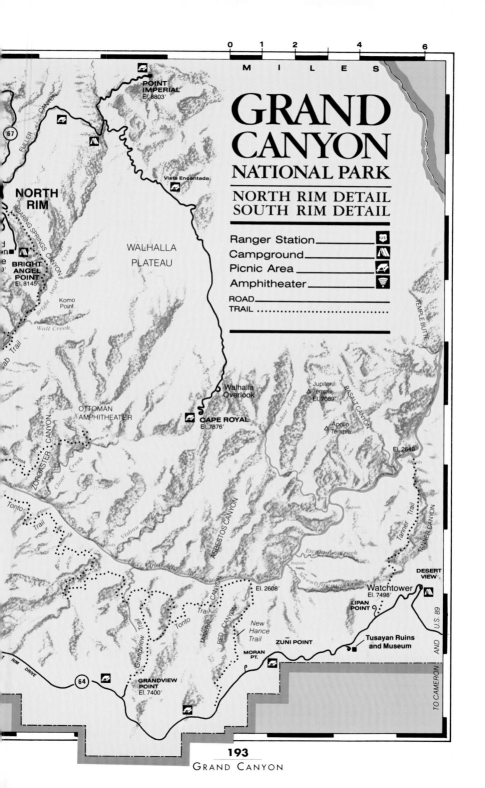

MILES

0 1 2 4 6

GRAND CANYON
NATIONAL PARK
NORTH RIM DETAIL
SOUTH RIM DETAIL

Ranger Station _____ US
Campground _____
Picnic Area _____
Amphitheater _____
ROAD _____
TRAIL ....

POINT IMPERIAL
El. 8803'

Vista Encantada

NORTH RIM

ROARING SPRINGS CANYON

BRIGHT ANGEL POINT
El. 8145'

Komo Point

WALHALLA PLATEAU

Bright Angel Creek

Wall Creek

Kaibab Trail

OTTOMAN AMPHITHEATER

ZOROASTER CANYON

Clear Creek

Tonto Trail

Vishnu

Rapids

Walhalla Overlook

CAPE ROYAL
El. 7876'

Unkar Creek

Jupiter Temple
El. 7089'

Apollo Temple

BASALT CANYON

TEMPLE BUTTE

El. 2640

Rapids

ASBESTOS CANYON

Rapids

Escalante Creek

Rapids

Seventyfive Mile Creek

Tanner Trail

TANNER CANYON

DESERT VIEW

Watchtower
El. 7498'

LIPAN POINT

El. 2608'

MINERAL CANYON

RED CANYON

New Hance Trail

ZUÑI POINT

Tusayan Ruins and Museum

U.S. 89

TO CAMERON AND

Tonto Trail

Grandview Trail

MORAN PT.

RIM DRIVE

64

GRANDVIEW POINT
El. 7400'

FULLER CANYON

67

First Inhabitants

In 1933, archeologists discovered a number of split-twig figurines—apparently representations of animals—inside caves within the Grand Canyon. These figurines were to alter their chronology of the human habitation of the canyon, pushing the known dates back to at least 2,000 years before Christ. These first inhabitants probably were hunters and gatherers from the deserts to the west; scholars do not know how long they stayed in the canyon, or why they left.

Prior to the discovery of the figurines, the earliest known inhabitants of the canyon were thought to have been the Anasazi, who entered the region around A.D. 500, during the Basketmaker phase of their culture. In addition to hunting, they cultivated corn and squash. By A.D. 1000, their culture had evolved to include the manufacture of pottery, the use of intensive cultivation methods, and the construction of pueblo dwellings.

The Cohonina, originally from what is now west-central Arizona, settled on the South Rim of the canyon around A.D. 700. Their material culture was strikingly similar to that of the Anasazi, although their social and religious life probably was very different.

Theodore Roosevelt designated the Grand Canyon a national monument in 1908.

Around 1150, due to prolonged drought, the Grand Canyon was abandoned by both the Anasazi and the Cohonina. About 150 years later, the Cerbat migrated to the South Rim from the deserts of the lower Colorado River. These hunters and gatherers (who also practiced agriculture) lived in rock shelters and brush wickiups on the Coconino Plateau and in the tributary canyons. The Cerbat were the direct ancestors of the Hualapai and the Havasupai, two tribes that still live in the western reaches of the canyon.

Also around 1300, ancestors of the present-day Southern Paiute settled in the heavily forested regions of the North Rim and its tributary canyons. They moved into old Anasazi ruins, mingling their artifacts with those already there and giving archeologists more material over which to puzzle.

Spanish Exploration

The Cardenas expedition of 1540 brought white explorers to the canyon for the first time. The Spaniards spent three days looking for a path down to the Colorado River before finally giving up.

Two hundred years later, another Spaniard passed through the region. In 1776, while the American colonists on the eastern shore of the continent were struggling for independence, a Franciscan padre named Francisco Tomás Garcés traveled alone from the lower Colorado River Valley into the country of the Havasupai at the western end of the canyon. After spending time with the natives, he traveled to the Hopi villages, where he was coldly rebuffed in his effort to spread the Word of God. Undeterred, Father Garcés returned to the Havasupai, who welcomed him with six days of feasting.

In the same year, two other Franciscan fathers, Francisco Atanasia Domínguez and Sylvestre Vélez de Escalante, started out from Santa Fe to find an overland route between New Mexico and California. They traveled a difficult path north through the Rocky Mountains and west into present-day Utah before turning south and crossing the Colorado River in Glen Canyon and circling back to Santa Fe. Although they did not actually see the canyon, Domínguez and Escalante helped to pioneer a route across the northern section of the region that later explorers and settlers would follow.

American Exploration

The first Americans to see the Grand Canyon were the intrepid mountain men—the fur trappers and traders whose wanderlust opened up many areas of the West. In 1826, a character named James Ohio Pattie may have passed through the region. Unlike most mountain men, Pattie was literate, and he kept a journal, which makes gloomy mention of the "horrid mountains" he encountered at Grand Canyon.

It was the mid-nineteenth century before news of the discovery traveled to the rest of the world. By the terms of the Treaty of Guadalupe Hidalgo of 1848, following the Mexican War, the future states of New Mexico, Arizona, and California became United States territories. During the 1850s, the federal government sent surveying parties led by military officers to map the new terrain, specifically to locate routes for future railroads. The most interesting of these expeditions, as far as the Grand Canyon is concerned, was led by Lieutenant Joseph Ives. In 1857, Ives and his party chugged up the Colorado River in a sternwheeler called *Explorer*. At Black Canyon, near the spot where the Hoover Dam now stands, the *Explorer* struck a sunken rock, and Ives had to abandon the damaged steamer. The party continued overland, into the depths of the "Big Cañon." While Ives admired the beauty of the place, he was pessimistic about its usefulness. "The region is, of course, altogether valueless," he said in his report. "Ours has been the first, and will doubtless be the last, party of whites to visit this profitless locality."

Prospectors and Tourists

After the explorers came the prospectors, in a pattern that characterized much of the development of the West. In the 1870s and 1880s, sizable deposits of lead, zinc, copper, and asbestos were found in the canyon, and enterprising miners staked out claims down in the depths. The difficulties of extracting the ore and transporting it to the rim were the main reasons that mining at the Grand Canyon was never very successful. By the early 1900s, most mines had been abandoned. The discovery of uranium at Orphan Mine near Powell Memorial Point in the 1950s stimulated new activity. In 1987, the claim at Orphan Mine reverted to the National Park Service.

Around the turn of the century, the sensibility of many Americans toward their natural heritage began to change. They began to realize that there was a dimension to the land other than the economic one. Artists like Thomas Moran and writers like Clarence Dutton and John Van Dyke depicted the Grand Canyon in terms that had far more to do with aesthetics than with utility.

In response to this shift in attitude, a whole new industry evolved. In the 1890s, the Bright Angel Trail was completed, enabling tourists to walk or ride down to the spacious mantle of the Tonto Platform. J. W. Thurber's stagecoach route between Flagstaff and the South Rim was made obsolete when the Santa Fe Railroad constructed a spur from Williams in 1901. Old miners soon came to

Conservationists John Muir and John Burroughs (fourth and sixth in line) descend by mule into the canyon.

see great potential in this new source of gold, and they built accommodations like Bass Camp and the Grand View Hotel. The Age of Tourism had begun.

A settlement of sorts, later to be known as Grand Canyon Village, sprang up on the South Rim. The El Tovar Hotel was built in 1905, followed by the Hopi House, Babbitt's General Store, and Verkamp's Curios. The North Kaibab Trail was carved from the North Rim in 1904, enabling hikers to reach Rust's Camp, the forerunner of Phantom Ranch, deep in the Inner Gorge.

With the construction of Bright Angel Lodge in 1935 and the completion of a road system along the South Rim, tourism increased dramatically. Grand Canyon Lodge, an imposing limestone structure, was built on the North Rim in 1928. On the Colorado River, at the mouth of Bright Angel Creek, Phantom Ranch, the hostel designed by Mary Jane Colter, was built in 1922.

The Colorado River and Its Runners

The identity of the first explorer to float the length of the canyon by boat has long been debated. James White may have done so in 1867, two years before the expedition of John Wesley Powell. White kept no record of his ordeal, and his memory was hazy. Be that as it may, Major Powell's expedition of 1869 was one of the most important of the century. Powell's expedition and a second trip through the canyon in 1871 filled in one of the last blank spots on the map of the continental United States.

In 1889, a party led by Robert Stanton shoved off on an expedition to determine the feasibility of constructing a railroad along the bottom of the canyon. The trip was badly organized, and the party lacked equipment; three men drowned. Other float trips followed, capped by the 1911 voyage of Ellsworth and Emery Kolb, two photographer brothers who had a studio on the lip of the South Rim. The Kolbs made the first film of the canyon—a flickering, sepia-tinted feature of the Inner Gorge and its ferocious rapids.

At the time of the completion of Glen Canyon Dam upstream from Lees Ferry in 1965, some 2,000 people were known to have made the journey between the granite walls. By 1972, more than 16,000 claimed the adventure, and the Colorado River was in danger of becoming overcrowded. In response, the National Park Service laid down stringent regulations to control the number of boaters.

The construction of the dam altered the Colorado's ancient pattern of flooding and subsidence. Instead of scouring the inner canyon every spring with its annual convulsion, the river is regulated by the dam. The Colorado is thus unable to rebuild its eroded beaches and to cleanse debris washed down from tributaries.

Establishment of the Park

In 1903, during a trip to the Grand Canyon, President Theodore Roosevelt called the canyon "the most impressive piece of scenery I have ever looked at." An ardent outdoorsman, Roosevelt was an early champion of a national policy of conservation. By 1908, part of the Grand Canyon already had been declared a game preserve and a national forest. In that year, taking advantage of his powers under the Antiquities Act of 1906, Roosevelt designated the Grand Canyon a national monument. Shortly after Arizona became a state in 1912, the more complicated process of transforming the monument into a park began in earnest. Woodrow Wilson declared the Grand Canyon a national park on February 26, 1919.

From the viewpoint of environmentalists and all those who loved the river in its natural state, the construction of Glen Canyon dam, which created Lake Powell and flooded one of the most lyrically beautiful stretches of the Colorado, was a tragedy. Then, seizing on a clause in the law creating the park that left open the door to the construction of dams inside the park, the U.S. government pressed plans to build two dams that would flood 146 river miles. The churning water that had carved the gorge for uncounted millenia would be silenced forever.

The Sierra Club had failed to prevent construction of a dam in Yosemite National Park early in the century. But the Club and its allies were now more adept at political infighting. In 1966, David Brower, the Club's executive director, ran ads in major newspapers: One said, " . . . there is only one simple, incredible issue here: this time it's the Grand Canyon they want to flood. *The Grand Canyon.*"

Dam supporters argued that the lakes could hardly be seen from the rims, and that visitors in boats could see the rocks up close. In a newspaper ad, the Sierra Club asked, "SHOULD WE ALSO FLOOD THE SISTINE CHAPEL SO TOURISTS CAN GET NEARER THE CEILING?"

Dam opponents stressed that the dams would only be cash registers, that power they generated would be sold to finance water development elsewhere. Other sources could provide cheaper power. Environmentalists refused to compromise, the public rushed to defend the canyon, and the plan for the dams was abandoned.

The Internal Revenue Service accused the Sierra Club of attempting in a "substantial" way to influence legislation, and took away its tax-exempt status. But the fight was a breakthrough for the Club in terms of its national influence, and membership soared.

A law signed by President Gerald Ford in 1975 almost doubled the size of the park. The new boundaries include all of the interior of the canyon, except for Indian reservations, from the Paria River near Lees Ferry to the Grand Wash Cliffs at the western end.

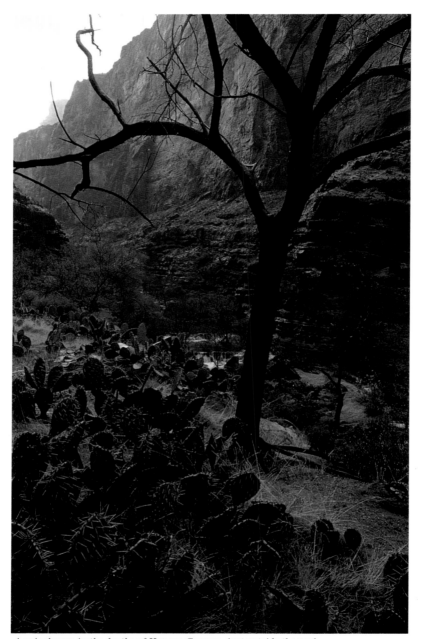

A rainshower in the depths of Havasu Canyon, just outside the park.

Vishnu Schist.

The rocks in the Grand Canyon illustrate 2 billion years of the earth's development, or nearly half of its total history. In few other places can one look so deep into the earth's crust or so far back into the planet's evolution. "Geology is an anthology of stories," says geologist Michael Collier, "the best in the world." And the geological layers of the canyon can be read like the pages of a book.

Metamorphic and Sedimentary Rock

The canyon is primarily composed of metamorphic and sedimentary rocks. The Inner Gorge, sections of which are visible from the South Rim, contains some of the oldest exposed rock surfaces in the world. The Vishnu Schist, as this rock is called, is all that remains of a once giant mountain range that existed about 2 billion years ago during the late Precambrian era. The vertical seams of dull rose quartz in the walls of the Inner Gorge were formed by molten material from the interior of the earth that penetrated into the base of the mountain range and forced its way into cracks in the rock before cooling and hardening. Gradually, the mountains were worn down by erosion, and the great sedimentary deposits that compose the rest of the canyon were laid down on the eroded roots millions of years later.

At various times during the Precambrian era (2 billion to 600 million years ago), wide, shallow seas covered most of northern Arizona. Shell-bearing animals had not yet evolved, and the most common rock types laid down during this period were sandstone and shale. A few limestone layers were deposited by algae, which grew abundantly in these seas. About 1 billion years ago, the land in the Grand Canyon region rose above sea level, tilting northeastward as it rose. The layers that are exposed at the top of the Inner Gorge were originally deposited horizontally; but as a result of the uplift, they now lie at a 10° to 12° angle.

This era of uplift was followed by an interval of erosion that lasted for perhaps 400 to 500 million years. Erosion was so severe that all traces of several earlier sedimentary deposits were obliterated. These gaps in the record are known as unconformities. Other types of uncomformities were created when the Grand Canyon was above sea level and no sediments were laid down and, as a result, no rocks were formed.

Vast seas again flooded the Grand Canyon region during the Paleozoic era, which began about 600 million years ago. The deposits they laid down as they receded were subjected to some erosion before being inundated by new seas. Unlike the earlier seas, those of the Paleozoic era were populated by a hard-shelled animal similar to the modern oyster, clam, and coral. The remains of these animals now form enormous limestone layers in the Muav and Redwall formations. This cyclical pattern of deposition and ero-

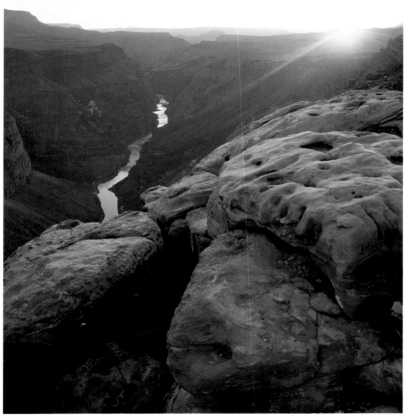

The Grand Canyon, with the Colorado River more than 3,000 feet below.

sion continued until about 70 million years ago, resulting in an accumulation of sandstone, limestone, and shale layers that amount to more than 3,000 feet.

In the Permian period, which began some 270 million years ago, the Grand Canyon region remained arid. Formations such as the Coconino Sandstone were created by desert conditions. Sand, blown by stiff winds, stacked up in shifting dunes covering thousands of square miles. The layers left by these dunes are easy to recognize by their buff color and their distinctive herringbone pattern, which geologists call dune cross-bedding.

The desert period was followed by one of warm, shallow seas that resulted in the Toroweap and Kaibab layers, the latter being the uppermost stratum of the canyon. Fossils of brachiopods and mollusks, as well as fossils of sponges and sharks' teeth, are found in these layers, indicating abundant marine life.

Little evidence remains of yet another chapter in the unfolding story of the Grand Canyon. During the Mesozoic era, which began 230 million years ago, additional layers of sediment, 8,000 feet thick in places, were deposited. Wind and rain took their toll, and only two remnants remain: Cedar Mountain, near Desert View and the eastern boundary of the park; and Red Butte, about 15 miles south of Grand Canyon Village.

The Cenozoic era, which began some 70 million years ago, was the last great formative period of the canyon's history. During this era, the region remained above sea level. The dominant geological process was a combination of widespread erosion and sustained volcanic activity. The San Francisco Peaks, 70 miles to the southeast, were created, and thousands of feet of rock deposited during the preceding Mesozoic era were stripped away. Later in this period, the Colorado River began to cut down in earnest through the rock layers to the Inner Gorge. The buttes that stand out in the canyon like lonely sentinels are a byproduct of the action of the river. The buttes, which are made up of once-continuous strata that stretched from rim to rim, are identifiable by the small caps or tips that rise from their flat tops. Over the years, various explorers and surveyors have given them exotic names such as Vishnu Temple and Wotans Throne.

The Colorado River

The formation of the Grand Canyon is intimately related to the complex development of the Colorado River system, which extends its tentacles—a far-flung array of tributaries—throughout much of the Southwest. The headwaters lie far away from the Grand Canyon, in southwestern Wyoming, western Colorado, and northwestern New Mexico. The tributary rivers—the Gunnison, the Green, the Yampa, the Upper Colorado, the San Juan, and the Little Colorado—merge into the Colorado River before it enters the Inner Gorge of the Grand Canyon; they drain much of the southern and central Rocky Mountains.

Geologists are divided in their opinions of how and to what extent the Colorado River influenced the creation of the Grand Canyon. There are several theories, one of which is the "stream-piracy" theory. The South Rim of the canyon stands at 7,000 feet, the North Rim at approximately 8,200. Why did the river cut through some of the highest country in the region? Why did it not seek the line of least resistance and go around the area?

One version of the "stream-piracy" theory suggests that more than 5 million years ago, the Colorado flowed southward into Marble Canyon (just upriver from the Grand Canyon) and then southeastward through the channel of the present-day Little Colorado River, into a huge lake. At some time less than 5 million years ago, a small drainage flowing westward through the Grand Canyon eroded its way upstream until it intercepted the canyon of the Little Colorado. The interception resulted in the "capture" of the waters of what was then the main channel of the Colorado. A new channel to the west opened up, and instead of flowing south-eastward, the river began to flow in the directions (west and north) the Little Colorado and the main Colorado flow today. This relatively sudden change in direction was to have a profound effect on the rock formations in the area, resulting in the cutting of the Grand Canyon to its present depth. According to this theory, the rapid erosion of the Grand Canyon was largely completed 1 to 2 million years after the shift in direction of the currents of the Colorado and Little Colorado.

During the past 6 million years, volcanic activity has also helped to shape the Grand Canyon. Much of this activity was contemporaneous with the cutting of the canyon by the river. Evidences of the tumult are still visible, especially in the Toroweap Plateau at the western end of the canyon. Great lava deposits cascaded over the area, temporarily damming up the Colorado River. Vulcan's Forge, at river mile 177.9, marks the remains of a volcano that erupted through the present riverbed.

The formation of the Grand Canyon is an ongoing process; the region still may be rising, and the Colorado River, despite having been dammed at Glen Canyon, is still eroding its bed. Heavy rainfall followed by flash floods in the tributary canyons tumble vast quantities of debris into the main channel, and this debris in turn is pulverized by the action of the current, which continues to deepen the canyon.

Kaibab squirrel.

Within the Grand Canyon are many ecological systems, as well as four of the seven major temperate zones of the North American continent. The difference in elevation—from 2,400 feet above sea level at the bottom of the canyon to 12,670 feet at the top of Mount Humphreys in the San Francisco peaks—is responsible for the wide variation. As the crow flies, only 90 horizontal miles separate those points, but at the Grand Canyon, distance is vertical. A 1,000-foot increase in elevation up the canyon walls is equivalent to a 300-mile move northward across flat country. As a result, the contrast in vegetation and animal life between the lowest and the highest points in the park is like that between Sonora, Mexico, and British Columbia!

Inner Gorge

The life zone at the bottom of the canyon is designated Lower Sonoran. In summer, the weather is steamy, and the temperature is 20° warmer on the average than that at the South Rim. Less than 10 inches of rain falls annually, and the vegetation is sparse. Willows and cottonwoods grow along watercourses like Bright Angel Creek and around seeps that form natural springs. Warblers, grosbeaks, and vireos make use of the leafy cover these trees provide. Hummingbirds flit among the shrubs searching for nectar. Under the surface of the Colorado River, the native fish that once flourished have nearly been annihilated as a result of the frigid change in water temperature created by Glen Canyon Dam. Squawfish, chub, and razorback sucker have been replaced by carp and rainbow trout.

Along the riparian corridor and on the Tonto Platform are found varieties of cactus, agave, and yucca. Lower Sonoran forms like mesquite, ocotillo, and creosote bush are also present. The black-throated sparrow, a popular desert bird, lives here. Blackbrush, found at similar elevations of the Mojave Desert, is a common shrub.

As in most arid environments, the mammals have adopted a

nocturnal way of life. Western pipistrelle bats search the air at night for insects. The spotted skunk steals forth in the moonlight to look for deermice. At midday, when the heat is suffocating, chuck-wallas and other lizards retreat to shadowy crevices. Located at this level, too, is the Grand Canyon rattlesnake. Over the millenia, this species has developed a protective adaptation—its salmon-colored skin blends in with the pink rocks.

Among larger animals, mule deer dip their delicate tongues into the cold river. Bighorn sheep move nimbly along the narrow ledges of the Inner Gorge. Colin Fletcher, in his book *The Man Who Walked Through Time*, tells of seeing beaver and wild burros. The burros are descendents of those used by miners in the 1800s to haul out ore from the canyon. They feed on grasses that normally provide forage for the mule deer and the bighorn sheep. When the herd expanded in the 1970s, the question of what to do about the burros became a topic of public debate. Some burros were adopted by human parents. Others became subject, in bureaucratic terminology, to "direct reduction."

South Rim

From the South Rim, the ground slants southward onto the broad slope of the Coconino Plateau, carrying most of the scant rain water and much of the soil with it. Due to the light rainfall—approximately 16 inches a year—trees do not grow very tall on the South Rim. Their abbreviated height has caused them to be termed a "pygmy forest." The ponderosa pine, which grows back from the rim, may reach 100 feet, but this is unusual. Common trees like the pinyon pine and the Utah juniper are no more than 20 to 30 feet tall.

Wildflowers grow in abundance on the South Rim. Cliffrose—a gnarled, shaggy evergreen with creamy, aromatic blossoms—is everywhere. Fernbush, another member of the rose family, flowers in August and September, which is late considering the warm climate. Three varieties of pentstemon are found in the park. The most prevalent on the South Rim is the Eaton pentstemon. Down in the canyon it flowers in April; on the South Rim, in June and July. Eight species of thistle are present, including the carmine thistle, which blooms from May to October.

Smaller animals that make the South Rim their home are the porcupine, the striped skunk, and the Abert, or tassel-eared, squirrel. Cliff chipmunks and rock squirrels scamper fearlessly along the rim.

Turkey vultures wheel in wide circles looking for carrion. Ravens with glossy black wings glide over the canyon, making peculiar croaking sounds. Violet-green swallows zoom overhead. In

Opposite: The prickly growth of spines covering the hedgehog cactus prevents animals from eating the soft pulp underneath.

the trees and shrubs along the rim are chickadees, nuthatches, scrub jays, and Steller's jays.

North Rim

The North Rim is more than 1,000 feet higher than the South Rim, and ecologically it is a much different place. The South Rim belongs to the Upper Sonoran and Transition life zones, the North Rim to the Canadian. The average annual rainfall on the North Rim is 28 inches, compared with half that on the South Rim; the North Rim receives around 140 inches of snow a year, compared with only 61 inches on its counterpart. The North Rim's higher elevation and additional moisture support two distinct coniferous forests—the spruce–fir–aspen and the yellow and ponderosa pines. The pin-yon pine and Utah juniper "pygmy forest" grows far below the rim, along the steep slopes of the canyon. Masses of warm air that rise out of the depths feed these growths. In the late summer months, the warm air, cooling as it rises, forms dark thunderheads that keep the North Rim liberally doused with rain.

Back from the canyon, the landscape of the North Rim is characterized by pristine forests and flowing meadows. Although the growing season is shorter than that of the South Rim, the variety of wildflowers is greater. Pink phlox blooms in early spring. Goldenrod, sunflowers, and mountain dandelions add a splash of color to the green meadows. Asters bloom in late summer, after many other flowers have wilted.

The soil on the North Rim is richer and deeper than that on the South Rim, and it supports a diverse group of burrowing animals such as voles, weasels, and pocket gophers. The lush meadows provide a perfect habitat for them; above their tunnels they beat tiny paths through the high grass, out of reach of predatory birds.

Shrews, skunks, wood rats, deermice, and horned toads add to the list of small animal life. Among the larger creatures are mule deer, coyote, porcupine, and an occasional mountain lion. Birds include wild turkeys, flickers, great horned owls, and red-tailed hawks.

Perhaps the most distinctive animal on the North Rim is the Kaibab squirrel. A large squirrel, with tassled ears and a bushy white tail, it is closely related to the Abert squirrel, which lives on the South Rim. The different coloration of the two squirrels evolved through speciation. As it cut down through the rock layers, the Colorado River gradually widened the gap between the rims. The squirrels, unable to cross the barrier, were isolated in different habitats and eventually developed different characteristics. Differences in climate between the two rims also influenced the evolution of the squirrels.

White-water rafting.

There are three kinds of trails in Grand Canyon National Park, classified according to use and condition—main trails, secondary trails, and routes. Secondary trails are not maintained and require some route-finding ability. They are infrequently patrolled by the National Park Service. Routes are difficult to follow, and for part of the way they may no longer even exist. To hike them safely, experience on Grand Canyon main and secondary trails is necessary.

All trails require twice as much time to hike up as to hike down. If it takes 5 hours to hike down a particular trail to the river, you should allow at least 10 hours to hike back up to the rim.

South Rim Sites

The canyon from the South Rim presents an awesome spectacle. It is from this side that most tourists enjoy their first view. There are a number of points on the rim that offer superb vistas. Within Grand Canyon Village, three points—Grandeur, Yavapai, and Mather—provide excellent overlooks. During the summer months only, shuttle buses follow West Rim Drive to Hermits Rest, 8 miles from the village. The route follows the lip of the canyon and passes through or near all the major overlooks—Pima, the Abyss, Mohave, Hopi, Powell, and Maricopa. These points are excellent locations from which to photograph sunsets; they also offer fine views of the Colorado River far below.

At Grand Canyon Village are several interesting old buildings. *Hopi House* was designed by Mary Jane Colter and constructed in 1905. The "house" is modeled after the Hopi Indian pueblo of Old Oraibi. The *El Tovar Hotel* was completed the same year, and offers the most luxurious accommodation on the South Rim. *Bright Angel Lodge*, also designed by Mary Jane Colter, was built in 1935. Among its many interesting features is a fireplace that was constructed out of all the types of rock in the Grand Canyon placed in proper chronological sequence. *Lookout Studio* was designed by Colter and built in 1914. Assembled out of rough-cut limestone, the

Overleaf: Watchtower at Desert View, constructed on the South Rim in 1933.

studio blends with the rim and is hardly visible from the Bright Angel Trail, which winds below.

From Grand Canyon Village to the eastern entrance of the park is 25 miles. Along the way are Yaki, Grandview, Moran, and Lipan points. Desert View is the easternmost overlook, and it offers an excellent view of Marble Canyon and the Painted Desert. At Desert View is the famous Watchtower, designed by Mary Jane Colter and constructed in 1933.

South Rim Trails

Bright Angel Trail. For hikers, strollers, and loiterers, Bright Angel Trail is the main thoroughfare, a wide and well-marked trail that snakes down into the canyon in a series of tight switchbacks to the Tonto Platform. This is also the trail that the famous Grand Canyon mules use for day trips or overnight treks to Phantom Ranch. The mule rides are fun, but very popular; it is best to make reservations well before you visit the canyon. Riders must be over 4 feet, 7 inches in height and weigh less than 200 pounds. Everyone, regardless of age, must have a tolerance for heights: although sure-footed, the mules skirt perilously close to the edge of the trail.

The trail slants through the Kaibab, Coconino, and Supai formations, offering clear and graphic views of their colors and textures. At the bottom of the Redwall Formation, the trail levels out at Indian Garden, and branches off in two directions. One branch leads to the rim of the Tonto Platform, and offers a dramatic overview of the Inner Gorge. The other follows Garden Creek until it dips down into Pipe Creek, and then veers away from the creek and drops into the Inner Gorge via a series of switchbacks known as the Devil's Corkscrew. Just before reaching the Colorado River, the trail branches east 1.7 miles to the Silver Suspension Bridge, which leads to Phantom Ranch and Bright Angel Campground.

It is 9.5 miles from the canyon rim to Bright Angel Campground. The descent is 4,400 feet and takes about 5 hours to hike down and 10 to hike back up.

South Kaibab Trail. The South Kaibab Trail was completed in 1928 and is part of a cross-canyon route that links the two rims. The trail, though well tended, is quite steep. No water is available along the way.

The trail descends quickly to Cedar Ridge, 1.5 miles below the rim. Because South Kaibab Trail follows ridge lines instead of side canyons, the view along the trail, unlike the view from Bright Angel Trail, is unobstructed for practically the entire distance to the river.

The descent from Cedar Ridge takes the hiker past O'Neill Butte and down through the Redwall Formation. At the Tipoff, the trail drops into the Inner Gorge to the Kaibab Suspension Bridge, which spans the Colorado River. This bridge was constructed in 1928. The thick cables that help support it were carried down intact on the brawny shoulders of forty-two Havasupai Indians. On the other side of the bridge are Phantom Ranch and Bright Angel Campground.

The South Kaibab Trail begins near Yaki Point just off East Rim Drive. From the rim to the Colorado River is 6.4 miles, and the trail takes about 4 hours to hike down and 8 hours to hike back up.

Secondary Trails

Before venturing onto any of the secondary trails, please inquire at the Backcountry Office or the Visitor Center about trail conditions, which vary a great deal. Please remember also that permits are required for all overnight hikes.

On the South Rim there are several interesting secondary trails: Boucher, Hermit, Tonto, Grandview, New Hance, and Tanner.

Boucher Trail. The Boucher Trail is very difficult and requires some route-finding ability. Access to it is by way of the Dripping Springs branch of the Hermit Trail. The trail crosses the drainage above Dripping Springs, winds around the base of Eremita Mesa, then plunges down a series of switchbacks through the Coconino Formation. A broad shelf of the Supai Formation is then traversed, followed by a difficult section of loose rock and steep grades that lead over White Butte Saddle. From the Redwall Formation, the trail descends to the Tonto Platform, where it links up with the Tonto Trail.

Both Boucher Trail and Boucher Creek, which are just beyond the junction with the Tonto Trail, are named after Louis Boucher, a French–Canadian prospector. The remains of his cabin can be seen on the east side of the creek, just south of where the trail enters the creekbed.

Hermit Trail. The Hermit Trail begins near Hermits Rest, the limestone curio shop and snack shop that was designed by Mary Jane Colter and constructed in 1914. The trail head is at the end of West Rim Drive. The trail drops down through the Supai Formation to Santa Maria Spring. The path leading away from the spring passes through an area of rock slides to the Redwall Formation, which is negotiated by a series of switchbacks known as the Cathedral Stairs. The Hermit Trail then intersects the Tonto Trail and proceeds west to Hermit Camp and Hermit Creek. The Colorado River can be reached from this point by hiking 1.5 miles

Overleaf: A canyon vista viewed from the El Tovar Hotel on the South Rim.

down Hermit Creek. The distance from the rim to the Colorado River is 8.5 miles and takes approximately 7 hours to hike down and 14 hours up.

Tonto Trail. The Tonto Trail, the main east–west route through the interior of the canyon, follows the Tonto Platform for 72 miles. The trail is seldom hiked in its entirety but is used to complete routes between various trails that lead into the canyon from the South Rim. For example, it links up with the Bright Angel Trail and the South Kaibab Trail, as well as with several secondary trails. The trail passes through desert terrain and is often difficult to follow in the western portion of the canyon.

Grandview Trail. The Grandview Trail goes as far as Horseshoe Mesa, a distance of 3 miles from the rim. After descending the north side of Grandview Point, the trail crosses a narrow saddle between Hance Canyon and Grapevine Canyon and continues down through the Coconino and Hermit formations. From there it eases out into Horseshoe Mesa, on top of the Redwall. From the western prong of the mesa, the trail drops onto the Tonto Platform, where it links up with the Tonto Trail.

New Hance Trail. The head of the New Hance Trail is located on East Rim Drive, about 1 mile south of the Moran Point turnoff. There are washouts in many places along the trail, so route-finding ability is a necessity. The trail zigzags down a shallow drainage to the base of the Coconino Formation. From there, it picks up a drainage that leads down the east side of the Coronado Butte to the top of the Redwall Formation. The descent off the rim of the Redwall is difficult to find; a large heap of stones indicates the proper trail. Once through the Redwall, the main trail is obscured by a maze of wild-burro trails, and to locate it requires a keen sense of direction. After the trail crosses a major drainage from the southeast below Moran Point, it heads down toward the bed of Red Canyon. By following this creekbed, you reach the Colorado River. Total hiking time, down and up, is 24 hours.

Tanner Trail. The Tanner Trail is at the east end of the canyon; its head is about 100 yards from Lipan Point on the east side of the road. The trail descends quickly to the base of Escalante and Cardenas buttes, around which it contours until it reaches a break in the Redwall Formation. From there, it leads down through Tanner Canyon to the Colorado River.

The route was once known as Horsethief Trail. Horses stolen in Utah were driven down from the North Rim to a low-water ford near the Tanner Trail. From there, the horses were driven out to the South Rim and sold to unsuspecting ranchers.

Total hiking time, down and up, is approximately 27 hours. There is no water along the way. Hikers are urged to avoid this trail in the summer, as it can be blazing hot.

North Rim Sites

Standing on the North Rim, looking over the Grand Canyon, is an exhilarating experience. On a clear day, the San Francisco Peaks near Flagstaff, 70 miles distant, are visible. The South Rim and the Inner Gorge seem far away. There is much about the North Rim that enforces a sense of isolation. The rim is 1,000 feet higher than its counterpart. The river, tucked out of sight, is twice the distance from the North Rim than it is from the South Rim. North of the river, the rate of erosion is greater because the precipitation that falls there drains to the south toward the canyon. The precipitation that falls on the South Rim also drains to the south, away from the canyon, and thus the erosive effect is minimized.

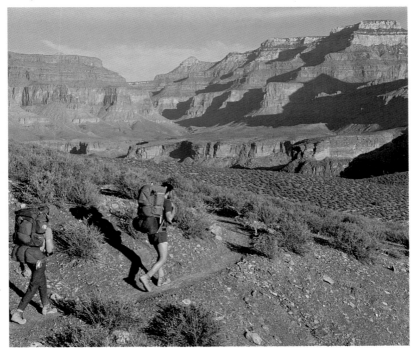

The 72-mile Tonto Trail is the main east–west trail through the canyon's interior.

TRAILS OF GRAND CANYON NATIONAL PARK*

SOUTH RIM TRAILS

RIM TRAIL: Starts at Hermits Rest; ends at Yavapai Point; 18 miles round trip; 10 hours; safe, easy hike along the edge of the South Rim for those who wish to view the canyon without hiking into it; passes through or near all the major overlooks along West Rim Drive.

BRIGHT ANGEL TRAIL: Starts at South Rim; ends at Bright Angel Campground; 19 miles round trip; 12 hours (not recommended for day trip); 4,400-foot ascent; wide, well-marked main thoroughfare (same trail used by mules); series of tight switchbacks to Tonto Platform; trail splits at Indian Garden: one branch leads to rim of Tonto Platform for view of Inner Gorge, other follows Garden Creek to Pipe Creek, then into Inner Gorge to Colorado River.

SOUTH KAIBAB TRAIL: Starts at Yaki Point off East Rim Drive; ends at Bright Angel Campground; 12.8 miles round trip; 12 hours (not recommended for day trip); part of cross-canyon route linking rims; unobstructed views almost entire distance; at Tipoff, drops into Inner Gorge to suspension bridge and on to Phantom Ranch.

HERMIT TRAIL§: Starts at Hermits Rest off West Rim Drive; ends at Colorado River; 17 miles round trip; 12 hours (not recommended for day trip); drops down through Supai Formation to Santa Maria Spring, from there to junction with Tonto Trail and on to Hermit Camp.

GRANDVIEW TRAIL: Starts at Grandview Point; ends at Horseshoe Mesa; 6 miles round trip; 6 hours; at western end of Horseshoe Mesa, drops onto Tonto Platform; carry water.

TONTO TRAIL: Starts at Garnet Canyon; ends at Red Canyon; 72 miles one way; main east-west route through interior of canyon; desert terrain with little shade.

TANNER TRAIL§: Starts east of Lipan Point on East Rim Drive; ends at Colorado River at Tanner Rapids; 16 miles round trip; 12 hours (not recommended for day trip); indistinct in places; low rock cairns mark difficult sections; little shade.

Boucher Trail§: Starts at Dripping Springs Trail (via Hermit Trail); ends at Boucher Creek; 22 miles round trip (from head of Hermit Trail); 14-16 hours (not recommended for day trip); one of the more difficult trails; route-finding ability required; 1 mile beyond Columbus Point, descends through Hermit and Supai formations; start of descent poorly marked by rock cairns, which must be located before proceeding down.

New Hance Trail§: Starts west of Moran Point turnoff on East Rim Drive; ends at Colorado River at Hance Rapids; 16 miles round trip; 12 hours (not recommended for day trip); difficult; indistinct in spots, rocky, and very steep; doubles around corners and plunges abruptly; some bad rockslides.

North Rim Trails

North Kaibab Trail: Starts at North Rim; ends at Bright Angel Campground; 28 miles round trip; 36 hours; 5,840-foot ascent; descends sharply first 4.7 miles; Phantom Ranch is 14.1 miles from trail head; open only between mid-May and mid-November.

Clear Creek Trail: Starts at Phantom Ranch; ends at Clear Creek; 18 miles round trip; 10 hours (not recommended for day trip); runs along Tonto Platform; branches off from North Kaibab Trail, switchbacks up talus slope, and ascends back to plateau; trout fishing in creek with license.

*Use permits, which are available at the backcountry office, are required for all overnight trips into the canyon. An infinite variety of off-trail hiking routes exist. Some are well known, used by several parties each year, and may even be marked with rock cairns. Others have been hiked once or twice. Still others remain to be discovered. If you are interested in hiking unmarked routes off established trails, talk with park rangers and be certain that your party has the equipment and experience necessary to handle inevitable problems associated with "bushwhacking," as well as potential emergencies. For permit information, write the Backcountry Office and request a Backcountry Trip Planner. Permits must be acquired by mail or in person.

§Do not attempt these trails unless you have tested your hiking ability on the Bright Angel or South Kaibab trails.

See map on pages 192–193..

Fewer people visit the North Rim than visit the South Rim. The North Rim is on the lip of the "Arizona Strip," an isolated section in the northwestern part of the state that abuts against the Utah boundary. Access to the North Rim by road is circuitous.

There are three main overlooks at the North Rim. From east to west they are Point Imperial, Cape Royal, and Bright Angel Point.

North Rim Trails

North Kaibab. The North Kaibab Trail originally was used by Indians and prospectors. François Matthes, a topographer working with the U.S. Geological Survey, improved the route for modern use in 1902. The path was so steep, Matthes reported, that his supply burros "fairly slid down on their haunches." When the first tourist camp was established at the mouth of Bright Angel Creek in 1903, the trail was further improved.

Because heavy snows blanket the North Rim, the North Kaibab Trail is open only between mid-May and mid-November. For the first 4.7 miles, the route descends at a precipitous angle through the sheer Redwall Formation, offering spectacular views of the canyon. At the junction of Roaring Springs Canyon and Bright Angel Creek, there are several good swimming holes. From the junction, the trail then drops down to Cottonwood Campground, 6.8 miles from the rim. Bright Angel Campground and Phantom Ranch are 7.3 miles beyond Cottonwood Campground. This portion of the trail is not as steep as the first miles; the trail winds over several high bridges that span creeks and chasms.

The total distance from the rim down to the river—14 miles—can be hiked in about 12 hours. It takes 24 hours to return to the rim, or 36 hours up and down.

Clear Creek Trail. In 1933, the Civilian Conservation Corps built this 8.7-mile trail from Phantom Ranch along the Tonto Platform to Clear Creek. The trail branches off from the North Kaibab just before Phantom Ranch. It zigzags 1,000 feet up to the rim of the Inner Gorge and onto the Tonto Platform. The trail remains on the plateau even after Clear Creek is sighted and contours along the drainage for some distance before descending to the Clear Creek streambed. The water in the creek is cold; when the Colorado River becomes muddy, trout swim up Clear Creek and other side streams.

From Clear Creek, it is 7 more miles to Cheyava Falls. *Cheyava* is the Hopi word for "intermittent." At most times of the year, the fall is a mere trickle; in the spring, when snow melts off the North Rim, it swells to a major waterfall.

The Colorado River Trip Through the Grand Canyon

"August 13 [1869].—We are now ready to start on our way down the Great Unknown. . . . We have but a month's rations remaining. . . . We are three quarters of a mile in the depths of the earth, and the great river shrinks into insignificance, as it dashes its angry waves against the wall and cliffs, that rise to the world above. . . . We have an unknown distance yet to run; an unknown river to explore. What falls there are, we know not; what rocks beset the channel, we know not; what walls rise over the river, we know not. Ah well! we may conjecture many things. The men talk cheerfully as ever; jests are bandied about freely this morning; but to me the cheer is somber and the jests are ghastly."

The Colorado River rises in the Never Summer Range in western Colorado, and carves a tortuous 1,450-mile corridor through many layers of rock to the Gulf of California. Through the miracle of erosion, the Colorado and its tributaries have created many beautiful canyons that attract river-runners seeking both whitewater adventure and a chance to exult in the enchantment of hidden worlds that other mortals can hardly imagine, even from photographs.

Major John Wesley Powell, who had lost an arm in Civil War combat, and his men were the first party known to have gone through the canyon on the Colorado River. Ten of them—mostly trappers and ex-soldiers—began their trip in four small wooden boats in Green River, Wyoming, on May 24, 1869, initiating the last major exploration within the "lower forty-eight" states. By the time the nine men (one had dropped out) reached the eastern end of the Grand Canyon, in August, they had already floated more than 1,000 miles through three future states.

After running many harrowing rapids, three more of Powell's men decided they had had enough, abandoned the trip, and struggled upward to the canyon rim—only to be killed by Indians. The remaining six explorers emerged from the canyon at the end of August.

Within the next 80 years, only 100 more people had traveled the length of the Colorado River through the Grand Canyon, some 277 miles, but thereafter the number grew rapidly. The availability of World War II-surplus rubber rafts stimulated a postwar boom in the exploration of America's bigwater rivers, including the Colorado. The enterprising Georgie White, a woman guide, lashed three pontoons together and steered them with an outboard motor, taking fifty paying customers down the river at once.

Today, would-be river runners may obtain a list of commercial guides from the park. Most trips begin at Lees Ferry, 6 miles northeast of the town of Marble Canyon, and vary in length from three days to three weeks. Some trips end, and others start, at Phantom Ranch, on the Colorado River, about midway through the canyon. (The Phantom Ranch option involves a hike up out of, or down into, the canyon.) The outfitters provide guides, food, and camping equipment. Commercial trips are available from April to October, and must be reserved well in advance. No motorized trips are allowed after September 15. A trip without motors takes about twice as many days as one in which motors are used. In some non-motor trips, participants do some of the rowing. Some outfitters offer trips in wooden or aluminum dories, boats that provide a bouncier ride through the rapids. Reduced rates may be available for families and groups. A trip without motors is the choice for any-

Anasazi granaries near Nankoweap Canyon. The float trip through the Grand Canyon is one of the greatest adventures in the world of nature.

one seeking a serene wilderness experience punctuated only by the sweet song of a canyon wren.

Any persons who plan to row through the canyon on their own must obtain permission from the National Park Service.

A guidebook, preferably one with detailed information on the rock formations, and U.S. Geological Survey topographic maps in waterproof covers are essential for a full appreciation of the natural and geological wonders that await a Grand Canyon rafter. What follows are only a few of the highlights:

All river miles are measured from Lees Ferry. The first real rapids, at Mile 8, occur at Badger Creek, and result from boulders washed into the river by tributaries; these moderate rapids are rated 4 to 6 on a scale of 1 to 10. This stretch of the river, to Mile 62, where the Little Colorado River enters from the left, is called Marble Canyon, for the tall, sheer, striped limestone walls. Natural features, at the river or up side canyons that may be hiked, include Silver Grotto, Redwall Cavern (a vast chamber Powell thought

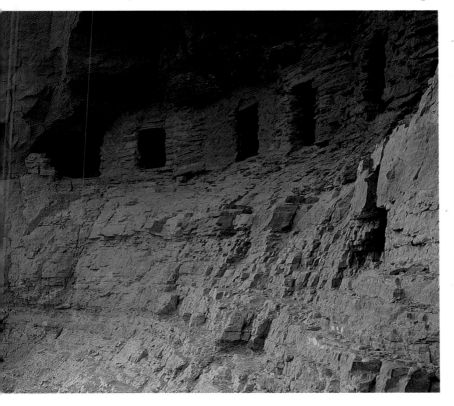

would seat 50,000 people), and Triple Arches.

Below the Little Colorado, the river flows past ancient ruins in several locations. In the granite gorge below Unkar Creek, heavy rapids—Hance, Sockdolager, and Grapevine—come in quick succession (Miles 76-82).

Powell's journal entry for August 15, 1869, reads: "Early in the afternoon we discover a stream entering from the north—a clear, beautiful creek, coming down through a gorgeous red canyon. We conclude to name it Bright Angel." Today, Phantom Ranch stands near the mouth of Bright Angel Canyon, at Mile 87.

Beyond the tree-shaded resort, heavy rapids loom. Huge standing waves at Hermit and Crystal rapids (Miles 95 and 98) crash over vessels, drenching passengers. Crystal became a major rapids in 1966, when a flash flood after a cloudburst washed large boulders into the river.

Elves Chasm (Mile 116) is a shady slot where Royal Arch Creek, nearing the river, spills over a travertine fall lined with ferns and flowers. Two miles up Tapeats Creek (Mile 133), hikers find Thunder River, and 1 mile up that river are hanging gardens, a cave, and Thunder River Spring in a limestone cliff.

Havasu Creek, entering from the left at Mile 157, features three high waterfalls—Mooney, Havasu, and Navajo. Above the falls is the secluded village of the Havasupai—"people of the blue waters." (The village and the falls, which are outside the park and in the Havasupai Indian Reservation, may also be accessed by a paved road leading north from U.S. 66 to Hualapai Hilltop, then a trail down Hualapai and Havasu canyons. For information, call 520-448-2961, or write the Havasupai Reservation, Post Office Box 10, Supai, AZ 86438.)

Most of the Colorado River whitewater occurs before Havasu Creek. However, at Lava Falls (Mile 179), rafters experience rapids rated at 8 to 10, the biggest navigation hazard in the canyon. Long ago, an outpouring of lava created a natural dam, over the rubble of which the river now tumbles. The canyon walls in this area contain impressive volcanic forms, including frozen cascades of lava and rivers of black basalt.

Most river travelers take out at Diamond Creek, Mile 225. Some continue on to Lake Mead.

—Donald Young

Opposite: Havasu Falls, in the western part of the canyon, is perhaps the most magical oasis in the Southwest.

GREAT BASIN
NATIONAL PARK

Shooting stars carpet the ground near Stella Lake and below Wheeler Peak.

GREAT BASIN NATIONAL PARK
BAKER, NEVADA 89311
TEL.: (702) 234-7331

HIGHLIGHTS: Lehman Caves • Wheeler Peak Scenic Drive • Stella and Teresa Lakes • Bristlecone Pine Grove • Snake Creek • Baker Creek • Lexington Arch

ACCESS: From U.S. 6 and 50, 6 miles south on Nevada 487 to Baker, then 5 miles west on Nevada 488 to park headquarters and Visitor Center.

HOURS: Open year-round, 24 hours, daily.

FEES: None for entrance; charged for Lehman Caves tour and camping in developed sites.

PARKING: At major points and trail heads.

GAS, FOOD: Limited but sufficient in Baker; complete services in Ely, Nevada, and Delta, Utah.

LODGING: Limited in Baker and at Utah–Nevada state line on U.S. 6 and 50; also in Ely and Delta.

VISITOR CENTER: At end of Nevada 488, one mile beyond park entrance. Closed on Thanksgiving, Christmas, and New Year's Day.

PETS: Permitted on leash, except on trails and in buildings. Horses and llamas are permitted on backcountry trails.

PICNICKING: Developed and primitive sites throughout the park.

HIKING: Many trails available; see ranger for information.

BACKPACKING: Permitted in all but a few day-use areas and bristlecone pine groves. Permits not required; registration at Visitor Center recommended.

CAMPGROUNDS: Developed sites at Wheeler Peak, Upper and Lower Lehman Creek, and Baker Creek campgrounds; primitive sites in Snake Creek area and other locations.

TOURS: Lehman Caves tours, hourly during summer, less often in other seasons. Ranger-led walks, evening programs, and other activities daily.

OTHER ACTIVITIES: Fishing (Nevada license required, no live bait allowed); in winter, cross-country skiing and snowshoeing.

FACILITIES FOR DISABLED: Visitor Center and restrooms, some campsites, selected ranger-led activities, and first room of Lehman Caves are wheelchair-accessible, or accessible with assistance.

For additional information, see also Sites, Trails, and Trips on pages 241–249 and the map on pages 230–231.

REAT BASIN NATIONAL PARK FEELS LIKE the edge of a continent. The southern Snake Range, which forms the heart of the park, rises like an island in a vast sea of space, but instead of water lapping at its shore, there stretches a desert of greasewood and saltbush inhabited by black-tailed jack rabbits, pronghorn, and raking winds. Summer temperatures commonly top 100 degrees. There are no shade trees except for what ranchers have planted. If all you do is drive across this part of Nevada, you might agree with the pioneer who wisecracked, "I reckon God knows what he made that country for—he hain't told anybody though."

Evidently, that pioneer never climbed into the cool beauty of the Snake Range, where high above the baking flats, snowfields give rise to icy streams. The water trickles through wildflower meadows, collects in sparkling alpine lakes, and spills in white cascades beneath a dark canopy of pine and fir. In most parts of the world, these streams would emerge from the mountains and join rivers flowing to the sea. But here they strike the valley bottom and vanish into one of the most compelling of North America's landforms, the Great Basin.

The Great Basin was named in 1844 by the explorer John C. Fremont, who described it as an area "surrounded by lofty mountains: contents almost unknown, but believed to be filled with rivers and lakes which have no connection to the sea." He wasn't far wrong. The Great Basin is indeed defined most simply by its

Wheeler Peak, elev. 13,063 feet, is the highest point in the Snake Range.

GREAT BASIN
NATIONAL PARK

Bristlecone Pine Area
Ranger Station 🆄🆂
Campground
Road
Picnic Area
Unpaved Road
Primitive Campsite
Trail

N

Baker

487

488

Lehman Caves 🆄🆂 Visitor Center

LOWER LEHMAN CREEK

UPPER LEHMAN CREEK

BAKER CREEK

POLE CANYON

STRAWBERRY CREEK

HUMBOLDT NATIONAL FOREST

LEHMAN CREEK

BROWN'S LAKE

GLACIER

JEFF DAVIS El. 12771'

S N A K E

BUCK MOUNTAIN El. 10972'

WHEELER CREEK

TERESA LAKE

STELLA LAKE

BAKER PEAK El. 12298'

BALD MOUNTAIN El. 11562'

WHEELER PEAK El. 13063'

PYRAMID PEAK

BAKER

M   I   L   E   S

0   1   3   6

RANGE

SHOSHONE

SNAKE CREEK

WASHINGTON PEAK
El. 11658

NORTH FORK

SOUTH FORK

LINCOLN PEAK
• El. 11597

GRANITE PEAK
• El. 11218

Lexington Arch •

ARCH
CANYON

H U M B O L D T   N A T I O N A L   F O R E S T

BIG WASH

LEXINGTON CREEK

VICINITY MAP

15

Baker
• Garrison

GREAT
BASIN
N.P.

21

318

93

50

BRYCE
CANYON
N.P.

56

ZION
N.P.

Utah
Nevada

Arizona

93

15

Las Vegas

INSET SCALE

0 15 30

M I L E S

231
GREAT BASIN

pattern of drainage. Covering most of Nevada and parts of California, Oregon, Idaho, and Utah, it is a 210,000-square-mile region with no outlet to the sea. Whatever streams originate here stay here.

Yet Fremont seems to have missed the more intricate structure of the region. It contains not just one basin but many, all separated by mountain ranges standing in parallel ranks, hence the term "basin and range," commonly used to describe the corrugated topography of Nevada. Anchored by 13,063-foot Wheeler Peak, the southern Snake Range holds an especially fine sample of this enigmatic, little-known, and surprisingly beautiful region.

HISTORY

People, from prehistoric desert cultures to miners and ranchers, have always been attracted to these mountains. The first wandering hunters and gatherers left behind little evidence of their passing. They were perhaps the same people who some 4,000 years ago placed animal figurines in caves deep within the Grand Canyon. Except for those fragile split-twig effigies, they left almost nothing to mark their long centuries of coping with what might be the continent's most challenging living conditions outside of the Arctic.

When white settlers began probing the Great Basin, the native people near what is now the park were mostly Western Shoshone, along with a smaller number of Utes and Paiutes. Like the vanished desert cultures, they lived by moving, following sources of food according to the season. Rabbits and pinyon pine nuts served as staples, yet just about anything encountered and caught could make a meal. Food sources included waterfowl nesting in brackish basin marshes, fish from lakes and mountain streams, lizards, roots, bulbs, berries, grass seeds, even ants, Mormon crickets, and grasshoppers.

Summer was a relatively fat time but winter could be desperate. Survival required a deep knowledge of the land and its growth cycles. Desert people needed to know exactly when to harvest oil-rich pinyon nuts before rodents took them, and which trees would produce the best harvest in a given year. They had to predict movements of migrating waterfowl, and know how to lure them with decoys made of wood or stuffed skins. Often their hunting involved teamwork. Pronghorn, deer, rabbits, and other animals could be driven toward plant-fiber nets. This technique worked even with crickets; huge numbers could be trapped by herding them toward trenches covered with wisps of straw. The crickets would fall through the straw, which, when ignited, would roast them.

All told, native people of the Great Basin sought out more than a hundred different plant species and a variety of animals that would challenge the most adventurous eater. Consider the legendary mountain man Jedediah Smith and two companions, who in 1827, starving and nearly dead from dehydration, were saved by a gift of ground squirrels and water rushes provided by the local inhabitants. Days later, hungry again, they were invited to share a feast of roasted scorpions, but these they could not face. It was common in the late 1800s for judgmental whites, who equated a lack of material possessions with cultural poverty and even laziness, to make disparaging comments about the desert people. Yet more than a century later, despite all their mechanical abilities and faith in development, the region's non-native population is still no larger than the native population was in the mid-1800s.

In the end, the Indians succumbed—not to their environment, but to encroaching white settlement. There was no fighting to speak of; the Shoshones were not an aggressive or warlike people. Instead, it was a matter of attrition. Ranchers appropriated water and the best land. Their cattle and sheep displaced wildlife. Miners captured the flow of entire streams and diverted them to high-pressure hydraulic nozzles. In the face of these changes, the ancient ways of the desert people were doomed.

Absalom Lehman

Starting with Jedediah Smith, travelers, prospectors, and adventurers came through the Great Basin, failed to find a reason to

A cabin off Baker Creek Road recalls the days when prospectors mined for silver.

stay, and left it behind. One of the few who settled permanently was Absalom Lehman. A miner and prospector for most of his life, he chased the 1849 gold rush from Ohio to California. Failing there, but drawn on by rumors of gold, he set sail for Australia, and this time found a measure of success. But a miner's luck rarely holds; along with other misfortunes, the death of his wife and daughter brought him back to California and eventually eastern Nevada. He came on a wave of silver excitement, and staked at least one claim in the Snake Range. But after twenty years of prospecting with scanty results, he put most of his energy into building a ranch. He knew that mining was a risky proposition, and that ranchers at least had plenty to eat.

Lehman homesteaded two ranches, one along Strawberry Creek just outside the current park boundary, the second in a relatively sheltered valley on the east slope of the Snake Range beside the creek that today bears his name. There was morning sun, plenty of timber, a pleasant climate, and enough water to grow an orchard. He didn't know it then, but two miles upstream there was also one of the country's loveliest and most richly decorated limestone caves.

How Lehman discovered the cave is a matter of conflicting legends, some of which are clearly tall tales. However it happened, he was not the first. In 1938, archeologists found a small number of native skeletons in the entrance chamber—dumped or buried there, no one knows which. But there were no signs of deeper explorations before Lehman took sledge in hand and hammered his way through impassable narrows. Truly, this is Ab Lehman's cave—his most successful prospecting venture.

Unfortunately, he never saw the complete results. Lehman died in 1891 still trying to make a commercial success of the cave. After that, the property passed through several private owners before 1922, when President Warren Harding declared it and 1 square mile of surrounding land a national monument. In 1959, the U.S. Forest Service designated the 28,000-acre Wheeler Peak Scenic Area, and made plans to build a paved road up the mountain. For years, the idea of a national park had been argued by supporters and opponents. The time finally came in 1986, when just over 77,000 acres, including the high peaks and much of the range's eastern slope, became national park land. It was an accomplishment of compromise, involving boundary gerrymandering around mining properties and the retention of cattle grazing as a historic use. Cows, decided Congress, were in this case an essential part of the scene. Unfortunately, the park boundaries did not encompass any significant portions of the valley floor itself.

In its 210,000 square miles, the Great Basin contains some 90 basins and 160 separate mountain ranges. Although the southern Snake Range claims some of the most impressive peaks in the region, it is just another chord in the larger repeating theme of basin and range, basin and range.

The Boring Era

Just about every geologic story in the West begins with a reference to a great inland sea that once covered the region, and this one is no exception. It happened during the Paleozoic, the era of sedimentary deposition. For geologists who deal with the enormous movement of continents and tectonic plates, who find great meaning in volcanic eruptions and vast upheavals, the Paleozoic was a singularly uninteresting time. For several hundred million years, water sloshed slowly back and forth as the sea advanced and retreated. Beneath the waters, sediment piled up to form sandstone, shale, limestone, and combinations of all three. The limestone is particularly important to Great Basin National Park. Whitish-yellow in color, it covers all but the highest parts of the Snake Range, and provided the matrix for Lehman Caves. It resulted from unthinkable numbers of sea creatures living and dying over some vast stretch of time, their shells and bones piling

Columns in Lehman Caves, a home to many beautiful and unusual formations.

up on the sea floor to form a thick bed of almost pure calcium carbonate.

The same things were going on not far away in the area that is now the Grand Canyon—layers of sediment piling neatly atop one another. So why are the canyon and the Great Basin such different looking places? It has to do with an accident of location. The Grand Canyon rests on the edge of the Colorado Plateau, a zone of relative geologic calm whose rock layers have lain essentially undisturbed since they were formed. Over time the canyon rocks have been uplifted, eroded, bent, and cracked, but nowhere near as much as in the Great Basin.

The Big Stretch

A geologic map or a satellite photo of the region clearly indicates that something important happened to the Great Basin. Bordered on the west by the Sierra Nevada, and on the east by the Wasatch Range of the Rocky Mountains, this region of parallel mountains, all about the same size and marching in military precision from east to west, seems to have been created by one overriding geologic event.

Actually there were two forces working together. The first was compression caused by the Farralon Plate (part of the Pacific sea floor) pushing beneath North America—a sort of slow collision in which one chunk of the crust slid under the other. This began about 70 million years ago, and lasted until about 50 million years ago. It caused the western half of the continent to crumple and rise thousands of feet above sea level. Bulges appeared in the once-flat surface, including one that eventually became the Rocky Mountains. The Great Basin might also have become a single mountain massif except for the second event.

This one began roughly 20 million years ago, and continues today. The Farralon Plate stopped sliding eastward beneath North America. A new movement became dominant, this one toward the northwest along the San Andreas Fault. Where there had been compression there was now tension. Uplift became collapse. The rocks of the Great Basin cracked along north-south lines, forming huge elongated blocks that foundered as pressure was released. Some fell, becoming valleys. Others tilted and pushed upward (or, to be more accurate, they fell less far; the whole area was subsiding), becoming mountains. The Snake Range is a block that tilted toward the east; that is, its steep side faces west.

The remainder of the geologic story is primarily one of shaping and polishing through erosion. A small amount of volcanic activity occurred, but with little impact on the overall appearance of the range. Beneath Wheeler Peak, for example, a body of molten rock forced its way through cracks toward the surface without actually breaking through. The heat of this intrusion might be what changed some of the limestone into the low-grade marble in which Lehman Caves was eventually carved. Meanwhile, erosion carried on with its slow but vast work. Water, ice, and wind scarred the mountain blocks, stripping off huge amounts of stone and carrying it into the valleys. The great continental ice sheets of the Pleistocene stopped far north of Nevada, but alpine glaciers grew on the summits and pushed downward under their own immense weight. In doing so, they carved out cirque basins and vertical cliffs in the high peaks. Wheeler Peak, the highest of all, was entirely stripped of its limestone cover, revealing the quartzite mountain that we see today.

Of the glaciers, only a token remnant of ice remains in the deep shadows of Wheeler's north face. Some call it a glacier, others an ice sheet. The distinction lies in whether it moves or not. But ice it is, the only thing of its kind in the Great Basin, and all around it are the tracks of its vastly more powerful ancestors. Yet, as strong as they were, those ancient glaciers never reached the valley floor. The glacier that carved the Lehman Creek drainage, for instance, smoothed its path down to about 9,000 feet, where the ice melted. Above that point, the valley is a classic glacial U-shape. Below, it becomes a steep-sided V, carved by water, not ice.

NATURAL HISTORY

In one sense, the Snake Range is a miracle of water. Because of elevation and coolness, the mountains attract and retain moisture in a region known for its aridity. About 25 inches of rain per year falls on the mountain peaks, while the valley floor sees a bare 5 inches annually. This great disparity of moisture, coupled with altitudinal temperature gradients, is largely responsible for the distribution of plants and animals.

A Desert Island

Biologists often refer to the mountain ranges of the Great Basin as islands—biological islands rising above a sea of aridity. Animals and plants that might die on the desert thrive on the adjacent mountains. Of the larger mammals, these temperate survivors include bighorn sheep, mountain lions, mule deer, and elk. They

Overleaf: Nevada consists of alternating basins and ranges, including the Snake Range.

are joined by smaller ones like water shrews, montane voles, porcupines, northern pocket gophers, and yellow-bellied marmots.

It wasn't always desert on the valley floor. Fifteen thousand years ago, during the last ice age, the overall climate was much cooler. Glaciers sprawled across the high peaks. Powerful rivers emptied into the valleys, where, in place of today's greasewood, there grew bristlecone and limber pine. Mammoths and ground sloths roamed where coyotes now chase jack rabbits, and long, sinuous lakes filled the basins. The enormous prehistoric Lake Bonneville, currently represented by a shrunken remnant called Great Salt Lake, pounded a beach just three miles from the Snake Range.

Things began to change around 12,000 years ago with the onset of a warming trend. Glaciers melted back and disappeared, lakes dried up, and desert plants moved into the desiccated valleys. Bristlecone pines, limber pines, and other temperate species retreated to the cooler heights. The Snake Range became a real-life Lost World, a refuge for creatures that would otherwise have disappeared from the region.

For some of them, it became a prison. While many species are able to move freely between islands—notably birds, large mammals, and plants that produce wind-driven seeds—other organisms have no means of transport, or no behavioral inclination to make the crossing. For them, the desert basins present impassable barriers. They are cut off from others of their kind as surely as if they were marooned in a real ocean.

One of the world's fastest animals, the pronghorn runs at 30 to 70 miles an hour.

Virtually all park sites are reached from the eastern side of the Snake Range. Although spectacular to look at, the west side is very steep, with almost no road access points. The east side is a gentler place, penetrated by several good roads. The main entrance road, beginning at the town of Baker, leads to the heart of the park. Major sites include Lehman Caves, Wheeler Peak Scenic Drive, the bristlecone pine grove, and the Baker Creek area. Most visitors begin here and go no farther, which is understandable considering the wealth of things to see and do. On the other hand, several outlying areas—particularly Snake Creek and Lexington Arch—appeal to the more adventurous.

Lehman Caves

Despite its name, Lehman Caves is a single cavern, and as dark holes in the ground go, a most friendly one—a good place to take someone for whom the appeal of caves is a mystery. This one is relatively small, and not especially deep. It does not contain the enormous disorienting rooms that frighten some people at Carlsbad Caverns. There are no scary black holes dropping off into mysterious nowheres, few bats, and only enough water to help park rangers explain how such caverns are created. An experience here could well lead to a new appreciation for the underground world. Best of all, Lehman Caves is one of the most richly decorated cav-

An immature mountain bluebird; it stays near the ground, watching for insects.

erns in the country. Along the half-mile walking tour all but a few spaces are filled with cave formations, or as cave scientists call them, speleothems. These include common cave objects like stalactites, stalagmites, flowstone, soda straws, drapery, and columns. There are also intriguing rarities: helictites, gypsum flowers, aragonite, and one of the best collections anywhere of the mysterious objects called shields.

Everything is the result of flowing water. Water in abundance carved the cave; water in trickles has made it beautiful to look at. In a manner of speaking, limestone caves are living things. They are born, they mature, and they die. First comes a period of enlargement, in which slightly acidic water dissolves the limestone, which consists almost entirely of calcium carbonate. Joining underground streams, the mineral-laden solution is carried away to emerge somewhere else through springs. At this early stage the growing cave is filled with water, and just keeps getting bigger. However, everything changes when and if the cave drains. Perhaps the water level falls because of climate shifts, or the groundwater finds a new outlet. Whatever the cause, air replaces water, and as mineral-rich seepage enters the cavern it loses carbon dioxide to the air, which makes it less acidic. Unable to retain its load of dissolved calcium carbonate, the water begins depositing new stone. Where it drips from the ceiling, it leaves tiny rings that gradually grow into stalactites. Where drops hit the floor, stalagmites appear. Where it flows in thin sheets down the walls, the water leaves behind mounds of flowstone.

So what about those strange shields? No one has ever come up with a convincing explanation of how shields are created. They resemble clam shells, a matching pair of disks separated by a hairline crack. Some are quite large, six feet or more across, and heavily laden with stalactites and flowstone. The Parachute, symbol of Lehman Caves, is a richly decorated shield. One theory about its origin involves water under high pressure periodically spraying out from cracks in the wall (a phenomenon once observed in a French cave), but why this would build symmetrical disks, and what maintains the hairline crack between them, is a continuing mystery.

Wheeler Peak Scenic Drive

Few roads in the country can boast such a rapid vertical rise as Wheeler Peak Scenic Drive. Although it officially begins at the park boundary, climbing 3,400 feet in 12 miles, the road actually continues a long ascent that begins in the nearby town of Baker. Measuring from there, visitors gain nearly a mile in elevation, and pass through all the park's major life zones except for the alpine. Nothing could be more illustrative of the park's major theme—the effect of altitude on climate and living creatures.

The first few miles traverse a broad ramp, or apron, of alluvial material that surrounds the Snake Range. Such deposits are typical features of desert mountains, especially old ones. Erosion wears them down, but in the absence of rivers to carry away the resulting debris, it just piles up. Eventually, if there is no change in climate, desert mountains can bury themselves in their own rubbish.

Climbing this apron, the road passes through sagebrush grassland until it approaches the park boundary, where it enters a forest of mixed pinyon pine and juniper. Just inside the park Wheeler Peak Scenic Drive turns off to the right. For several miles it follows Lehman Creek, which provides a fine example of riparian vegetation along its banks. This is especially evident at the Upper Lehman Creek Campground, where pinyon pine, juniper, ponderosa pine, aspen, willow, white fir, and many other plants mingle in a sort of natural arboretum arranged along the creek.

From here the road leaves the creek and climbs steeply through changing belts of vegetation. First comes a belt dominated by mountain mahogany, a shrub that here grows the size of apple trees and forms a miniature forest too thick for people to walk through. Above that is a deep forest of Engelmann spruce and Douglas-fir. Aspens are the real democrats of the forest, seem-

Wheeler Peak is not difficult to climb; high winds may cut short a stay at the summit.

Top: *The world's oldest known tree, a bristlecone pine.*
Above: *The U.S. Forest Service cut it down in 1964 in order to find out how old it was (4,950 years).*

ing to do as well at 10,000 feet as at 7,000, consorting with all sorts of other plants, including juniper, at its lower range, all the way to limber pine just below the alpine tundra. Yet it cannot reach as high as the true stalwarts of the boreal world—bristlecone pines.

If you take only one walk in Great Basin National Park, a visit to the bristlecones is perhaps the best choice. Conveniently, several other interesting hikes also begin at the same trail head. A pleasant day can be made by following optional routes.

Bristlecone Pine Grove. The trail (3.5 miles round trip) begins near the campground at the top of Wheeler Peak Scenic Drive. Along the way, it wanders beneath the mighty, gnarled branches of limber pines, impressive trees in their own right, but mere striplings in comparison with their ancient neighbors. It is impossible to enter the bristlecone grove without a sense of wonder. The trees' polished surfaces have the feel of marble. When tapped, they ring. Many of these trees have stood on Wheeler Peak's windblasted flanks for almost 4,000 years, and some for much longer than that. They were old trees when the Egyptian pyramids were built. Even their needles live 40 years.

Until recently, the oldest known tree on earth grew in this grove. It had survived 4,950 years and was still living when in 1964 a U.S. Forest Service crew cut it down for a researcher who, believing it to be one of the oldest bristlecones, wanted an accurate count of its age. It was killed to prove how long it had lived. This was not an accident. The cutting was carried out against the objections of the superintendent of Lehman Caves National Monument (who had no legal authority over the bristlecone grove). Others agreed with him. The first chainsaw operator, when ordered to begin cutting, refused to even start up his saw. He was replaced the next day by someone more compliant.

Not surprisingly, the loss of that ancient tree, called Prometheus by the few who knew it alive, sparked national outrage and reinforced support for creation of a national park. Currently, the oldest known bristlecone pine (4,600 years old) stands in California's White Mountains. There is the possibility that an older tree still survives in the Wheeler Peak grove, or somewhere else in the Snake Range, but scientists are understandably reluctant to suggest cutting down another tree to find out, and the Park Service is not eager to focus attention on the possible candidates. The purpose of scientists would not be simple curiosity. Tree-ring dating provides concrete evidence of past climatic conditions, and allows exact dating of a variety of events—droughts, fires, good growing years, and more. Prometheus, in death, provided a continuous record of conditions in Nevada for five millennia. In fact, the record goes further than that. Chunks of wood from long-dead bristlecones, preserved in the cold climate of Wheeler Peak, have added their rings to a sequence that reaches back longer than 7,000 years.

Bristlecone pines do not require arctic winds and thin soil to grow. At lower elevations—down to 8,000 feet in some cases—they become straight and tall. Almost unrecognizable, they look more like normal trees. But here's the rub: In easy surroundings, they live no longer than other species—usually a few hundred years. Why is it that these trees achieve great age only under the most difficult of growing conditions? It seems there must be a lesson in that, something about strength in the face of adversity, and adversity giving rise to strength. Realistically, a more probable explanation is that slow growth develops an exceptionally hard wood with concentrated resins that resist rot and insect attack.

Wheeler Peak Rock Glacier. Is it a talus slope or a glacier? Perhaps both. Beginning about 300 vertical feet and 1.25 miles above the bristlecone grove, the glacier is a sheet of ice covered with quartzite boulders lying at a steep angle beneath the towering crags of Wheeler Peak. It's an odd, alien place echoing with wind, seemingly devoid of life, buried under snow for much of the year.

Stella and Teresa Lake Loop Trail. Beginning at the same trail head near the Wheeler Peak Campground, this 3-mile loop wanders through forest and meadow among rounded quartzite boulders on its way to visit two small but lovely glacial tarns. Teresa is surrounded by forest; Stella mirrors a steep cliff that rises virtually from its western shore. There are no fish in these shallow lakes. The winters are too long, the ice too thick. Summer comes in July with a burst of wildflowers that will be brown and gone to seed before the end of August.

Climbing Wheeler Peak. Five miles each way and 3,000 feet up on a good trail—for a major peak, Wheeler is relatively easy to climb. The trail begins at the Summit Parking Area, and for the first mile contours gently through a forest of mixed aspen and conifers. Where it crosses meadows, the views of Wheeler Peak are unsurpassed, and in warm weather, hikers tend to linger here before starting the actual ascent. The real work begins past the Stella Lake Trail junction. Here the path abandons all whimsy and climbs steadily to the saddle between Wheeler Peak and Bald

Mountain. One can take a breath to enjoy the view westward, then follow the trail as it shoots straight up the ridge to the distant summit, which is visible for most of the climb. The footing is good and the view is the best for many miles in any direction. Wheeler's western flank drops all the way to the valley bottom. The eastern face is a 2,000-foot cliff ending on the rock glacier. If the air is clear, you can see all the way to Mount Nebo, near Nephi in central Utah. On a windy day, however, the natural inclination is to turn and head for shelter as soon as you touch the summit.

Lehman Creek Trail. Those wishing to get a closer look at the various forest habitats of the Snake Range should consider walking down the Lehman Creek Trail. Following the creek, the trail descends 2,100 feet in four pleasant miles. The music of water is always present as it tumbles through aspen groves and occasional open spaces, sometimes disappearing into dense stands of "black timber"—Douglas-fir and Engelmann spruce casting dark shadows. At about 9,000 feet, the creek bed changes shape, becoming a sharp V. Glacial ice, after smoothing the upper valley, melted here. The difference in erosional styles is clearly evident. Lower, and warmer, the trail passes through manzanita and curl-leaf mountain mahogany. The latter, usually a shrub but here growing the size of apple trees, has extremely dense and hard wood that quickly dulls a chainsaw. Near the end of the trail, towering ponderosa pines add their elegant presence to the forest mix. Their long needles pile up on the ground, forming a deep cushion that feels good beneath sore hiking feet.

Baker Creek

Baker Creek tumbles cheerily down from the alpine lake at its source, past the Baker Creek Campground, and out across a broad alluvial fan toward the basin. At its head, tucked into a steep-walled alpine cirque at an elevation of 10,600 feet, lies Baker Lake. The trail to the lake (5.5 miles, 2,600-foot elevation gain) generally follows the creek, but makes many interesting side trips away from the riparian zone. Its course provides an object lesson in microclimates. In one section it winds through a stand of mature mountain mahogany, the trees so old and venerable they resemble small oak trees. At another point it follows the dividing line between the damp soil of an aspen grove and the drier substrate of a pinyon-juniper forest. Vegetation changes continually, and a variety of animals can be seen. Mule deer graze the forest edge. Rock squirrels race through the boulders. Flickers call from the aspen groves. There are even trout among the boulder-lined pools of the creek. At just over 10,000 feet stands the decaying cabin of Peter Dieshman. A prospector, he built the cabin in the 1920s, but never found much of the gold he sought. One and a half miles farther, tall conifers shade the shoreline of Baker Lake. On a warm summer afternoon, it's very pleasant sitting here. You might wish you had brought a tent and a sleeping bag so you could spend the night.

Snake Creek

The gravel Snake Creek Road starts several miles south of Baker on Nevada 487. It bumps along for five miles to the park boundary at 6,200 feet elevation, then 8 miles farther to a trail head and the primitive Shoshone Campground at around 8,000 feet. The first few miles traverse what appears to be a flat sagebrush plain. It's only when you turn and look back that you realize how far above the basin you've come. Rugged outcrops of yellow and white limestone rise above the pinyon-juniper forest, while cottonwoods, wild rose, and rabbitbrush follow the riparian zone of Snake Creek. The creek is small but lovely, tumbling through glades and thickets with just enough strength to support minnow-sized trout. The road ends in mature aspen groves, with a full view of 11,926-foot Pyramid Peak and a series of high rock-walled cirques.

Johnson Lake Trail. From the campground, an old mining road leads steadily uphill through aspen glades mixed with white fir, mountain mahogany, and manzanita. After 5 miles and 2,480 vertical feet, the trail reaches Johnson Lake. Perched where the forest gives way to the steep walls of a rocky cirque, it was named for Alfred "Timberline" Johnson, who established a tungsten mine above the lake in 1912. The mine is long closed, but some relics remain. Despite many attempts on the part of prospectors, this was the only mine to actually produce commercial minerals in what eventually would become the park. This trail is part of the Baker Lake Loop; by running a vehicle shuttle, hikers can continue over the pass to Baker Lake and from there to the Baker Creek trail head.

Lexington Arch

An excursion to this far corner of the park takes most of a day and gives visitors a distinctly different view of the Snake Range. If you go, take water and other supplies. The rough dirt road, suitable for high-clearance vehicles, begins south of Garrison on Utah

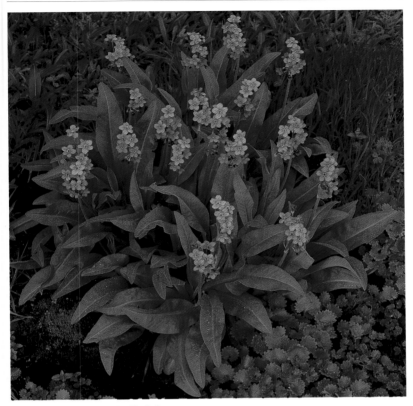

Parry's primrose near Stella Lake.

21, just south of Pruess Lake. From here it is 12 miles to a parking area where the hiking trail sets off through pinyon and juniper trees into the narrow gully of Arch Canyon. The creek bed is dry much of the year, as is the surrounding country. Fir trees grow on the north-facing side of the gully, while pinyon, chokecherry, and mountain mahogany join branches to create a dense thicket on the opposite side. Nearing the arch, the trail fades away into narrow game trails, mostly the work of deer. If you climb up to stand beneath the arch itself, the 2-mile hike is moderately strenuous. On a hot day it can be downright challenging. The best view of the arch, however, is from the canyon bottom, and many hikers will choose to remain there, admiring its graceful shape from the shade of a fir. What made the arch? Carved into limestone, it might be the last remnant of a large cave tunnel that collapsed and eroded in the distant past. Flowstone at its base supports this idea, but no one knows for sure.

GUADALUPE MOUNTAINS NATIONAL PARK

El Capitan, at 8,078 feet, anchors the southern end of the park and is one of the Southwest's most famous peaks.

GUADALUPE MOUNTAINS NATIONAL PARK
HC 60, BOX 400
SALT FLAT, TEXAS 79847
TEL.: (915) 828-3251

HIGHLIGHTS: Smith Spring • McKittrick Canyon • Devils Hall • Guadalupe Peak • The Bowl • El Capitan • Williams Ranch • The Pinery • Dog Canyon

ACCESS: From Carlsbad, 55 miles southwest on U.S. 62/180. From El Paso, 110 miles east on U.S. 62/180. From Van Horn, 65 miles north on Texas 54.

HOURS: Daily, year-round. Visitor Center, 8 A.M.–4:30 P.M., later in summer; closed Christmas day.

FEES: For camping.

PARKING: At each public-use point.

GAS, FOOD, LODGING: In Whites City, Carlsbad, Van Horn, and El Paso.

VISITOR CENTER: Headquarters Visitor Center, on U.S. 62/180, offers exhibits, information; maps for sale. McKittrick Canyon Visitor Center, 4 miles from U.S. 62/180. Dog Canyon Visitor Center, on north side of park, accessible on New Mexico 137. Interpretive handouts in French, German, Japanese, Spanish.

MUSEUM: Exhibits in Headquarters and McKittrick Canyon Visitor Centers, and in Frijole Ranch History Museum.

PETS: Permitted on leash in campgrounds, not on trails or in public buildings. Horseback riding permitted on designated trails; no rentals; no backcountry camping with horses; call in advance. Frontcountry horse camps at Frijole and Dog Canyon.

PICNICKING: At Headquarters Visitor Center, Pine Springs Campground, McKittrick Canyon, Frijole Ranch Museum, and Dog Canyon.

HIKING: On 80+ miles of trails; water at trail heads only.

BACKPACKING: Permit required. Camp only at 10 designated backcountry campgrounds. Carry water.

CAMPGROUNDS: Pine Springs, 20 tent sites, 19 RV sites, 2 group sites. No hookups or showers. No open fires, including charcoal, allowed; containerized fuel stoves only. Dog Canyon, 9 tent sites, 4 RV sites.

TOURS: Nature walks, evening programs in summer.

FACILITIES FOR DISABLED: Headquarters and McKittrick Canyon Visitor Centers and 1 campsite at Pine Springs Campground.

For additional information, see also Sites, Trails, and Trips on pages 266–276 and the map on pages 254–255.

GUADALUPE MOUNTAINS NATIONAL PARK IS a study in contrasts. What was once a reef awash on the edge of the sea is now a mountain range baking in the desert sun. Yet in a few hours' climb, a hiker can leave the desert behind and, almost miraculously, enter a cool forest that seems as though it should be hundreds of miles north. There are other contrasts and extremes: hidden places where water transforms the desert into a leafy, bird-filled oasis; hot summer days with comfortable evenings and, at high elevations, cool nights; harsh winters with fierce winds that whip through canyons and passes and threaten the existence of man and his vehicle.

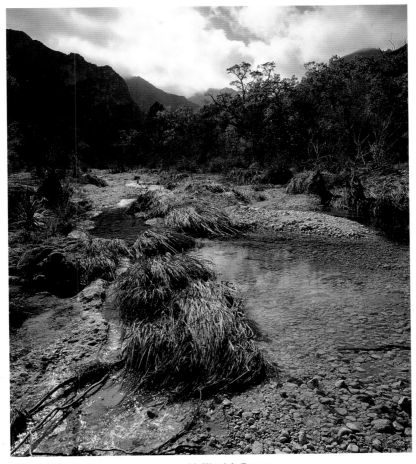

Clouds lift after a heavy rainstorm in McKittrick Canyon.

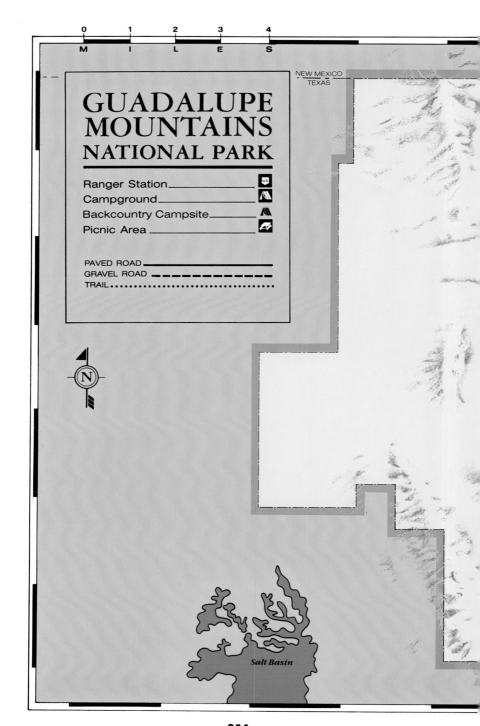

GUADALUPE MOUNTAINS
NATIONAL PARK

Ranger Station _____ US
Campground _____
Backcountry Campsite _____
Picnic Area _____

PAVED ROAD _____
GRAVEL ROAD — — — — — — — — —
TRAIL ••••••••••••••••••••••••••••

NEW MEXICO
TEXAS

N

Salt Basin

TO NEW MEXICO 137

Indian Meadow Nature Trail

DOG CANYON

Permian Reef Trail

McKittrick Canyon Visitor Center

TO CARLSBAD

Tejas Trail

Marcus Trail

LOST PEAK
El 7834'

McKittrick Canyon Trail

South McKittrick Canyon

Blue Ridge Trail

Mountain Trail

Bush Mountain Trail

PINE SPRING CANYON

Juniper Trail

Bowl Trail

HUNTER PEAK
El 8362'

Bear Canyon Trail

Smith Spring Trail

Smith Spring

FRIJOLE RANCH
HISTORY MUSEUM
Frijole

180
62

Devils Hall Trail

THE PINERY
Historic Site

Visitor Center

Guadalupe Peak Trail

PINE SPRINGS

GUADALUPE PEAK
El 8749'

El Capitan Trail

Visitor Center
and Park Headquarters

WILLIAMS RANCH
Historic Site

EL CAPITAN
El 8078'

VICINITY MAP

NEW MEXICO
TEXAS

180
62

Salt Basin

GUADALUPE MOUNTAINS N.P.

180
62

Salt Flat

54

TO VAN HORN   TO EL PASO

INSET SCALE
0   5   10
M I L E S

Native Americans

When humans first saw the skyline of the Guadalupe Mountains, it probably looked pretty much as it does now; El Capitan was just as awesome. But in human terms that was long ago, perhaps 10,000 years. The mountain was similar, but the flora and fauna were different. People who lived and hunted in these mountains saw and knew the taste of mammoth, of four-horned antelope, of camel—all extinct now. The early hunters left enough signs of life that we know they were here, but not much more. Undoubtedly they sought shelter in the mountains' many caves, and were familiar with the streams and canyons. But until the desert gives up some of its secrets, these early people will remain ghostlike.

Not so the Apache! Occupying the Guadalupes when Europeans arrived, the Apache played a major role in the history of the Southwest and perhaps an even greater role in southwestern literature. They deserve the recognition, if only for having been so successful in wresting a living, and a culture, from the desert. The Apache appear to have come from the north, and even without the horse (which came later, from the Spanish) they ranged far, following seasons and food sources. Their houses were temporary brush *jacales* and occasionally a teepee-like leather tent, suitable for people who moved often. The Apache traded with the more sedentary Pueblo farmers to the northwest near the Rio Grande, from whom they no doubt learned about the Spaniards, a new people who came from the south in the 1500s bringing such miracles as the horse and the gun. The few Spaniards who got this far from the river were collecting precious salt from the nearby salt flats. The Guadalupe Mountains remained the domain of the Apache.

The Road West

Because of faraway events, the Guadalupes passed into American control in 1848. Few people yet knew they existed, but the young country was spilling west. Texas miners in the California gold rush may have passed the range in 1849, and certainly army expeditions did in the next few years. The young country was exploring its new land, especially seeking a way to connect its east and west coasts. The Guadalupes seemed to lie in the path of progress.

Faced with the urgent need for rapid and reliable mail service to the burgeoning west coast, the United States Congress in 1857 gave a profitable contract to John Butterfield; overnight the

A way station on the Butterfield Overland Mail Line, around 1875.

famous Butterfield Overland Mail Line was born. The route stretched from St. Louis to San Francisco, and under the terms of the contract the company was granted 320 acres for each way station. One was built in the Guadalupes; its stone walls are still visible near the Pine Spring Campground—the same spring that supplied water to the station. Exhausted horses were replaced by new teams here, while motion-dazed passengers bolted a meal of venison pie, coffee, and the inevitable baked beans.

The cross-country stage became history and then legend in just a few years. More Americans arrived, looking for minerals or establishing ranches. The Apache saw what was happening and resisted, but the new culture was a powerful one. Devastating encounters between the Apache and the army occurred within the borders of the present park. At Manzanita Spring, near the historic Frijole Ranch Museum, on December 30, 1869, the army drove the Indians from an encampment and destroyed the winter's cache of food and supplies. The tactic was effective, and slowly the Indians were pressured and weakened. For a while the Apache kept up a guerrilla effort—Geronimo often rode the Guadalupes, and so did Victorio—but the newcomers prevailed. The Apache today, famed for their skill as cattlemen, live on a reservation to the northwest in the Sacramento mountains.

Establishment of the Park

After the Civil War and the Indian wars, ranching came to the Guadalupes. The area was desert, and times were hard. Few imagined the boom that was to come to the area east of the mountains—the Permian Basin oil field. The mountain range was crucial to an understanding of the geologic history of the oil-bearing basin, so many of the people who were involved in the new industry began working in the Guadalupe region. One geologist who knew and came to love the area was Wallace Pratt. During an immensely successful career in oil exploration, he bought huge tracts of land in the Guadalupes, including beautiful McKittrick Canyon. There he built a house, which still can be seen by hikers in the park. Due largely to Wallace Pratt's efforts and donations of land as a start, as well as the influence of Judge J. C. Hunter, the other large landowner, in the 1960s a movement was organized to have this unique area set aside as a park. Congress passed the bill in 1966, and the Guadalupe Mountains became a national park in 1972.

GEOLOGY

The Resurrection of a Reef

Guadalupe Mountains National Park encompasses the southern, highest part of the 50-mile-long Guadalupe Mountain Range. Rising gradually from the broken plains around Carlsbad, New Mexico, the long, narrow block has spectacular drop-offs on both the east and west sides. At the southern end, it abruptly drops back to the desert; El Capitan, the last, massive promontory, is one of the famous peaks of the Southwest.

It is a curious coincidence that erosion has revealed the mountain in this particular way, for it resembles to some degree the form in which it was created about 250 million years ago. Then part of it was a largely submerged sea wall, bordering an arm of a shallow Permian ocean. Today it is a wall thrown across the Texas desert, and travel routes must skirt it at one end or the other.

The Rocks Form

The Guadalupe Range is a study in the rocks that form where a shelf meets the sea, and is especially famous for its exposure of a section of an ancient reef. *Reef* is the correct word, and is used by geologists; but the ancient reef was not a barrier reef like those around South Sea atolls.

The area to the south and east of the present-day town of

Boulders and pool in upper McKittrick Canyon

Carlsbad was a basin of the trilobed Permian ocean; today it is called the Delaware Basin. (The Midland Basin to the east and the Marfa Basin to the west are the remains of the other lobes.) The Glass, Delaware, and Apache mountain ranges are other exposures of the rocks that surrounded the basin, although they are not as geologically clear as the Guadalupes. Oil-well borings have traced underground sections of the formation in a circle 400 miles around!

According to current geological thinking, an imaginary Permian explorer who was traveling from dry land to open ocean would first have encountered a restricted lagoon that was slowly filling with erosional debris from the land. Next, separating the lagoon from the ocean, was an area of tidal flats, in some places tens of miles wide, that sloped down to the sea. Finally, deep underwater, the shelf ended in a lip, and the bottom dropped toward the ocean depths. It was along this underwater "edge" that the reef formed.

Much of it was the remains of tiny organisms, mostly algae. Some donated the limy part of their own bodies, while others secreted lime that cemented the sediment together. In addition, a remarkable amount of lime precipitated from the water and thus further contributed to the growing reef. In some places, the amount of precipitated lime greatly exceeded the amount of organic material.

The Permian Reef has no known counterpart among the "active" reefs in the world. South Sea reefs are made up largely of coral and calcareous algae; the Permian Reef was composed of sponges and calcareous algae. South Sea reefs are themselves "walls" between the open ocean and lagoons; in Permian times, the highest point was the tidal flat, which was shoreward from the reef. The reef itself was submerged; if the Permian explorer had had a Permian boat, he could have sailed right over it! Finally, coral reefs are derived mostly from living creatures. While the ancient reef was partially composed of organic remains, it was largely formed of precipitated limestone. The origin of other parts of the Permian Reef still puzzle geologists.

The Time Between

Even seas are only temporary. Eventually the sources of the sea became blocked, and the process of evaporation began. It was remarkably rapid in geologic terms, perhaps as short as a few million or only 1 million years. As water evaporated into the drying air, it left behind salts and minerals that became the great gypsum beds that underlie the surface, while in some places special circumstances produced the potash deposits that are so valuable as a source of fertilizer. With successive geologic ages came slow burial in sediments that became massive. For 200 million years (compared with the perhaps 50 million years that the sea existed), the whole complex lay buried. Weight and heat did their slow work. The sediments in the tidal flats and in the lagoon became rock adjoining the reef rock. In some places petroleum formed, as it had ages earlier in layers beneath even these. No hint of the buried complex appeared at the surface, where strange creatures evolved, dominated for a while, and then disappeared. The weight of the overlying sediments was enormous, and even though the reef was basically intact, a 100-mile-wide limestone bracelet in a gypsum setting deep in the earth, it cracked. The cracks formed a pattern that would be identifiable millions of years later.

Reemergence

The land lifted again. In the complex, slow churning that changes the earth's surface, the whole region was uplifted. Uplift led to more erosion, as water rushed faster to the sea. Layer after layer of the overburden was stripped away. The removal was rapid in geologic terms, beginning a "mere" 10 or 12 million years ago. Had there been a film, run now at fast speed, it would show the reef emerging, its limestone resisting the erosion that quickly took away the softer surrounding gypsum.

Limestone is not immune to erosion, though; it is soluble. Slightly acidic water seeping in along the cracks that had developed when the reef was underground slowly carried away tiny amounts of the lime. As a result, the Guadalupe Mountains are laced with caves. Many are known, and certainly hundreds more are unknown, for a cave does not have to have an opening to the surface. One cave may be the most famous in the world—Carlsbad Caverns, a major hollowing of the reef that is now a national park about 40 miles north of Guadalupe Mountains National Park.

Geological processes did not occur just to get to where we are now; the earth is always en route to something else. Today the ancient fossil reef is a mountain range in a desert, clothed in desert garb. But each flash flood and each rockfall, even a tiny one, reduces it some small amount. It is a great mountain range, and a great display of the earth's history.

NATURAL HISTORY

Water! In the Guadalupe Mountains it is water that determines where life will be and what form it will take. The winds that blow across western Texas carry little water, but they do carry some. The mountains cause the winds to rise and cool, dropping their moisture. Thus the top, including the fine basin known as "the Bowl," gets more than 20 inches of precipitation a year, compared with half that amount down in the surrounding desert. But the water does not stay at the top, where there is no natural permanent surface water. It sinks into the porous limestone and eventually comes out in springs at the base of the mountains. Life flourishes around each of these springs, and from the road it can be seen as a band of green along watercourses.

The park has three distinct life zones: the desert, the wet places, and the forest at the top.

The Desert

In the desert is the least water and the most evaporation, and a glance at the creosote bush points up these conditions. If these stingy bushes seem rather evenly spaced across the desert floor, there is good reason; each has staked out its own territory, just as

Clockwise, from top: Texas horned lizard; Columbine; Maple leaves, McKittrick Canyon; Great horned owl.

far out as its roots can reach the precious little moisture that falls. And that is where the next one survives, and so on. The plant's small, leathery leaves impede evaporation and thus help hoard what water the plant gathers.

Cactuses are here in prickly profusion; these highly specialized desert plants have all but forsaken leaves, modifying some into spines and performing photosynthesis in the green stem. The cholla produces waxy, purple flowers in June. It is a bad cactus to bump into, because the outer segments are only loosely attached. The plant self-prunes, dropping those segments during droughts.

The agave, or century plant (locally sometimes called Spanish bayonet), looks like the yuccas, though fatter. The plant does not flower for years, but stores energy in the fat leaves. Each leaf has a needle-like point that can puncture a tire, and has a chemical that gives even a small prick to the skin an odd, chilling effect. Then after fifteen years or so, the plant suddenly sends out a stalk, actually growing several inches a day. It reaches higher than a one-story building and produces great bunches of pale blossoms that are lovely, especially in the moonlight.

The animals of the desert are specially equipped for dryness too. The adaptation seems to reach an extreme in the various rodents that *never* drink water. They need it, of course, so they manufacture it chemically from seeds in their diet.

Wildlife have habits to protect against the heat. Most desert mammals are nocturnal. Deer are common in the park, and can be seen virtually every dusk coming out to browse. Coyotes are heard then too, but primarily in the early, early morning. Skunks and badgers make their way at night, almost never seen by visitors. The night is busy, but the day is largely left to the lizards and the insects.

The Wet Places

Smith Spring is a wonder, a Japanese garden tucked away in the desert. It is one of the wet places, where water is the magic ingredient in transforming the desert into an oasis of green.

The plants change in such places. Even as you enter you can see it, smell it, and feel it; there are ponderosa pine, walnuts, maples, and oaks. McKittrick Canyon is justly famous for its autumn foliage, which is unusual in this part of the country. And there are Texas madrones, trees that most people have never seen before visiting Guadalupe. The distinctive red tree looks as though it were bursting out and growing *over* its own bark, inside out. Insects and, of course, birds abound. There are wrens, found tanagers, and sparrows. The seldom-seen desert reptiles are not found in the wet places, but garter snakes and newts are.

These are very special areas, properly hidden behind a curtain of grapevine. Perhaps they are appreciated because they almost always appear at the end of a hot desert hike—quite unexpected and most welcome!

The Forest at the Top

That the springs are beautiful is at least predictable, as water in the desert is almost always beautiful. But the forest at the top is unexpected. The long block of the Guadalupes is avalanche-steep on the sides but flat on top—at least in comparison to the sides. Actually the top has considerable relief, cut primarily by South McKittrick Canyon. A special place is "the Bowl," a large, heavily timbered, basinlike area that is quite invisible from below. The dense forest in the Bowl seems to belong somewhere else; Douglas-fir, limber pine, and ponderosa pine make the hiker feel hundreds of miles north. Many of the plants and animals here—including elk (reintroduced after extinction by hunting), bear, even mountain lion, and birds, such as mountain chickadee, nuthatch, and war-bler—are at the southern limit of their ranges.

This is a relict forest. A few tens of thousands of years ago, ice sheets covered much of North America. They did not reach the Guadalupe region, but their effect did. A great coniferous forest extended this far south and perhaps even a little farther. But when the ice sheets retreated, the forest could not take the warming, drying climate, and junipers and other plants that are now common in the area took over. But the conditions changed by altitude, not just by distance from the receding ice sheets, much as water rises in a tub in which a child has made an irregular pile of stones. At first a nonswimming insect might have the run of the pile, but as the water rises, high places gradually become islands. If trapped on one, our nonswimming insect would find itself stranded, perhaps able to continue but only in isolation, far from others of its sort. The great forest has long since retreated far northward, but here on the Guadalupes is an island left behind, a relict forest.

Of course, the life-zone divisions are not clear cut, though some-times they appear to be. Along the trails that rise rapidly up a cliff face, the change at the rim from desert to the relict forest is aston-ishing. But along a natural pathway up, such as McKittrick Canyon, there are all possible combinations of trees, shrubs, and animals, some of them quite unlikely. The Guadalupe Mountains, by the cir-cumstances of their creation and location, provide a bewildering array of conditions for life, and life has moved in accordingly.

SITES, TRAILS, AND TRIPS

There are two kinds of hiking experiences in the Guadalupes: on roads that go around the base of the mountains and occasionally poke in a short way, and in the deserts and desert mountains. Hiking is especially rewarding, and in walks of just a few hours, visitors will find the quiet and natural beauty of Guadalupe Mountains National Park.

Guadalupe Pass. U.S. 62/180 passes the foot of El Capitan in Guadalupe Pass, the break between the Guadalupe Range and the Delaware Mountains to the south. The Mescalero Apache knew and used this pass. Forty-niners heading for the California gold fields traveled through it, and the famous Butterfield Overland Mail Line stagecoaches struggled over it. After a hundred years of improvements, the road has become a comfortable paved highway, but El Capitan probably looks much as it did when the going was tough.

Williams Ranch. A four-wheel-drive road on the west side of the range leads to the old Williams Ranch. Interested persons may get a map and the gate key at the Visitor Center. The road is rough, and the abandoned ranch house strikes most visitors as a lonely place—perhaps as desolate as any they will see on their whole vacation. Yet people did homestead here, and grass grew. Bone Spring, free-flowing pools of water that soon disappear into the ground, is about 1 mile behind the ranch house. A hiking trail (El Capitan Trail) goes from the Pine Spring Campground to the Williams Ranch; but it is long, and overnight camping is recommended.

Low Hikes into the Backcountry

Smith Spring Trail. About 1.5 miles east of the Headquarters Visitor Center on an old dirt road is a shaded ranch complex, with a small main house and some outbuildings. The spring that supplies it is called Frijole Spring, named after the beans that were the staple for the early ranchers. It was not luxurious, but it was, and is, beautiful. It is now maintained as a cultural history museum with displays and exhibits of early local artifacts and lore.

The trail to Smith Spring is an easy one. It goes gently uphill through waist-high scrub brush, and hikers think they can see the whole mountainside and wonder where the spring could be hidden. Then in less than 1 mile, the trail crosses a gentle shoulder, heads up a canyon, and suddenly comes upon the spring. It is green here, with small pools, as exquisite as a Japanese garden. The trees are walls and a roof that keep the desert out. There are dragonflies and birds, and large animals come to drink at dawn and dusk. This is fragile land, and the hiker should stay on the trail, but the trail itself is in the heart of the oasis.

Coming back down, the trail passes Manzanita Spring. This quiet spot, another watering place—one may even see elk—has not always been so peaceful. It was here that the cavalry surprised an Apache rancheria and in a brief battle destroyed their winter supplies.

The Smith Spring Trail is about 2 miles round trip, ideal for a

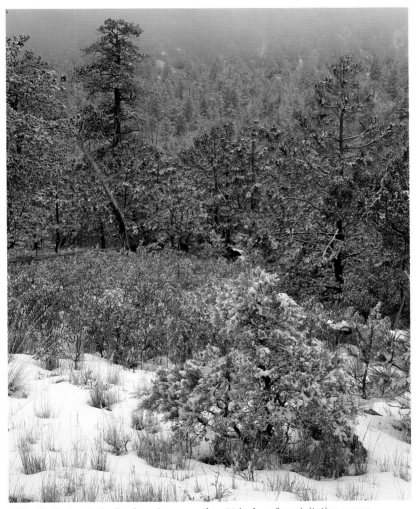

Heavily timbered, the Bowl receives more than 20 inches of precipitation a year.

TRAILS OF GUADALUPE MOUNTAINS NATIONAL PARK*

No water is available on trails.

GUADALUPE PEAK TRAIL: Starts at Pine Spring Campground; ends at Guadalupe Peak; 8.4 miles round trip; 6 hours; 3,000-foot ascent; leads to highest point in Texas (8,749 feet); magnificent views of surrounding peaks; 5,000-foot drop to the salt flats to the west. (Strenuous)

DEVIL'S HALL TRAIL: Starts and ends at Pine Spring Campground; 4.2 miles round trip; 4 hours; walk along wash floor between narrow canyon walls of clearly stratified sedimentary rock; no climbing. (Moderate)

TEJAS TRAIL: Starts at Pine Spring Campground; ends at Dog Canyon Campground; 11.7 miles one way; 8–10 hours; 2,000-foot ascent; main route to the high country intersects Bush Mountain, Marcus, Juniper, McKittrick Canyon, and Bowl trails; excellent views of all the Guadalupe peaks; one highlight is view from 7,830-foot Lost Peak; good view of Bowl and the reef structure as it slopes downward to the northeast. (Moderate to Strenuous)

BEAR CANYON TRAIL: Starts at Pine Spring Campground; ends at Bowl trails; 3.4 miles one way; 3–4 hours; 2,000-foot ascent; alternate route to the high country (used more often for returning from high country); connects with Bowl trails; steeper and more rugged than Tejas Trail. (Strenuous)

BOWL TRAIL: Starts at Tejas Trail and loops past Bear Canyon and Juniper trails, with a spur to Hunter Peak, while passing through the thick fir and pine forest of the Bowl, with its variety of mammals, birds, and reptiles. (Moderate)

JUNIPER TRAIL: 2-mile forested Bowl route connecting the Bowl Trail with the Tejas Trail. (Moderate)

BUSH MOUNTAIN TRAIL: Starts at Tejas Trail (3.7 miles up from Pine Spring Campground); ends at Dog Canyon Campground; 11.4 miles one way; 8–10 hours; 3,000-foot ascent; passes Bush Mountain, second highest peak in Texas (8,676 feet) and Cox Tank, an earthen dam; excellent views to Cutoff Mountain. (Moderate to Strenuous)

FOOTHILLS TRAIL: Horse trail that links the Frijole Trail with Frijole Ranch; 1.9 miles. Public horse corral on this trail. (Easy)

MARCUS TRAIL: Starts at Tejas Trail; ends at Bush Mountain Trail; 3.8 miles one way; 2 hours; 1,800-foot ascent; historic abandoned jeep trail into the high country; gradual climb into heavily forested area. (Strenuous)

MCKITTRICK CANYON TRAIL: Starts at McKittrick Canyon parking area; ends at Tejas Trail; 9.6 miles one way (most one-way hikes start at Dog Canyon and end at McKittrick Canyon); 8–10 hours; 2,380-foot ascent; arduous climb, but spectacular views; follows floor of McKittrick Canyon for 4 miles, then climbs steeply out; walk into canyon and back is excellent 1-day introduction. (Easy to Strenuous)

SMITH SPRING TRAIL: Starts and ends at Frijole Ranch Museum; 2 miles round trip; 1.5 hours; 500-foot ascent; gentle climb up hill from historic site to oasis overlooking desert; best introduction to terrain of park. (Easy)

PERMIAN REEF GEOLOGY TRAILS: Starts at McKittrick Canyon information station; ends at north park boundary; 4.9 miles one way; 8 hours; 2,000-foot ascent; leads up north wall of canyon through ponderosa pine forest; close look at major formations of the Permian reef. Geology guidebook available. (Strenuous)

EL CAPITAN TRAIL: Starts at Pine Spring campground; ends at Williams Ranch; 9.8 miles one way; 16 hours; gently rolling hike, skirting base of El Capitan (8,078 feet) and under the west cliffs of Guadalupe Peak; spectacular views of salt flats. (Moderate)

*The Guadalupe Mountains National Park trails are interconnected; a "hiker's guide" and trail map are essential.

SEE MAP ON PAGES 222–223.

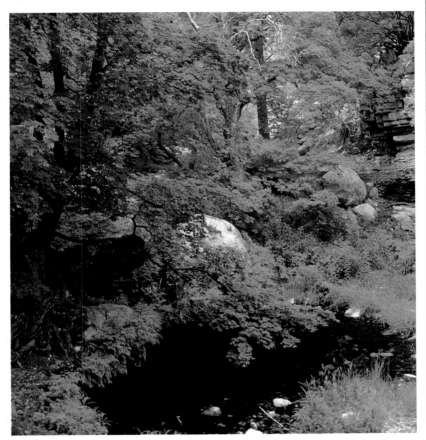

Smith Spring, north of Frijole near the eastern boundary of the park, is an oasis in the desert.

visitor with limited time. It gives a small taste of the desert and shows the miracle of water, all in less than 2 hours.

Devil's Hall Trail. Starting at Pine Spring Campground, the Devil's Hall Trail leads along a wash in the canyon. More strenuous paths branch off to climb the canyon walls on either side, but the main trail continues on the canyon floor. In just over 2 miles, with very little rise, the canyon walls close in dramatically, thus the name "Devil's Hall." Pools of water are often found; the rock formations are clear, and fossils abound.

El Capitan Trail. The El Capitan Trail begins at the Pine Spring Campground and leads off to the west around El Capitan and Guadalupe Peak, passing directly beneath the sheer cliffs of both. This is a long trail, but it is one that offers a taste of the desert.

Hikes into the High Country

The following hikes lead into the high country with considerable climb, and they are all strenuous. The Guadalupes rise abruptly; so do the trails. Hikers must be in reasonably good physical condition, wear sturdy shoes, and carry plenty of water.

Guadalupe Peak Trail. The Guadalupe Mountains emerge from the broken country around Carlsbad, 50 miles north in New Mexico, and slope upward to reach 8,749 feet at Guadalupe Peak, the highest point in Texas.

Leaving from the Pine Spring Campground, the Guadalupe Peak Trail begins to climb abruptly and seems never to stop. It is only a little more than 4 miles to the peak, but the climb is 3,000 feet. On the way up, there are views back over the plains to the east—great reasons to stop and rest. Walking up is like walking north. Scrub brush gives way to a few ponderosa and then a pine forest. About .5 mile before the top is a side trail that leads a few hundred yards to a campground with fine views, but no water. Finally the trail breaks out of the forest and climbs onto the rocky, windy peak itself. The view—or rather the 360° panorama—is dramatic. To the east are the plains, broken by isolated mountain ranges blue-gray in the distance. To the south is the famous massif of El Capitan, which looks quite different when viewed from *above.* To the west and far below are the salt flats, scene and cause of the bloody El Paso Salt War of 1877. To the north are the jumbled peaks and ridges of the Guadalupe Range, stretching toward Carlsbad.

Do not treat lightning casually. Afternoon thundershowers are common and awesome to watch as they build and move, but hikers should leave if they get even close. The peak is struck often.

Tejas Trail. The Tejas Trail is the hiker's main route into the high country, and like those that branch off here and there along the way, it is spectacular. It begins at the Pine Spring Campground and climbs the north canyon wall in a rapid rise that soon reveals incredible views of the canyon and the plains to the east.

It is 11.7 miles on to the Dog Canyon Campground, where the Tejas Trail ends. Along the way it intersects first with the east end of the Bush Mountain Trail, the Bowl trails to the east, the Marcus Trail to the north, and the west terminal of the McKittrick Canyon Trail. About 3 miles from Dog Canyon, the Tejas Trail passes Lost Peak, one of the more impressive landmarks in the park. The view from this 7,830-foot mountain is worth the climb, or, as one park booklet understates, it is "especially noteworthy."

The dramatic change in the "personality" of the Guadalupe terrain along this trail cannot be overstated. The climb up from Pine Spring Campground is rather steep in comparison to the gentle up-and-down rolling of the trails in the high country, and the environment is just as different—from hot, dry desert to thick, green forest.

Bush Mountain Trail. The rugged Bush Mountain Trail begins about 2.5 miles up the Tejas Trail—already in the high country—and branches off to the west along a ridge toward Bush Mountain, the second highest peak in Texas (8,676 feet). Later it passes the Cox Tank, an earthen dam that supplied the early-twentieth-century goat ranching operation with water, crosses the Marcus Trail, and then drops down into Dog Canyon, where it again meets and ends with the Tejas Trail.

Blue Ridge Trail. This is a short connecting trail between the Bush Mountain and Marcus trails.

Marcus Trail. This is an old jeep road that leads into the park from the north and rises into the high country to join the Tejas Trail.

McKittrick Canyon Trail. A good introduction to the Guadalupes is the walk into McKittrick Canyon, long famous for its beauty. In 1912, a young oil geologist, Wallace Pratt, made the then-rough trip in to see it and realized that the canyon was a slice through an ancient reef that would give geologists an "inside look" at what had been largely theoretical. (Along the road to the trail head are the remains of some concrete tables, "The Arm-waving Spot." A fine cross section of the reef is visible just there, and Pratt's employees noticed that the place "just naturally seemed to make geologists want to wave their arms around!")

Overleaf: Gypsum dunes, remnants of an evaporated sea, produce potash, which is a source of fertilizer.

There is an information station with exhibits at the trail-head parking lot, but it may not be manned. A trail brochure is available there. Almost immediately, the trail enters the canyon. It stays on the canyon floor, is shaded, and has much to delight the eye. The trees are maples and oaks, stark contrast to the desert just "outside." In autumn, the colors can be breath-taking. The stream runs year-round, but there is a geological oddity in the canyon. Dissolved limestone in the water coming off the old reef is deposited on the streambed as travertine, which cements the rocks together and seals the streambed. Breaks are common, however, and there are sections where the stream runs *under* the streambed, which then appears to be dry.

About 2.75 miles in is Pratt Cabin, the home that geologist Wallace Pratt built of selected native stone. Water and restrooms are found here in summer.

About 1 mile beyond Pratt Cabin is a trail to the Hunter cabin and "the Grotto," replete with dripping water, ferns, and cave formations. From the grotto trail junction the McKittrick trail begins to climb out of the canyon on a very steep grade. This is a good place for the day hiker to turn around, or perhaps to climb another .5 mile to Turtle Rock, with its great views. The trail continues up into the high country, but that is a more formidable hike that requires planning.

The total hike—from the parking lot, past Pratt Cabin and the Grotto to Turtle Rock, and out again—is about 10 miles; but there are so many glens and special places that the hike deserves a whole day.

Bear Canyon Trail. Years ago, rancher J. C. Hunter (for whom Hunter Peak is named) wanted to provide for animals he had introduced into the high country. His men built a pump station far below at upper Pine Spring and laid a pipeline to the top. The pumping system has long been abandoned, but the pipeline can still be seen along the trail.

A half-moon rises behind a sotol, a yuccalike plant commonly found in the park. Its flowers were eaten by Indians and the leaf fibers were used for rope.

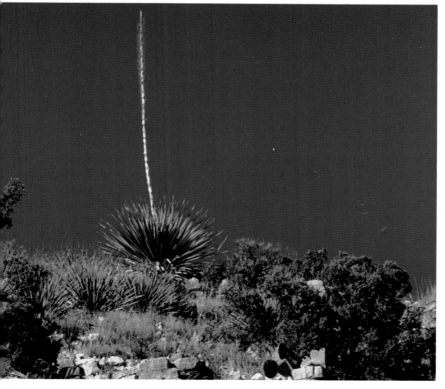

This is an alternative trail to the high country, but it is used more often for returning rather than climbing; the route is more strenuous than the Tejas Trail. It rises more than 2,000 feet in less than 2 miles.

Bowl Trails. A loop trail in and around the oasis called the Bowl connects the Tejas Trail with the head of Bear Canyon Trail, and passes by a spur to Hunter Peak on the east edge of the ridge. (Hunter Peak offers an exciting view of Pine Canyon and the eastern plains on one side and the Bowl on the other.) About halfway along this trail, a path leads down into the thick fir and pine forest of the Bowl and intersects the Juniper Trail, which leads to the Tejas Trail.

Permian Reef Geology Trail. This special trail is for those who are interested in the geology of the Guadalupes. The Permian Reef Geology Trail takes the explorer through a ponderosa pine forest along a canyon wall where the features of the reef are revealed—clear exposures of layered rock that was formed about 280 to 230 million years ago. A geologic guidebook is available.

Overnight Hikes

Many Guadalupe trails into the high country are long and arduous and require more than just a few hours or a day to appreciate; there are campsites on all the major trails. Permits, required for overnight hikes, can be obtained at the Headquarters Visitor Center and at the ranger station at Dog Canyon. Both day hikers and overnight hikers must sign trail-head registers before departing; the registers are checked regularly. The rugged Guadalupe backcountry can be dangerous for the inexperienced. There are regulations for the hikers' protection and for the preservation of the park and its flora and fauna. One gallon of water per person per day is recommended.

El Capitan. To have entered into legend, to have a train and even a rousing march named after it, a rock must be dramatic—and El Capitan is. It is the last towering monolith at the southern end of the Guadalupes, where they abruptly break off and drop back down to the desert. It seems almost a mountain by itself. At 8,078 feet, El Capitan is not the highest point of the range; Guadalupe Peak (8,749 feet), just behind it, is. But from many points, "El Cap" blocks the higher peak from view, and it is El Capitan that has become the symbol of the Guadalupes.

Opposite: McKittrick Canyon's autumnal colors brighten the desert landscape.

MESA VERDE
NATIONAL PARK

Cliff Palace, with its many rooms and towers, is the largest site at Mesa Verde.

MESA VERDE NATIONAL PARK, COLORADO 81330
TEL.: (970) 529-4461

HIGHLIGHTS: Cliff Palace • Balcony House • Spruce Tree House • Long House Ruin • Weatherill Mesa • Ruins Road Drive • Step House • Badger House Community

ACCESS: From Cortez, take U.S. 160 east to entrance. From Mancos, take U.S. 160 west to entrance.

FEES: At entrance for each vehicle and bus rider, and for campgrounds.

PARKING: At Far View, Morefield, Wetherill Mesa, and Chapin Mesa.

GAS, FOOD: In park from mid-May to mid-October. Off season, in Cortez and Mancos.

LODGING: In park from mid-May to mid-October. Off season, in Cortez and Mancos. Limited food service available off-season at Chapin Mesa.

VISITOR CENTER: Open only during summer at Far View.

MUSEUM: Open year-round in headquarters area.

GIFT SHOPS: From mid-May to mid-October at Far View, Spruce Tree Terrace, and Morefield Campground.

PETS: Permitted on leash, except on trails, at archeological sites, or in public buildings.

PICNICKING: In museum area, Ruins Road, Weatherill Mesa, and Morefield Campground.

HIKING: Restricted to 5 trails only; 2 require permit.

CAMPGROUND: Morefield Campground, open May 1 to October 16, both tents and trailers. No reservations, no wood gathering. Showers available.

TOURS: During summer months, all sites open; 3 have guided tours. In fall, winter, spring, 1 or 2 sites open for guided tour, weather permitting.

OTHER ACTIVITIES: Bicycling. Guided tours require free tickets, available at the park.

FACILITIES FOR DISABLED: At Far View and Chapin Mesa, some campgrounds.

For additional information, see also Sites, Trails, and Trips on pages 296–304 and the maps on pages 282–283 and 301.

MESA VERDE NATIONAL PARK LIES between Cortez and Durango in southwestern Colorado. A 21-mile drive from its entrance leads to the finest collection of prehistoric cliff dwellings preserved in the United States. The dwellings, occupied by the Anasazi Indians until A.D. 1300, are so rich in history and beauty that in 1978 the United Nations declared Mesa Verde a World Heritage Site.

Numerous vista points overlook an unbroken panorama of the Four Corners states. The park lies between the 14,000-foot peaks of the San Juan Mountains in Colorado and the Navajo Reservation in Arizona. It is home to Rocky Mountain mule deer and a variety of other large mammals. Occasionally cougars, bears, and elk are sighted. More than 160 species of birds have been observed in the park, nesting among the Douglas-fir of the northern slopes, the pinyon and juniper of the mesa tops, and the sagebrush of the canyon bottoms.

Park elevations range from 5,000 to 8,500 feet above sea level. The mesa is a great block of Cretaceous sedimentary rock, mostly shale and sandstone, that was deposited 90 million years ago and has been tipped gently to the south.

HISTORY

The cliff dwellings of Mesa Verde have been empty since the last years of the thirteenth century. The inhabitants, a people called the

John Wetherill, whose family rediscovered Mesa Verde, at Cliff Palace in 1891.

MESA VERDE
NATIONAL PARK

Ranger Station
Amphitheater
Campground
Picnic Area
Information
Archeological Sites
ROAD
TRAIL

TO DURANGO

160

VALLEY

MANCOS

WEBER
MOUNTAINS

Mancos River

RIM

Whites

Waters Canyon

Eas

EAST

PARK
ENTRANCE
El. 6954

Point
Lookout
Trail

Knife Edge Trail

MOREFIELD
CAMPGROUND
El. 7803

Prater Ridge Trail

MOCCAS

RIM

School Section Canyo

NORTH

PARK
POINT
El. 8572

Soo

Navajo Hill
FAR VIEW
El. 8040

We

N

MILES

TO CORTEZ AND U.S. 666

VICINITY MAP

BIG MESA

WHITES MESA

Morefield Canyon

Prater Canyon

Canyon

Monticello

Dove Creek

Cahone

Pleasant View

566

163

Blanding

UTAH
COLO.

Bluff

Aneth

262

HOVENWEEP

NAVAJO RES.

Cortez

Mancos

160
666

MESA VERDE
N. P.

UTE MTN. INDIAN RES.

INSET SCALE

0   10   20
M I L E S

VIEW
SITE

Far View
Site Trail

(See trail map)

Navajo Canyon

Wickiup

Canyon

Long
House
Site
Trail

STEP
HOUSE

Step
House
Trail

MESA

WILDHORSE

LONG
HOUSE
El. 7000'

WETHERILL MESA

MESA

LONG

MESA

CEDAR TREE
TOWER

Soda

CHAPIN

Canyon

Spruce
Canyon
Trail

PARK
HEADQUARTERS
El. 6969'

Petroglyph
Point Trail

MESA

Soda
Canyon
Trail

BALCONY
HOUSE
El. 6720'

UTE
MOUNTAIN
INDIAN
RESERVATION

Anasazi, who lived not just at Mesa Verde, but throughout the Four Corners region, walked away from the home that had been theirs for 700 years, leaving no sign of turmoil, fanfare, or regret. They simply left. And the entire Four Corners region lay silent, seemingly empty for 300 years.

The Anasazi

Who were the people who lived in the cliffs? The Navajo, who live south and west of Mesa Verde, call them Anasazi—"Ancient Ones" or "Enemy Ancestors." Navajos of historic time have hesitated to tread amid the unquiet spirits among the cliff dwellings. (Although the term *Anasazi* is used in this and other chapters of this book, objections to the term is growing among some Native American groups because "enemy ancesters" is one of the translations.)

The comings and goings of a people are difficult to trace. Twelve thousand years ago, hunters and gatherers stalked deer and elk, and gathered pinyon nuts and prickly pear, across the region that is Mesa Verde. Four thousand years ago, an event occurred that would alter southwestern life at least as much as the invention of the steam engine altered European civilization. Corn was introduced, probably from Mexico or Central America. At first people would merely drop kernels in favorable places and return months later to see if anything had grown. But slowly these people learned to tend their plants and cultivate their land. Perhaps by the year A.D. 500, they could be called an agricultural people, relying for their subsistence more on the seeds they sowed, which by then included beans and squash, than on the animals they hunted or the nuts and fruit they gathered.

The Anasazi evolution to agriculturalism probably occurred well south of Mesa Verde. It was not until A.D. 550 that the Anasazi arrived there. The Green Mesa, covered with juniper and pinyon, offered plentiful firewood, and there were seeps and springs along the cliff edges. The people stayed.

These people, the Basketmaker Anasazi, built permanent pit houses, singly or in small clusters. With wood or stone they dug out a pit 10 to 15 feet across and 3 feet deep. The roof and walls, which were supported by four corner posts, were made of mud-covered juniper and pinyon branches. Attached to one side of the pit house was an antechamber used for storage. Entrance was by ladder through a hole in the roof of the main room.

The Basketmaker people, secure in their Mesa Verde home, began to experiment. Finely woven baskets of yucca fiber and rabbitbrush had been used for storing seeds, carrying water, and even

Opposite: A reconstructed Basketmaker pit house in Step House on Wetherill Mesa.

cooking; but pottery, once introduced, was gradually developed into the traditional black-on-white ware typical of Mesa Verde. The atlatl (a spear-throwing device) and the throwing stick were replaced by the more accurate bow and arrow. Turkeys were domesticated.

Around A.D. 750, the Anasazi underwent social changes that are perhaps best reflected in their architecture. The pit house communities of the Basketmakers evolved toward the many-roomed pueblo. Situated above ground, living quarters faced a central ceremonial room called the kiva, which was built below ground. The kiva served as a social gathering place or as a religious center. Archeologists, twelve centuries later, used these changes in building methods to mark the end of the Basketmaker period and the beginning of the Pueblo period.

Changes in Anasazi social order are further underscored by the development of trade with neighbors to the south and by the communal water projects undertaken near Far View Site and south of Morefield Campground. Many hands were needed for the construction of Mummy Lake Reservoir near Far View, and the catchment channel that fed it. Work was begun around A.D. 950 and continued as long as the Pueblo Anasazi occupied the mesa top. Success may have swollen their numbers, and the subsequent crowding forced them to farm land that previously had been considered too poor to cultivate. Many small check dams were built at this time to catch silt and to hold water that would otherwise have been wasted.

The Classic Pueblo period, the culminating chapter of the Anasazi story at Mesa Verde, began around A.D. 1100. Mesa-top villages were consolidated into larger communities. A good example is Far View Site, which is surrounded by sixteen satellite villages within a half mile. Archeologists have observed but not explained this concentration of population at Mesa Verde. Perhaps there was a need for defense. External walls of these pueblos were built without doors. Kivas were drawn into courtyards within the pueblos. Towers were built more often, frequently connected by tunnels to a nearby kiva.

The Anasazi art of masonry reached its zenith with the construction of these mesa-top cities. Stones were worked into rectangular blocks; their surfaces were distinctively pecked or dimpled. These and other refinements provided the strength needed to build to a height of three or four stories. But they also satisfied aesthetic yearnings. The Anasazi of Mesa Verde, at the height of their success as farmers and traders, had earned time for the arts.

Almost all the great cliff dwellings of Mesa Verde—Cliff Palace, Spruce Tree House, Long House—were built and occupied only during the thirteenth century. In some cases, these fortress sites grew out of the walls of the mesa, made of the same rock. Though

The 1,700-foot-high volcanic plug Shiprock, south of the park.

hastily built, the dwellings are a graceful presence that comple-
ments the cliffs.

What triggered the move? We may never know. Certainly the
cliff dwellings were more defensible. Had the Anasazi acquired real
or imaginary enemies? No increase in burial sites, which would
suggest fighting, has been found, and the mummies and skeletons
that have been found usually indicate death by natural causes.
Firewood, harvested continually for six centuries, was surely

growing scarce. Perhaps the caves required less heating. Water sources may have dried up. Intensive agriculture, coupled with droughts such as that from 1090 to 1101, may have forced the people to seek and protect springs located in the canyon walls and in the back of the alcoves in which they built their new homes.

And having built the cliff dwellings, the Anasazi simply disappeared from this area before the year 1300. They left mugs, pots full of corn, bows and arrows, and jewelry scattered about their homes with a casualness that implied their intention to return later in the day. Archeologists believe that they migrated to the upper reaches of the Rio Grande and the Zuñi villages in New Mexico, and to the Hopi mesas in Arizona.

A severe drought, recorded in the shrunken rings of trees, struck the Mesa Verde region from 1276 until at least 1299. But these people had survived worse droughts. The mesa top, cultivated more and more intensively for seven centuries, may have grown too alkaline—too nutrient-poor—to be farmed any longer. Perhaps . . . Archeologists, if pressed, hypothesize that a combination of any or all of these or even more complex factors may have led to the evacuation of Mesa Verde.

The Spanish

Sylvestre Vélez de Escalante and Francisco Atanasia Domínguez, two Franciscan priests, stumbled across the foot of the La Plata Mountains and down into the Mancos Valley in August 1776, while looking for a route from Santa Fe to the missions of California. They were the first Europeans to see much of the parts of Colorado, Utah, Arizona, and New Mexico now called the Colorado Plateau. Certainly, they were the first to see the great green highland lying to the west of the Mancos; years later it was to be named Mesa Verde. Although they discovered none of the dwellings of the mesa, they did find the site complex near Dolores, Colorado, that bears Escalante's name.

The Spaniards who followed Escalante and Domínguez, and the occasional nineteenth-century geologist who surveyed the great Colorado Plateau, just missed, perhaps by several miles, the treasures known only to a few Native Americans.

The First Settlers and Discovery

The Ute Indians occupied western Colorado when the early explorers and trappers moved through. For the most part, the Utes were not threatened by these transient men. But in the 1870s, silver was discovered in the nearby San Juan Mountains, and people flocked to the Colorado Territory to seek their fortunes. Among them was

Benjamin Wetherill, a Quaker from Missouri who was down on his luck. His story was that of most—he found little, if any, silver. So he staked out some land and, in 1879, took up cattle ranching in the Mancos Valley. The Utes were slowly pushed back onto a fraction of the land they once had roamed. But, unknown to Wetherill and his neighbors, the Indians held the real treasure—Mesa Verde and the remains of a civilization long since vanished.

In 1874, members of the Hayden Geological and Geographical Survey, who were sporadically exploring the Mancos River at the foot of Mesa Verde, had discovered dwellings in the canyon walls. William Henry Jackson found Two Story House; a year later, W. H. Holmes discovered Sixteen Window House. In some, they found corncobs and bits of pottery. Their curiosity was piqued: Who were

Pottery made by the Anasazi, who lived at Mesa Verde between A.D. 550 and 1300.

the people who had lived in the cliffs?

Richard, Benjamin Wetherill's eldest son, learned from a Ute of a large stone house up one of Mesa Verde's side canyons. The Utes considered it sacred and, like the Navajos, never visited it. Richard's curiosity grew unbearable when the Indian refused to tell him how to find the dwelling.

In 1887, another son stumbled across what he described as a vast cave filled with an entire city of ruins—towers and multistoried buildings reaching beyond sight. The hour was late, however, and he had to continue on his way. Once again, discovery had slipped by.

Cliff Palace, Spruce Tree House, Square Tower House—these sites had remained undisturbed for 600 years. But on December 18, 1888, Richard Wetherill and his brother-in-law, Charlie Mason, while tracking stray cattle on Chapin Mesa during a heavy snow-storm, walked to the edge of Cliff Canyon. Through the swirl of blinding snow, they spotted the site now called Cliff Palace. Lashing logs together in a makeshift ladder, they scrambled down the sheer face of the cliff and across to the ruins and stepped into the past.

The Wetherills—generous perhaps to a fault—wanted all the world to know of their discovery. They guided reporters, tourists, and pot hunters through the sites, and unlucky was the visitor who left without a souvenir. They sold pottery, baskets, sandals, axes, and arrowheads—all from Mesa Verde. But the Wetherills also worked with Baron Gustaf Nordenskiold, who, in 1891, conducted the first systematic archeological survey of the sites of the Mesa Verde. As the significance of the sites came to be appreciated, a new ethic of preservation slowly emerged. The Wetherills ceased selling artifacts to tourists in 1895; from then on they contracted only with privately funded research expeditions for the excavation of intact collections. By good fortune, the great majority of the treasures they found ultimately ended up in the collections of four major institutions. Such were the beginnings of the science of archeology in southwestern Colorado.

Establishment of the Park

In 1891 and 1894, the Colorado General Assembly called on the United States Congress to preserve Mesa Verde as a national park; a sense of national heritage was evolving to replace the blunter instincts of free enterprise. In 1901, the Colorado Cliff Dwelling Association managed to persuade the Ute Indians and Congress to give it control of Mesa Verde; in return, the Utes were to receive an annual sum of $300 from Congress. On June 29, 1906, President Theodore Roosevelt signed a bill granting Mesa Verde the status of a national park; what was left of a civilization was preserved.

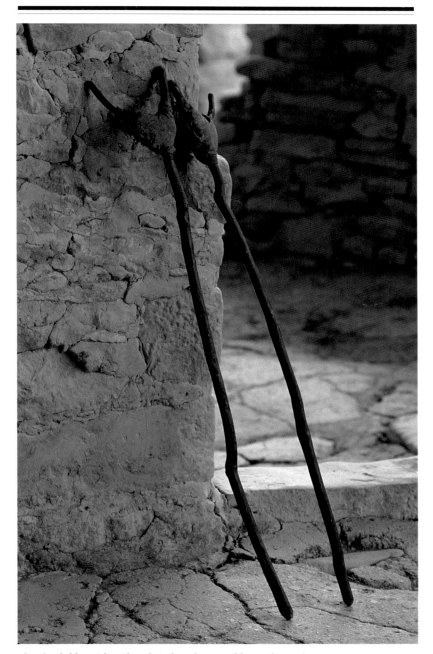

A pair of old crutches, thought to have been used by an Anasazi.

To see this expanse of almost empty land is to grasp at intangibles. How old are these rocks? How were they placed here? How were they sculptured into their present form? Wallace Stegner, writing about the Colorado Plateau, once said, "This is country that leads one to think in terms of geologic time, which if I am not mistaken is about the same as thinking in religious terms." Certainly the Navajos would agree. According to them, Shiprock, to the south, is Tse-bi-ta-i, the winged rock that brought their ancestors to this land. Sleeping Ute Mountain, just west of the park, is a Ute god, asleep on his back.

The geology of Mesa Verde, taken one step at a time, is really quite simple. Some 90 million years ago—before the Colorado Plateau or the Rocky Mountains had been lifted far above sea level—this land was under water. As the sea floor subsided, 2,000 feet of mud and sand were deposited. Upon hardening, this mud became the Mancos Shale.

Above the Mancos lie the sand and shale of the Mesa Verde Group. Within the park, this is composed of three distinct layers. The lowest layer is the Point Lookout Sandstone, which forms the lower of two prominent cliffs visible in canyon walls throughout the park. As the sea that deposited the Mancos Shale retreated to the northeast, sandy beaches were continuously deposited along the shoreline. Eventually, 250 feet of sand accumulated.

As the sea withdrew, the land became a swamp, crossed by river flood plains. Trees lived and died, and in time were compressed into coal. Along with sand and silt, they became part of the Menefee Formation, a 400-foot layer of rock named for a pioneer family of the Mancos Valley. Coal within the Menefee is found in two zones near the top and bottom of the formation. Many outcrops of coal have burned naturally when ignited by lightning or forest fires. Modern men have mined the coal in recent past, but the Anasazi apparently left well enough alone and did not use the coal as fuel.

The sea returned once again following deposition of the Menefee. The swamps were flooded, and rivers carried into the area the sand and clay that compose the 400-foot-thick Cliff House Sandstone—the third and final layer of the Mesa Verde Group in the park area. This rock, when eroded millions of years later, formed distinct cliffs that were punctuated by alcoves with high, vaulting roofs. The Anasazi would put to good use these alcoves of the Cliff House Sandstone.

The Mancos Shale and Mesa Verde Group were deposited toward the end of the Cretaceous period. At the close of this peri-

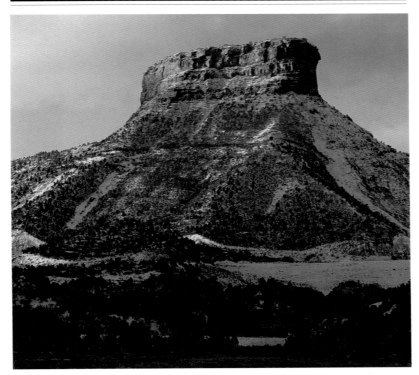

Butte seen from Point Lookout near the entrance to the park.

od, some 65 million years ago, a mountain-building epoch began that was to change the face of the West. The land was compressed, folded, and thrust upward. The Rocky Mountains began to rise. Over the next 40 million years, Sleeping Ute Mountain and the La Platas popped up like mushrooms overnight, geologically speaking. The San Juan Mountains were uplifted, gently tipping the surrounding countryside, including the Mesa Verde. These mountains were pushed up by a core of rising molten rock. Erosion was accelerated by the uplifts; the Mancos Shale and Mesa Verde Group, once extending in great sheets in all directions, were whittled down to their present extent at Mesa Verde.

Seen on a map, Mesa Verde is composed of many narrow mesas that run north and south. The mesas are separated by canyons that drain south to the Mancos River. Because the whole mesa tips to the south, canyons that flow in that direction have grown in length much faster than their counterparts that drain to the north. As a result, the south-flowing canyons have cut all the way back to the mesa's great northern escarpment. Geologically speaking, the canyons of the Mesa Verde are being cut deeper and wider at a frightful clip. The two sandstone formations at the bottom and top of the Mesa Verde Group form resistant cliffs that protect the soft underlying shales. Whenever blocks of sandstone are removed by erosion, the vulnerable shales beneath quickly melt away with the next rainfall.

Geology is the study of rocks—nothing could seem more down to earth. But this science lends itself to the consideration of space and time. Sitting at Park Point, one wonders about nature's grand design.

Natural History

Climate and Precipitation

Mesa Verde can get mighty cold and pretty warm. Mesa-top temperatures in the vicinity of the park headquarters on Chapin Mesa range from an average low of 18° F in January to a high of 88° F in July, although extremes of -20° F and 102° F have been observed. Summer temperatures can easily plummet 35 degrees after sunset. The dry air of the Southwest will surprise the unprepared visitor.

Both people and animals feed off the juicy fruit of the prickly pear.

The park's 18 inches of annual precipitation are delivered on a yearly installment plan—divided almost equally between winter snowstorms and late-summer thundershowers.

Flora

Mesa Verda, the Green Mesa, got its name from the pinyon and juniper stands that cover its top. The mesa tops, with elevations of between 6,800 and 7,400 feet, have been called the Anasazi cornbelt by some archeologists. Conditions at this altitude lent themselves to increasingly intensive agricultural development during the Pueblo period. In addition to farming, the Anasazi gathered the wild-growing prickly pear cactus, Indian rice grass, and Rocky Mountain bee plant.

Toward the north end of Mesa Verde grow stands of Douglas-fir on the cooler, north-facing slopes. In the canyon bottoms of the south-flowing creeks is found the big sagebrush that is better suited to the dry, warm canyons. Growing in the canyons and on the mesa tops is the versatile *Yucca baccata*, a member of the lily family. Its roots, fruit, and fibers were used by the Anasazi, the fibers to make sandals, baskets, ropes, and other useful items. A fascinat-

Above: The Anasazi made sandals, baskets, and rope from tough yucca fibers. Right: Mule deer are browsers, preferring to feed off leaves and twigs of shrubs and trees rather than grass.

ing symbiotic relationship has evolved between the yucca and an otherwise nondescript, papery-winged moth. The yucca is completely dependent on the pronuba moth for pollination. In turn, the moth lays its eggs only in the fruit of the blossoming yucca. Without the other, each would be frustrated in its efforts to reproduce.

Fauna

A surprising diversity of wildlife can be found at Mesa Verde. Rocky Mountain mule deer commonly forage near Morefield Campground around dusk and dawn. Coyotes sing their mournful songs after dark. Cougars, bears, and bobcats are seen on rare and special occasions. Birds are especially numerous within the park. Owls, hawks, eagles, and falcons hunt along the canyon walls and along the mesa's northern escarpment. The canyon wren is more often heard than seen, filling the air with its laughing, descending trill.

SITES, TRAILS, AND TRIPS

Mesa Verde, like an island in the sky, rises 2,000 feet above the surrounding Mancos Valley, Dolores Plateau, and Montezuma Valley. The most important decision, on entering Mesa Verde National Park, is which mesa sites to see.

Park Point. Entering the park from the north, drivers climb the steep shale face of the northern escarpment to the highest elevations of the park. Park Point is 8,572 feet above sea level. From here the mesa drops sharply to the north and more slowly to the south. The Mancos River, flowing south and then west, holds the mesa in the crook of its arm. Beyond the river, beyond the valley floors at the foot of the mesa, mountains are scattered across the desert. To the north are the Abajos and the La Sals of Utah. To the east rise the La Plata Mountains, and Lone Cone and Mount Wilson of the San Juan Mountains. Shiprock, the Lukachukai Mountains, and the Carrizo Mountains rise up from the Navajo Reservation to the south. Take the time to sit and soak in this country. The wind that always seems to blow here will rustle through the Gambel oak, Rocky Mountain juniper, and Utah juniper. Arrowleaf balsamroot, blooming in June, will turn the hillsides below you yellow. Try to imagine how this country seemed to the people who lived here a thousand years ago.

Far View. The Far View Visitor Center houses an exhibit that illustrates and describes historic Indian life styles and cultures. A park ranger at the information desk can suggest sites to visit and trails to hike. The Wetherill Mesa road begins across from the Visitor Center and is open during summer months. One mile to the south, along the road leading down Chapin Mesa, is Far View Site, which contains examples of some of the finest mesa-top architecture in the park. The site was excavated and stabilized by archeologist Jesse Fewkes in 1916.

Chapin Mesa. People visit Mesa Verde to see the cliff dwellings, but it is too easy to see only the major sites and then leave. Take a little time to acclimate to the park. Chapin Mesa offers a number of ways to ease into an understanding of the Anasazi.

The Chapin Mesa Archeological Museum is an excellent place to begin learning about the ancient people who once lived here. Dioramas depict all the phases of Indian habitation of the mesa. There are displays of pottery, weaving, toolmaking, and jewelry. Dendrochronology—the science of tree-ring dating—is explained in detail. The museum can suggest a bit of the richness of Anasazi life.

Next door to the museum is the main ranger station. Here visitors sign up for a hike to either Spruce Canyon or Petroglyph Point. The trails begin immediately below the ranger station; each is a little more than 2 miles long and will take 2 or 3 hours to hike at an easy pace.

The mesa top is covered by the uniformly green pinyon and juniper forest that gave Mesa Verde its name. When the Anasazi lived here, much of this forest would have been cleared for cultivation or carried home for firewood. Visible on top is the ever-precious yucca.

Spruce Canyon Trail. Spruce Canyon Trail drops off Chapin Mesa and descends to the bottom of Spruce Canyon. Morning hikers are more likely to be following Rocky Mountain mule deer tracks than those of fellow hikers. Of 600,000 people visiting the park in one recent year, only 600 registered to hike this trail. Hikers are likely to have the trail all to themselves.

The Anasazi walked this canyon searching for pinyon nuts. The pinyon pine bears a crop of nuts once or twice out of every seven years. Many years after the Anasazi, the Wetherill boys climbed up these canyon bottoms after their cattle, not yet realizing the incredible ruins that lay silent so near by.

Overleaf: Decorated interior of an Anasazi dwelling. The figures on the walls may be of religious significance.

TRAILS OF MESA VERDE NATIONAL PARK

SPRUCE TREE HOUSE TRAIL: Starts and ends at museum; .5 mile round trip; 1 hour; 200-foot ascent; ranger-guided tour in winter, self-guided tour in summer (114 rooms, 8 kivas), constructed between 1204 and 1278.

CLIFF PALACE TRAIL: Starts and ends at Ruins road loop; .5 mile round trip; 12 hour; 500-foot ascent; Cliff House (217 rooms, 23 kivas) was constructed between 1200 and 1300; narrow, winding, strenuous trail; not accessible to disabled. Guided tour only, ticket required.

BALCONY HOUSE TRAIL: Starts and ends at Ruins road loop; .5 mile round trip; 1 hour; 400-foot ascent; ranger-guided tour of cliff dwelling (45 rooms); access by 32-foot ladder, exit by 12-foot tunnel and 100-foot climb up cliff face; open May through September. Ticket required.

STEP HOUSE TRAIL: Starts and ends at Wetherill Mesa kiosk; .5 mile round trip; 1 hour; 500-foot ascent; self-guided tour of pit house/cliff dwelling; very strenuous.

LONG HOUSE TRAIL: Starts and ends at Mini Trail trail head; .75 mile round trip; 1 hour; 400-foot ascent; ranger-guided tour; strenuous, with 50 steps; not recommended for disabled.

SPRUCE CANYON TRAIL: Starts at Spruce Tree House; ends at Spruce Canyon picnic area; 2.1 miles round trip; 2 hours; 700-foot ascent; drops off Chapin Mesa to bottom of Spruce Canyon and then turns up canyon; registration at chief ranger's office.

PETROGLYPH POINT TRAIL: Starts at Spruce Tree House; ends at museum parking area; 2.3 miles round trip; 2 hours; 200-foot ascent; runs below edge of plateau; excellent views of Spruce Canyon and Navajo Canyon; registration at chief ranger's office.

PRATER RIDGE TRAIL: Starts and ends at Morefield Campground; 7.5 miles round trip; 4 hours; 700-foot ascent; changes in elevation and vegetation types.

KNIFE EDGE TRAIL: Starts and ends at Morefield Campground; 1.5 miles round trip; 1 hour; 100-foot ascent; follows old road alignment toward Montezuma Valley overlook; excellent place from which to watch sunsets.

SODA CANYON OVERLOOK TRAIL: Starts and ends at turnout north of Balcony House; .75 mile round trip; 1 hour; three overlooks of Soda Canyon; the southward facing overlook provides only good view of Balcony House.

FAR VIEW SITE TRAIL: Starts and ends at Far View Site; 1 mile round trip; 1 hour; 5 surface ruins of dwellings constructed between 900 and 1300.

POINT LOOKOUT NATURE TRAIL: Starts and ends at Morefield Amphitheater; 2 miles round trip; 2 hours; panorama of the surrounding area, including the Mancos and Montezuma valleys, Mount Wilson, the Dolores Peaks, and the La Plata Mountains.

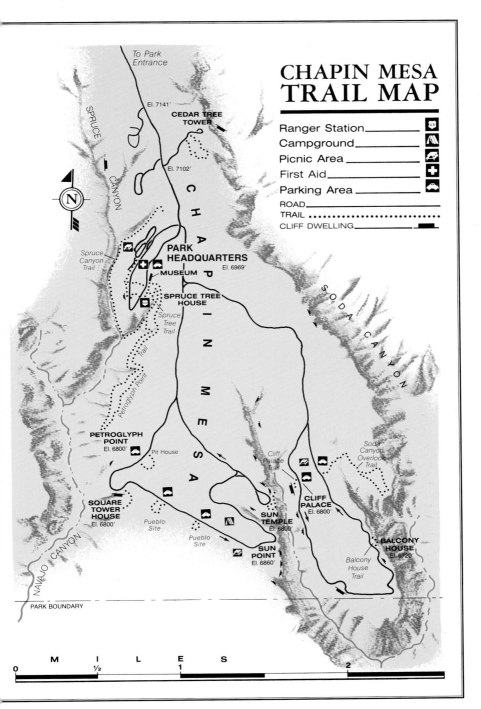

CHAPIN MESA TRAIL MAP

To Park Entrance

El. 7141'

CEDAR TREE TOWER

El. 7102'

SPRUCE CANYON

N

CHAPIN MESA

Spruce Canyon Trail

PARK HEADQUARTERS El. 6969'

MUSEUM

SPRUCE TREE HOUSE

Spruce Tree Trail

Petroglyph Point Trail

SODA CANYON

PETROGLYPH POINT El. 6800'

Pit House

Cliff Palace Trail

Soda Canyon Overlook Trail

SQUARE TOWER HOUSE El. 6800'

Pueblo Site

Pueblo Site

SUN TEMPLE El. 6800'

CLIFF PALACE El. 6800'

SUN POINT El. 6860'

BALCONY HOUSE El. 6720'

Balcony House Trail

NAVAJO CANYON

PARK BOUNDARY

Ranger Station

Campground

Picnic Area

First Aid

Parking Area

ROAD

TRAIL

CLIFF DWELLING

M I L E S

0   ½   1   2

Petroglyph Point Trail. The Petroglyph Point Trail is longer than the Spruce Canyon Trail, but it does not descend to the canyon floor. It winds along the base of the Cliff House Sandstone, leading past alcoves and a small cliff dwelling. Since much of this trail is shaded by the sandstone cliff, temperatures are lower and the ground is wetter than if it were not shaded, and trees like Douglas-fir are able to grow at this 6,700-foot elevation. Also found along this trail is the chokecherry bush, whose fruit was eaten by the Anasazi. Near the end of the trail is Petroglyph Point, where an excellent example of Anasazi rock art can be admired. The trail returns to the museum area along the top of Chapin Mesa.

Spruce Tree House. Spruce Tree House is directly across from the main ranger station on Chapin Mesa. The hike down to the ruin will take approximately 15 minutes. Just before reaching the site, hikers will pass the spring that served the 100 or so people who lived in the 114 rooms of the ruin. The National Park Service has reconstructed a roof over several of the eight kivas at this site; visitors are able to climb down the ladder in the roof of one of these kivas and view the interior. Kivas are used by men of the modern-day Zuñi and Hopi tribes, thought to be descendants of the Anasazi. Similar use is therefore ascribed to the Anasazi.

Mesa Top Drive. Pit houses constructed during the Basketmaker era (A.D. 575), several early Pueblo period villages (A.D. 950), and cliff dwellings can be seen along the Mesa Top Drive. The pit houses were built at the beginning of the Anasazi's seven-century occupation of Mesa Verde. There are few places in the United States that allow us to view the systematic evolution of a culture over so long a span of time. European-based culture has been established in the United States for only half the time spent by the Anasazi in the Southwest.

Cliff Palace. Cliff Palace contains 217 rooms and 23 kivas. Its towers, some four stories high, reach toward but just miss the alcove roof soaring overhead. Cliff Palace can be seen in a panoramic view from Mesa Top Drive across Cliff Canyon. Guided tours are conducted at Cliff Palace; tickets are required.

The masonry of Cliff Palace is fascinating. The Anasazi placed small chinking stones in the mortar to prevent cracking. Some walls adjoin others in an ill-fitting manner resulting from sequential rather than simultaneous construction. It is possible to roughly trace the growth of this site room by room as it filled up its cave. Construction of Cliff Palace occurred between 1209 and 1273, dates arrived at by archeologists using tree-ring dating methods on wood found in the ruin.

Because of the protective cave roof, the walls of Cliff Palace have resisted the effects of seven centuries of wind, rain, and snow. Pot hunters took their toll around 1900, but the site is now protected. The walls in front of the site are periodically stabilized to counteract the effects of hundreds of thousands of visitors walking across the base of the site each year.

Balcony House. Balcony House is a forty-room dwelling that nests in the cliffs above Soda Canyon. Entrance to the site in Anasazi times was possible only by hand- and toeholds down a cliff and then through a narrow tunnel. No intruder could have hoped to force an entry into this village. Like most other Mesa Verde cliff dwellings, Balcony House was built only in the last few decades of the Anasazi's long occupation of the mesa. Even though Balcony House has an extreme defensive posture, there is no specific evidence that the Anasazi were threatened by enemies.

A ranger-led tour of Balcony House involves a 1-hour hike down to the site and back up to the mesa top. Along the way, visitors climb a 32-foot ladder to enter the site, and squeeze through the original access tunnel to leave. Those faint of heart or afraid of heights may do well to pass this tour by. Tickets are required for the tour.

Soda Canyon Overlook. A little farther down the road is the .75-mile Soda Canyon Overlook Trail. It leads past prickly pear cactus (blooming in May and June) to a delightfully quiet view of Balcony House. Across Soda Canyon lies Moccasin Mesa, which burned in 1972. In many parks, lightning-strike fires are allowed to burn through their natural course, but fires at Mesa Verde are actively suppressed to protect the sites.

Wetherill Mesa. The science of archeology took a great step forward in 1959 when the five-year Wetherill Mesa Project began. The project's survey documented 800 Anasazi sites. Taking part in the study, in addition to archeologists, were geologists, meteorologists, biologists, botanists, and ecologists. Even an orthopedic surgeon became involved, examining deformities in the skeletons discovered in the ruins. Never before had such a fully integrated investigation of American prehistory been attempted. The results gave the clearest, most well-rounded picture of Anasazi life ever pieced together.

Wetherill Mesa was opened to the public after the completion of these elaborate excavations. Visitors drive the 12 miles from the Far View Visitor Center to Wetherill Mesa, where they may take a self-guided tour of Step House or a ranger-led tour of Long House, second largest of the park ruins. Each tour is about 1 hour long.

One out of fifteen visitors to Mesa Verde comes to Wetherill Mesa, just about the quietest corner in the park. The peacefulness is conducive to soaking in a bit of this land and its history. The Wetherill Mesa Nature Walk begins and ends at the bus parking lot. Along it hikers will see some of the 168 species of birds found in the park—perhaps a violet-green swallow rocketing across the wind, or a prairie falcon or sparrow hawk dropping like a falling star toward an unlucky scrub jay.

Wetherill Mesa is open from about June 1 through Labor Day.

Morefield Campground and Prater Ridge Trail. Morefield Campground, 4 miles past the park entrance, is a funny little town; between May 1 and mid-October, its few hundred residents move in, claim their homesites, and leave the next morning—a high turnover rate. There is drinking water at the restrooms, and a store and gas pump are up the hill. If you plan to camp at Morefield, the park's only campground, it is wise to choose a site early in the day. Occasionally in the summer Morefield will be quite crowded; certainly the better campsites will be taken by noon. Every summer evening the rangers put on a campfire talk—a National Park Service tradition that Jesse Fewkes began in 1915 at Mesa Verde.

Two trails start at Morefield Campground. The shorter one leads about .5 mile north to the escarpment overlooking the Dolores Plateau and Montezuma Valley—a good walk that can be rewarded by a memorable sunset.

The Prater Ridge Trail, the longer of the two, slants up and to the north along the hill just west of the campground, making a 7.5-mile loop around the cliffs of Prater Ridge. This is the longest, and possibly the prettiest, hike to be found at Mesa Verde. Along the way are extraordinary overlooks of the northern escarpment. Golden eagles patrol the ridgeline; Clark's nutcrackers crash noisily through the oak thickets. Out of the corner of your eye you might glimpse a mule deer raising its head to watch you pass. The turkey, reintroduced to Mesa Verde about 1990, is doing very well in this area of the park. On the southern end of the Prater Ridge loop, look down into the valleys where a black bear or two is sighted nearly every year. The tranquility of this trail offers the perfect ending to a day spent in Mesa Verde National Park.

Opposite: Cliff Palace, built in the 1200s, is protected from bad weather by a steep, overhanging shelf.

PETRIFIED FOREST
NATIONAL PARK

Pebbles and small rocks, washed down from "tepee" formations, represent final stages of erosion.

PETRIFIED FOREST NATIONAL PARK
P.O. BOX 217, ARIZONA 86028
TEL.: (520) 524-6228

HIGHLIGHTS: Kachina Point • Chinde Point • Puerco Pueblo • Newspaper Rock • The Tepees • Blue Mesa • Jasper Forest Overlook • Crystal Forest • Long Logs • Agate House • Giant Logs

ACCESS: From west, take U.S. 180 from Holbrook to south entrance. From east, leave I-40 at north entrance. See map on pages 310–311.

HOURS: Daily, 8 A.M.–5 P.M.; longer during spring, summer, fall. Road closed during bad winter weather. Closed, Christmas Day and New Year's Day. *Note:* Arizona is on Rocky Mountain Standard Time throughout the year.

FEES: At entrance, for each vehicle and each bus passenger. Golden Age, Golden Eagle, Golden Access passes available and honored.

PARKING: Ample at each public-use point.

GAS, FOOD: In park at Painted Desert Oasis and Rainbow Forest Curios. Also in Holbrook.

LODGING: In Holbrook.

VISITOR CENTER: Painted Desert Visitor Center, just off I-40 at north entrance, offers information and 17-minute film on petrified wood every half hour.

MUSEUM: Rainbow Forest Museum exhibits petrified wood and other paleontological features.

GIFT SHOPS: At Painted Desert Oasis and Rainbow Forest Curios.

PETS: Permitted on leash, except in public buildings and wilderness areas. Horseback riding permitted throughout park, no grazing; no rentals or stables.

PICNICKING: At Chinde Point, Rainbow Forest areas only. No open fires.

HIKING: Throughout park. Water must be carried. Topographical maps advisable outside developed areas. Permit needed for overnight.

BACKPACKING: Backpack camping permitted in wilderness areas with free permit from rangers. Permits available up to one hour before park closes. Carry water.

CAMPGROUNDS: None.

FACILITIES FOR DISABLED: At Painted Desert Visitor Center, 17-minute film and information in large script. At Puerco Ruin, restrooms, summer only.

For additional information, see also Sites, Trails, and Trips on pages 323–330.

PETRIFIED FOREST NATIONAL PARK IS A CURIOUS place. Where once stood tall trees and lush vegetation, there is now arid terrain. Where once reptiles roamed and huge rivers spread their waters, there are now ravens and lizards, dry washes and rivers. The earth has undergone many changes since that time. The area has been weathered over millions of years into sparse shapes and configurations. From the approaching highways, we see no outstanding features—yawning canyons or majestic mountains—that might give the park a familiar identity. Only a marker on Interstate 40 informs us that we are entering one of the most unusual landscapes on the continent.

First wagon trails, then the railroad, and finally, in the twentieth century, old U.S. 66 followed by Interstate 40 conducted travelers from east and west across this vast, empty land. The early explorers and pioneers suffered it all—the heat, the lack of water, the endless expanse, the eroded washes and gullies. Today, sealed

Banding of badlands indicates different sedimentary layers.

VICINITY MAP

666

191 Sanders

Chambers 40 Navajo St. Johns

PETRIFIED FOREST N. P. 180 Hunt

77 Sun Valley

Joseph City Holbrook

77

INSET SCALE

0 10 20
M I L E S

Black Knoll

Puerco Indian Ruin El. 5375'

Blue Mesa El. 5600'

Newspaper Rock

The Tepees

THE HAYSTACKS

RAINBOW FOREST

Jasper Forest

Crystal Forest El. 5530'

PUERCO RIDGE

The Flattops

Long Logs

Agate House

Rainbow Forest Museum El. 5475'

Giant Logs

Twin Buttes

Puerco River

Dry Wash

Adamana

Wash

180

TO ST JOHNS

TO HOLBROOK AND GRAND CANYON N. P.

in air-conditioned capsules, we speed across the terrain along four-lane highways. To experience a sense of the land, its swoop and roll, and the contours that distinguish one geological marvel from another in the American Southwest, we should follow the older roads that cling to the mantle of the land; or, better still, step out of the car and walk away from the road into the burnished palette of the Painted Desert, into the lunar hills of the Blue Mesa, or among the tangle of fallen logs that marks the petrified forests.

Because it is tucked away in folds and crevices of the desert highlands, Petrified Forest National Park is an easy place to miss. And yet for ninety years, until its full protection as a national park, this remote corner of Arizona was nearly ravaged into extinction by explorers, settlers, and turn-of-the-century entrepreneurs. A land as exposed and mysterious as this is especially vulnerable to exploitation. There are no mountains to guard it or rivers to conceal its treasures or canyons down into which prospectors with picks and shovels must laboriously descend. The accessibility of the land is part of its attraction, as well as its greatest weakness.

HISTORY

Human beings have been present in the Petrified Forest National Park area for at least 8,000 years. Within the boundaries are more than 600 archeological sites, varying in size from a few potsherd finds to pueblo complexes. It is believed that the oldest sites were occupied around A.D. 500. Some are oval pit houses 9 to 12 feet in diameter; they are scattered on top of a mesa in the southern portion of the park. Ruins of pit houses—with the added features of ventilation shafts and outside storage areas—in the Twin Buttes area indicate a more highly developed culture. Sherds of decorative pottery have been found there, along with sea shells and semiprecious stones, indicating trade with tribes on the Pacific coast and in the heart of Mexico.

The Anasazi

One of the larger ruins, and the one most easily accessible to the public, is on a windswept hill above the Puerco River. Here, for intermittent periods over three centuries, resided a people known as the Anasazi (Navajo for "Ancient Ones"), whose civilization at the end of the first millenium of the Christian era extended over the Four Corners region. The Anasazi were one of the most fascinating peoples of this continent. Over an 800-year period, from A.D. 500 to A.D. 1300, they evolved from a tribe of pit dwellers and food gatherers into a culture of sophisticated farmers and architects of

Before the park was established, souvenir hunters, attracted by the rainbow colors, removed thousands of tons of petrified wood.

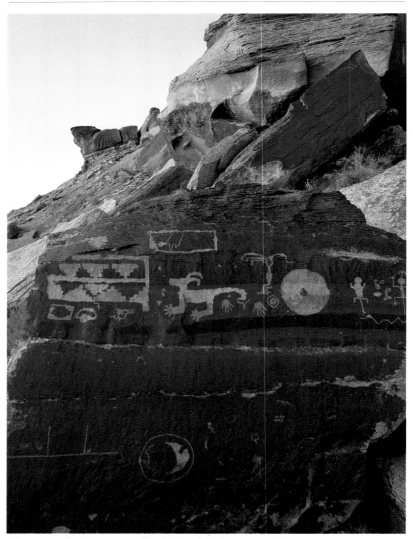

These petroglyphs were carved by Native Americans centuries ago.

complex housing projects like Chaco Canyon and Mesa Verde. They flourished in their Classic phase for a couple of centuries, and then for reasons still unknown, they vanished.

Archeologists estimate that during two occupations over three centuries (1100 to 1400), as many as 75 rooms were constructed at what is now called the Puerco Ruin. Here, perhaps 50 to 100 Anasazi cultivated corn, beans, and squash, made baskets and pottery, and lived a remarkably civilized existence in a hostile, arid environment. By 1540, when Spanish explorers first passed through the region, these early Americans had moved elsewhere, perhaps to the north and the heart of the Hopi nation, to the southeast where the Zuñi now dwell, or to the east where they may have become the ancesters of the modern-day Pueblo Indians.

Exploration and Exploitation

The first Spaniards in the area poked around a bit and then moved on. The Indians had left behind no gold, and the petrified wood chips that littered the ground had little monetary value. By contrast, the explorers of the mid-nineteenth century were excited by the petrified wood. A German artist named Baldwin Mollhausen, traveling with the Whipple survey expedition in 1853, wrote that "all the way we went we saw . . . great heaps of petrification gleaming with such splendid colours that we could not resist the temptation to alight repeatedly and break off a piece . . . ."

The temptation proved irresistible to just about everybody who followed. In 1883, the Atlantic and Pacific Railroad was completed across northern Arizona, and new settlers poured in. Part of the attraction was "Chalcedony Park," as the area was then known. During the 1890s entrepreneurs sawed and polished thousands of tons of fossilized wood into handsome pedestals and table tops, for which people back east were willing to pay high prices. In 1899, Arizona territorial governor N. O. Murphy declared that "the so-called Petrified Forest . . . is not attractive in the way of natural scenery . . . . Much expense on the part of the Government in creating a reserve for scenic purposes does not seem to me justified."

Establishment of the Park

But also by 1899, a counteroffensive against the exploitation of the Petrified Forest had gained momentum. Charles Lummis, a well-known southwestern writer, reported the depredations in one of his travel books. In 1895, Representative Will Barnes persuaded the Arizona Territorial Legislature to ask the United States Congress to set aside the Petrified Forest as a national park. The request was seconded in 1899 by U.S. Geological Survey paleontologist Lester Ward. The battle for preservation was on, and it was to last until 1906, when President Theodore Roosevelt established the Petrified Forest National Monument. The incorporation included only the Rainbow and Jasper forests in the southern portion of the park. In 1932, a large portion of the Painted Desert and the Blue Mesa area were added to the monument. And in 1962, Congress established the Petrified Forest National Park.

Two hundred and twenty-five million years ago, Arizona was a tropical land some 1,700 miles closer to the equator than it is today. According to the theory of plate tectonics (better known as the theory of continental drift), all the continents of the earth were once joined together into a supercontinent called Pangaea. Pangaea eventually cracked into blocks that drifted to the positions they occupy as the present-day continents. Thus Arizona shifted north and west, along with the entire North American continent, to its current position. During this long period, the land was shaped and built up by repeated inundations by warm, shallow seas and by metamorphic activity from deep within the earth's molten core.

Sedimentation and Erosion

Chinle badlands.

Mesozoic northern Arizona was a low, flat stretch of country, what today would be called a flood plain, across which rivers and streams meandered, depositing pebbles and sand. Eventually these deposits reached a thickness of several thousand feet and formed a mantle, or covering, called the Chinle Formation. It is the exposed sections of this formation—denuded by wind and water—that form the topographical features of the park.

Following the era of sedimentary deposition that resulted in the Chinle Formation came yet another that lasted until approximately 70 million years ago. Streams and rivers flowed northward from high mountains in southeastern Arizona toward a sea to the west of the present-day Colorado River (where southern California is now). On occasion these streams and rivers formed lakes and swamps, the remains of whose animal life formed deposits of muddy limestone 3,000 feet thick on top of the Chinle Formation. Gradually the weather changed, the climate grew arid, and these sedimentary rock layers above the Chinle Formation began to erode.

During the Tertiary period of the Cenozoic era, approximately 65 million years ago, an uplift occurred in the region that raised the strata of sedimentary rock approximately 7,000 feet. So gradual was this uplift that few faults and folds developed, the land rising with the uniformity of a table top. To the east, the uplift was higher, causing a natural barrier that trapped the waters of the ancestral Colorado River flowing down from the north. Over a long period of time, these waters spread in all directions, forming an extensive impoundment. Sand, silt, clay, and sediments flowed in with the current to create a vast body of water that geologists call Lake Bidahochi.

Some 10 million years ago, an expanding drainage to the west of the lake intercepted the route of the ancestral Colorado and caused it to flow westward, away from Lake Bidahochi. Eventually the lake dried up, and new geological influences appeared. Around 4 million years ago, volcanoes erupted in the area, blanketing the lake bed with lava and volcanic ash. This period was followed by another era of meandering streams and rivers, after which erosion became the dominant geological factor. The mantle of the Bidahochi Formation, laid down by the deposits of the former lake and the ash and lava from the volcanic activity that followed, was swept away. Only a few places within the park boundaries, such as Pilot Rock, remain to indicate the remnants of millions of years of sedimentary and metamorphic activity. The erosion also cut deep into the strata of the underlying Chinle Formation, uncovering the petrified wood and fossils.

Badlands

Nature is full of paradoxes. At Petrified Forest National Park, where there is virtually no water, practically all the landscape has been produced by the action of water and wind. The carving of the Chinle Formation—once a relatively flat series of sedimentary layers—into the gnashed and rounded topography of today took many millions of years. The popular term for this kind of terrain is *badlands*, and its creation is the result of a process that geologist William Lee Stokes has called "the principle of differential erosion." Hard rocks, such as sandstone, limestone, and lava, withstand erosion better than soft ones, such as clay and shale. Once, a long time ago, the low, rounded hills of the Painted Desert were protected by layers of hard rock. When this rock disappeared, the softer materials underneath were exposed, and erosion took place at a faster rate, geologically speaking. The hills we see today are composed primarily of soft, porous bentonitic clays. When they are soaked by a summer thundershower, these clays expand to eight times their original thickness. The sun then bakes them, causing the expanded surface to crack and crumble. The next rain washes the fragmented surface into a gully.

To appreciate the natural history of Petrified Forest National Park, we must first look back millions of years and try to visualize what the area once looked like. Two hundred and twenty-five million years ago—during the twilight portion of the Triassic period, early in the Mesozoic era—Arizona was a lush forest of exotic trees, plants, and flowers. Today, that forest is totally fossilized as a result of the effects of time and erosion. This is not to say that there are no plants and animals in the park; indeed, there are. But to truly understand the vast spectrum of natural history represented in the Petrified Forest, we have to reverse our perspective.

Petrified Trees

While walking through the Rainbow Forest in the southern portion of the park, where most of the colorful fossilized wood is found, it is difficult to imagine what the region looked like when the trees were alive and standing. Ninety percent of the fossilized trees in the park are remnants of the cone-bearing *Araucarioxylon*, relatives of which can still be found in parts of South America and Australia. Many of the trees were 200 feet tall, with straight trunks and few limbs. The location and density of the petrified wood have led some scientists to conjecture that the trees grew elsewhere, perhaps to the south and southeast, and that after they fell they were carried into the area by streams and rivers and formed enormous logjams.

But how did these trees harden into fossilized wood? Science has an answer—and a most intriguing one—for that question. After they die, trees and animals usually rot away to renew the cycle of nature. The parts that resist dissolution the longest are the hard trunks and bones. In the case of the towering *Araucarioxylon*, the decay rate was slowed because many of the trees were submerged in silt and water. The water not only excluded much oxygen, which is necessary for the process of decomposition, but also was rich in mineral-laden silica, which soaked through the logs and formed minute crystals of quartz within the cells of the tissues. In some trees, the process of petrification duplicated the original microscopic structure of the wood. In others, the cell walls dissolved as the silica percolated through them, forming amorphous petrifications. Cavities caused by decay or disease eventually filled with large crystals. The various mineral impurities in the silica produced the various colors of the fossilized wood: irons, the reds, yellows, and browns; manganese, the black; other minerals, other colors.

Opposite: The black-tailed rabbit's huge ears help it detect predators.

Fossilized Plants and Animals

Petrified Forest National Park has been described as a "geological textbook with the pages not only illustrated in full color, but three-dimensionally as well." While the most extensive chapters deal with the rock formations and the petrified trees, other passages are worthy of mention.

Fossils of more than forty plant species have been found in the layers of the Chinle Formation. The most common of these is the fern, ancestor of the ferns that grow profusely in tropical areas today. Some 250 million years ago, strange insects with wingspans the size of hawks' flew among the trees, but the only insect fossils that have been found are of cockroaches. Plenty of hardened vertebrate remains have been found, however. The most prevalent of these is the *Phytosaur*, a crocodilelike creature that had a narrow snout and bony-plated body. Other fossils include the *Placerias*, one of the largest land animals of its day—a herbivore with a broad, barrel-shaped body similar to that of a hippopotamus. A variety of fish fossils have been uncovered, including the skeletons of the ancient (though not extinct) coelacanth and the lungfish.

Erosion reduces petrified logs to chunks, then to chips, eventually to grains of quartz.

Flora

Despite an annual rainfall of less than 9 inches, a surprising variety of vegetation grows in Petrified Forest National park. Prickly pear and cholla cactus are common. Flowers include the mariposa lily, Indian paintbrush, and desert primrose. Sunflowers and asters flourish in the summer, and frequently can be seen from the main park road. Saltbush is found in the Blue Mesa region and throughout the Painted Desert. The tiny salt crystals that form on the leaves help the plant conserve water. Buckwheat, a shrub similar to rabbitbrush, turns a distinct orange-brown in the fall. Cliffrose, with its aromatic white blossoms, can be found along the rim overlooking the Painted Desert.

Wildlife

Because the park lacks significant bodies of water, wildlife is sometimes difficult to detect. The larger animals include pronghorn, coyotes, and bobcats. Porcupines are in evidence, and striped skunks are common. Jack rabbits, cottontails, and prairie dogs are everywhere. The most colorful of the many lizards is the collared lizard.

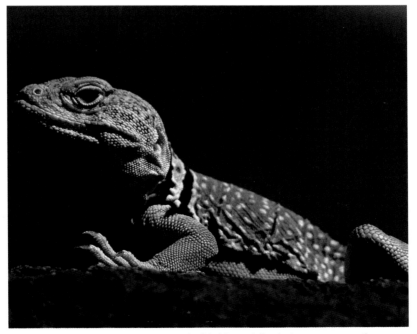

The collared lizard sometimes runs on its hind legs, giving it the appearance of a dinosaur.

Birds include rock wrens, horned larks, Bullock's orioles, and ravens.

The Park's Precious Resources

Animal fossils are difficult to find in the park, but fossilized wood is everywhere and easy to pick up. This deceptive abundance is the greatest single threat to the park's natural resources. Each chip or piece that disappears into an otherwise honest visitor's pocket leaves just that much less for future generations to enjoy. Today, despite strenuous efforts on the part of the park rangers, small pieces that "will never be missed" are illegally pocketed by park visitors. These "small pieces" add up to an estimated twelve tons every year.

Other threats to the park include tampering with archeological sites and vandalizing petroglyphs. Sites like the Puerco Ruin or Newspaper Rock or Jasper Forest are among the most treasured possessions of the United States. They constitute significant chapters in the human and geological history of the continent; when they are vandalized, we are all losers. The history of the United States is not to be measured solely by the accomplishments of the pioneers who settled it. There is an older heritage that has nothing

An early bloomer, the desert primrose flowers in the unlikeliest places.

to do with forebears. This heritage centers on landscape as the shaping factor; it relegates humanity to its preindustrial position among the variety of creatures that have inhabited the earth.

Sites, Trails, And Trips

There are few trails of any great length at Petrified Forest National Park. Several short trails lead through patches of petrified wood. One, for example, winds down through the Blue Mesa area. At sites overlooking the Painted Desert, you can get out of your car to enjoy the view; but even in this area of the park there are few regularly marked trails. And that is really part of the magic. If you choose to hike in the Painted Desert, you can go anywhere. You are free to roam like an Anasazi or a conquistador—to go wherever your feet may lead you.

The Painted Desert. The majority of westbound visitors enter the park at the north gate off Interstate 40, at Exit 311. The Visitor Center provides orientation to the park in the form of printed matter and a 17-minute film entitled *The Stone Forest.* A gas station and a gift shop and restaurant are also at the north entrance.

Once past the gate, the road loops onto a volcanic escarpment that rises over the edge of the Painted Desert. Situated at various points along this stretch of road are overlooks that provide excellent views of the landscape, even from the comfort of a car seat—Tiponi Point, Tawa Point (short sloping path to overlook), Kachina Point (where the Painted Desert Inn is located), Chinde Point (picnic area), Pintado Point (short steep path to the highest point along the main park road; excellent place for taking photographs), Nizhoni Point, Whipple Point, and Lacey Point.

For many, this stretch of road is the grandest in the entire park because the appeal of Petrified Forest National Park is not just in the shape of its landscape or in the fossilized trees. Spread out below, sweeping north and west, are the incredible colors of the Painted Desert. Various hues of red mingle with crusty alkali patches to create a livid, scaly palette. Red is the predominant color here, varying in degree (depending on the time of day) from a metallic sheen to a dull rust. The presence of iron oxides in the soil is responsible for the distinctive red tones. When the flood plains that originally produced the Chinle Formation dried out, the iron minerals in the mud oxidized. Rarely has a vista been so vividly lacquered by nature. In the late afternoon, the rounded formations cast dark,

Overleaf: The dazzling colors in the Painted Desert result from iron oxides.

silky shadows that deepen and define the prominent reds.

Kachina Point. Kachina Point is the starting place for hikes into the desert. A trail leads down the steep face of the escarpment, but it vanishes at the bottom, and the hiker is free to walk anywhere. Pilot Rock, the highest point in the park, is about 6 miles away. Permits are required for overnight backpack camping, which is allowed only in the wilderness areas.

There are many natural wonders to see in that magnificent desolation, though perhaps the most interesting encounter is with the profound and mysterious silence that reigns there. Climbing a cracked and shaly hill, scuffing through a sandy wash, watching the wind kick up spurts of sand brings us into contact with the awesome stillness that lies at the heart of nature in the southwestern United States.

The Painted Desert Inn. The inn, at Kachina Point, has been designated a National Landmark. A classic adobe structure, it was built in 1924 and reconstructed and enlarged during the 1930s by the Civilian Conservation Corps. The inn originally served as a waystop for travelers along old U.S. 66. After World War II, it no longer accommodated overnight guests, but functioned as a restaurant, curio shop, and park museum. Two of the rooms are decorated with murals by Fred Kabotie, the renowned Hopi artist. The inn now is being refurbished as a museum. The National Park Service has installed exhibits that illustrate the human and natural history of the park.

The design of the Painted Desert Inn, and the materials from which it was constructed, make it uniquely representative of southwestern architecture. A mixture of Spanish and Indian pueblo styles, colored a ruddy pink, it is a prime example of how human habitations can blend harmoniously with a landscape.

Puerco Pueblo. The main park road slopes gently off the escarpment, heading south. It crosses Interstate 40, the Santa Fe Railroad tracks, and the Puerco River. At the river, the road starts up the incline of another escarpment. A short distance away is the Puerco Indian Pueblo, the most easily accessible archeological site within the park. A short paved path leads from the parking lot up a knoll. Ahead are the ruins of the pueblo. The right-hand branch of the path has two lookouts from which petroglyphs can be seen. Both paths can be negotiated by wheelchairs.

The walls of the ruins have been ground down by erosion, but it

Opposite: Petrified logs and the Chinle Formation in the Blue Mesa section.

is easy to imagine how they looked 800 years ago. There was perhaps more moisture then, and a variety of small and large game inhabited the banks of the Puerco. Back from the river there were cultivated patches where the Anasazi grew vegetables.

Below the ruin, on the slope of the escarpment, figures have been pecked out of the rocks. One in particular, a large wading bird—an avocet, perhaps—with what appears to be a frog in its beak, rivals in artistry the figures at Newspaper Rock. These petroglyphs are easy to see from the edge of the ruin.

Newspaper Rock. Near the top of the escarpment the road passes Newspaper Rock turnout. A short walk from the parking area leads to an overlook. Newspaper Rock is one of the finest petroglyph sites in the Southwest. A dense cluster of Indian rock carvings is located here. Presumably, they were carved by the Anasazi. The exact date is difficult to determine; desert varnish forms slowly, and it is impossible to tell from the depths of the incised figures how old they are.

Scholars are still baffled about the meaning of these figures. It has been speculated that some of the marks indicate time periods. Some figures seem to represent animals being hunted or, perhaps, killed in a hunt. Still other figures are hauntingly anthropomorphic, indicative of gods and spirits.

Whatever their significance, the range and variety of the carvings are extraordinary. The Anasazi and those who preceded them had no written language, and these figures are the closest thing to a written language they possessed. Many of the petroglyphs were utilized as solar calendars. Perhaps the Anasazi equivalent of the Rosetta Stone will be found, enabling scholars to decipher these symbols. We can admire their artistry, and the care with which they were chiseled into the rock. These tantalizing figures deepen the riddle of the Anasazi.

The Tepees. Southeast of Newspaper Rock on the park road are the tepees, erosional formations colored by iron, manganese, and other minerals. Visible to the west are low hills with steep, sloping sides, called haystacks; they are banded in various colors—blue, gray, red—indicating different sedimentary deposits.

Blue Mesa. Midway through the park the road passes through a fascinating area known as Blue Mesa. It is a severely eroded badlands area, sprinkled with remnants of petrified wood. A 3-mile, one-way, spur road leads to the mesa top, on which pullouts offer a 360° view. Pedestal logs can be found throughout this area. A .75-mile paved loop trail leads steeply down into the heart of the bad-

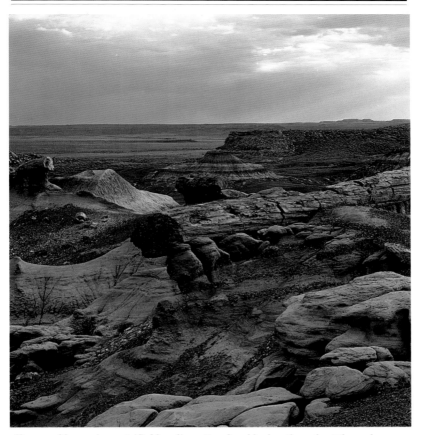

Uncovered by erosion, petrified logs lie scattered and broken throughout the park.

lands formation. To walk down the trail is to descend into some of the most unearthly terrain in the Southwest. Low hills with steep, sloping sides, called "haystacks," are the dominant formation. The haystacks are banded in various colors—blue, gray, red—indicating different sedimentary deposits.

Agate Bridge. This site is a graphic illustration of the bizarre effects that erosion can have on petrified logs. The log here is suspended across a gully with both ends implanted in sandstone. In 1917, concern that the log might collapse led to actions to shore it up and to a prohibition on foot traffic across it.

Jasper Forest. A short spur off the main road leads to Jasper Forest. The view here, especially to the north and west, is commanding. Chunks and pieces of petrified wood are strewn everywhere. The effects of erosion are especially evident, revealing vast deposits of fossilized wood buried in the Chinle Formation. The Navajos thought that the wood was the bones of Yietso, the great monster their ancestors slew when they first arrived in northern Arizona.

Crystal Forest. A .79-mile paved loop trail winds through the Crystal Forest, one of the densest accumulations of petrified logs in the park. "Crystal" is an apt description for this location, since it once contained innumerable examples of how the wood fossilized into solid chunks of quartz as a result of silica-rich water dissolving its cellular structure. The colors here on a sunlit day are marvelous to behold. It is easy to understand why the wood at the southern end of the park has been described as a "rainbow forest."

Long Logs Trail. The trail is a .5-mile loop, an easy 20-minute walk. Here may be found the largest concentration of petrified wood in the park. The logs are the remains of an ancient logjam that was buried in river deposits of mud, sand, and volcanic ash some 225 million years ago. When the tall *Araucarioxylon* trees that grew then toppled over from decay or old age, they congested together in certain areas—perhaps on sand bars or in shallow lagoons—where they were gradually covered by sediments and eventually petrified. Many of the logs in this section exceed 100 feet in length.

Just off the Long Logs Trail are the remains of an old dwelling known as the Agate House. It is perhaps the most unusual pueblo in the Southwest, made out of blocks of petrified wood. Archeologists estimate that it was once a "house" of seven rooms that was last occupied 700 years ago. To give visitors an idea of the original size and shape of the Agate House, two of the rooms were partially rebuilt in 1934 by the National Park Service.

Rainbow Forest Museum and Giant Logs Trail. The exhibits in the Rainbow Forest Museum depict how the tall trees became petrified. The museum also has a mural that shows the variety of unqiue creatures that roamed northern Arizona 225 million years ago. Behind the museum the .5-mile Giant Logs Trail leads past numerous examples of petrified wood. Due to the uneven terrain, there are many steps along this trail. Located here is "Old Faithful," one of the largest petrified logs in the park. Walking along this path, it is easy to imagine yourself tramping across a "lost continent" where strange creatures once thundered and where jewels lie in mute testimony to the earth's riches.

Opposite: The rainbow colors of a pedestal log in Blue Mesa are produced by the minerals iron, copper, and manganese.

SAGUARO
NATIONAL PARK

The flowers of the saguaro open at night; bats, birds, and insects seek the nectar.

SAGUARO NATIONAL PARK
3693 SOUTH OLD SPANISH TRAIL
TUCSON, AZ 85730
TEL.: (520) 733-5100

HIGHLIGHTS: Cactus Forest Drive • Desert Ecology Trail • Freeman Homestead • Tanque Verde Peak • Rincon Peak • Mica Mountain Peak • Bajada Loop Drive • Amole Peak • Wasson Peak

ACCESS: (East Section) From I-10 at Houghton Road (Exit 275) and from Tucson via the Old Spanish Trail at East Broadway. **(West Section)** From I-10 via Speedway Blvd. (Exit 248). Trailers and motor homes must use Avra Valley Road (Exit 242), Ina Road (Exit 248), or Ajo Way (Exit 99) off I-19. No public transportation is available to either district.

HOURS: Visitor Center open 8:00 A.M. to 5:00 P.M. daily. Closed Christmas day. **(East)** Cactus Forest Drive is open from 7:00 A.M. to sunset, year-round. **(West)** Roads are open 6 A.M. to sunset.

FEES: (East) For vehicle or walk-in. **(West)** No fees.

PARKING: At each Visitor Center.

GAS, FOOD, LODGING: Tucson.

MUSEUMS: (West) Arizona–Sonora Desert Museum just outside the park.

PETS: Must be leashed at all times; are not allowed on trails.

PICNICKING: (East) Two areas along Cactus Forest Drive. **(West)** Four areas along park roads, a fifth located in backcountry.

HIKING: Trails available. Carry water, shade hat, and sun cream.

BACKPACKING: (East) With camping in designated areas. Permits required. **(West)** No backcountry camping.

CAMPGROUNDS: (East) Coronado National Forest on Catalina Highway north of Tucson. **(West)** Gilbert Ray Campground in Tucson Mountain Park, near the Red Hills Visitor Center on Kinney Road. **(East)** Six backcountry camping areas.

TOURS: Ranger walks and hikes.

OTHER ACTIVITIES: Horseback riding, bicycling, scenic drives.

FACILITIES FOR DISABLED: Restrooms, some paved trails.

For additional information, see also Sites, Trails, and Trips on pages 345–347 and the map on pages 336–337.

A NATIONAL PARK IS BORN! CONGRATULATIONS to the proud parents—the two Saguaro National Monument sections, East and West.

In October 1994, with the help of Congress and the signature of President Bill Clinton, the two monument sections became the fifty-second national park.

This new kid on the block, initially set aside to protect the vast saguaro cactus acreage it houses, is a virtual living kaleidoscope of plant and animal diversity—displaying six vertical plant communities of overlapping flora and fauna. This diversity is comparable to that found along a 900-mile journey north into Canada.

In addition to the vast natural history assortment that attracts botanists, zoologists and birdwatchers, the park beckons poets, painters, writers, and sculptors who soak up inspiration from the ever-changing array of color, texture, shadow, and light.

The park occupies the lushest part of the Sonoran Desert, on either side of Tucson. The two districts are about an hour's drive apart by way of the cross-city route. Ringed by 8,000- and 9,000-foot "sky island" mountains (including its own Rincon Mountain District), Saguaro National Park provides a place of peace and sanity amid an ever-expanding metropolitan area.

The saguaro grows in southeastern California, southern Arizona, and northern Mexico.

SAGUARO
NATIONAL PARK

Backcountry Campsite

Campground

Picnic Area

Ranger Station

Unpaved Road

Trail

SAGUARO WEST

MILES

0 1 3 5

VICINITY MAP

SAGUARO N.P. (EAST)

Houghton Rd.

Tucson

Tucson International Airport

SAGUARO N.P. (WEST)

INSET SCALE

Ina Road
TO 10

Wade Road

Safford Peak El.3563

Picture Rocks Road

Golden Gate Road

Sendero Esperanza Trail

Amole Peak El. 4422

Wasson Peak El. 4687

Sweetwater Trail

King Canyon Trail

Hugh Norris Trail

Bajada Loop Drive

RED HILLS

Red Hills Visitor Center

Desert Discovery Nature Trail

Wildlife Viewpoint

Waterhole

TUCSON MOUNTAINS

TUCSON MOUNTAIN COUNTY PARK

Kinney Road

ARIZONA-SONORA DESERT MUSEUM

McCain Loop Road

Gates Pass Blvd.

Old Tucson

TO TUCSON

GILBERT RAY

Signal Hill

Valley View Overlook Trail

Sandario Road

AVRA VALLEY

Mile Wide Road

TO 10

TO 86

TO 10

SAGUARO EAST

CORONADO NATIONAL FOREST

CORONADO NATIONAL FOREST

CORONADO NATIONAL FOREST

RINCON

MOUNTAINS

Italian Ranch Trail

ITALIAN
SPRING

East
Slope
Trail

SPUD ROCK
SPRING

SPUD ROCK
DEER HEAD
SPRING

Turkey Creek Trail

Miller
Creek
Trail

Rincon Peak Trail

HAPPY
VALLEY
SADDLE

Heartbreak Ridge Trail

Mica Mtn.
El. 8666'

Reef
Rock

Rincon Peak
El. 8482'

North Slope Trail

Spud
Rock

Manning
Camp

Cow Head
Saddle Trail

Manning Camp Trail

Madrona Canyon

Chimenea Canyon

Rincon Creek Trail

DOUGLAS SPRING

GRASS
SHACK

MADRONA

RINCON VALLEY

Douglas Spring Trail

Wild Horse Canyon

Tanque Verde Peak
El. 7049

JUNIPER
BASIN

Box Canyon

TANQUE VERDE RIDGE

Tanque Verde Ridge Trail

TO COLOSSAL CAVE

Desert
Ecology
Trail

Cactus Forest Drive

Cactus Forest Trail

Freeman Homestead Trail

Old Spanish Trail

Visitor
Center

Speedway Blvd.

Broadway Blvd.

Freeman Road

Old Spanish Trail

Escalante Road

Houghton Road

TO TUCSON

N

TUCSON

337

SAGUARO

Drawings of running bighorn sheep suggest that early Native Americans were hunters.

In the bill establishing the park, 3,460 acres of cactus-studded land were added to the west side as a buffer against encroaching residential expansion.

Saguaro West, the Tucson Mountain District, embraces the most dense stand of saguaro cacti in the world. This district contains tenacious varieties of Lower and Upper Sonoran Desert flora and fauna—impressing the visitor with the miraculous survival adaptations of desert life forms.

The Arizona–Sonora Desert Museum, adjacent to the west-side boundary, contains a world-famous array of desert critters housed inside lifelike enclosures of fabricated stone and desert landscape. You can almost touch the hummingbirds and cactus wrens in the walk-through aviaries.

Saguaro East, the Rincon Mountain District, starts off with the same Lower and Upper Sonoran Desert landscape, then takes in the long ridgelines of the huge Rincon Mountain mass that angles up through grasslands, chaparral, oaks, pines, and junipers—finally topping out at 8,000 feet amid firs and aspens.

Saguaro National Park has been blessed by the restless spirits of sun, sky, and rain, as they continuously interact to populate the landscape with endless varieties of life forms. This many-jeweled desert kaleidoscope does indeed present the visitor with a different circle of colors every day.

History

By around 9000 B.C., Paleo-Indian groups carved out hunting grounds in the Tucson Basin, spearing Pleistocene mammoths and gathering wild foods. These early hunters stayed on the move, leaving only isolated examples of leaf-shaped and fluted spear points known as Clovis points.

From about 8000 B.C. to the time of Christ—the Archaic period—the inhabitants of the Tucson Basin became more settled, as evidenced by remnants of large base camps and quarries along major drainages in the Rincon Mountain District. Handstones and metates point to a more sedentary lifestyle.

By A.D. 700, groups known as *Hohokam* (those who have vanished) lived in the park area. They grew corn, beans, squash, and cotton, and supplemented their diet with wild game. They developed complex ceremonial and trading systems, as evidenced by pottery, human effigies, and underground religious structures. By 1450, the Hohokam culture had disappeared, perhaps because of soil deterioration, drought, or hostile invasion.

In 1694, European contact began when Spanish Padre Eusebio Kino visited the vicinity of the future park and encountered the *Tohono O'odam*, also known as the *Papago*, or desert people. The Tohono O'odam cultivated beans, corn, and squash. They gathered the fruits, seeds, buds, roots, and flowers of paloverde, mesquite, saltbush, acorns, ironwood, wild potatoes, and yucca. They hunted mule deer, antelope, peccaries, rabbits, wild turkeys, herons, lizards, snakes, and insects.

Spanish influence on the Tohono O'odam was both good and bad. Introduced diseases took a heavy toll. New methods of religion, agriculture, dress, and speech changed their life styles forever.

The Mexican period, 1821–54, brought a migration of farmers, ranchers, miners, and merchants from the south.

The American period, 1854 to the present, has seen dramatic population increases and economic development in the Tucson area. In 1933, the Rincon Mountain District of the Saguaro National Monument was established by presidential proclamation—followed by the addition of the Tucson Mountain District in 1961.

Tucson Mountain District (West Section)

In the West Section, granite forms the two highest peaks of the Tucson Mountains—Wasson Peak, highest at 4,687 feet, and Amole Peak.

The Wasson Peak granite formed from molten rock material that originated deep below the earth's surface. As a liquid, the material was lighter and slowly rose toward the surface. Additional tectonic action and crustal uplift moved the mass even closer to the surface. Subsequent cooling, crystallizing, and surface erosion exposed the granite peaks and surrounding terrain.

Sandstones, limestones, shales, and siltstones are also evident on the flanks of Wasson Peak. These sedimentary deposits are evidence of ancient seas that once covered the area, coming and going over millions of years.

Rincon Mountain District (East Section)

You can touch rocks that are more than a half billion years old while hiking up the Tanque Verde Ridge Trail on the flanks of the Rincon Mountains. Those rocks, called Catalina Gneiss, are part of the predominant metamorphic (changed over time by heat and pressure) rock exposures of the east section. They were formed deep below the earth's surface during the Precambrian era, when the parent rock was melted, then recrystallized into its present form. Subsequent uplift and erosion have exposed colorful outcrops of this white, gray, brown, and black banded rock. The gneiss contains alternating layers of quartz, feldspar, hornblende, and mica—giving it a banded appearance.

Mica is a main ingredient in the metamorphic complexes on the eastern side of the park, reflected in the naming of its highest peak—8,666-foot Mica Mountain.

Another metamorphic rock, called schist, underlies the flatter Cactus Forest area alongside the gneiss ridgelines. The same processes of heat, pressure, and time transformed the earlier parent rock into its present layered and platy appearance during the Cretaceous period—more than 65 million years ago. Most of the schists are found along desert wash exposures.

A limited amount of igneous rock is found in the east section, seen mainly as scattered volcanics in the Cactus Forest area.

The latest geologic event (still forming the park topography) is that of erosion. Wind, water, ice, snow, gravity, and time slowly grind down the uplifts, fill the valleys between them, and, in the process, trap ground water in the deep alluvial valleys. That's the ground water that slakes the thirst of Tucsonians today.

Desert Plant Adaptations

The Tucson Mountain District (west side) is home to the Lower and Upper Sonoran plant-life communities that we call desert scrub. But it wasn't always desert scrub.

The earth's climate has gone through cycles of hot and cold changes over millions of years. Plants (and some animals) slowly adapted to those changing environments. The present desert plants evolved from larger, bigger-leafed, and more abundant species that once grew in wetter, cooler climes. Only the strongest and most adaptable plants survived the almost 60 million years of trial-and-error evolution that we see in today's arid landscape.

There are basically three categories of desert plant adaptations. First are those plants that evade the hot and dry climate—like creosote bushes, which can lose up to 50 percent of their normal water supply and still survive, and the ocotillo plant, which reduces its water loss by dropping its leaves and "playing dead"

Left: Eggs of the great horned owl in a saguaro cactus.
Right: The red-tailed hawk may sit quietly for hours, then glide down to strike a rodent or lizard.

until the next rainstorm, after which it again sprouts leaves and flowers.

Next are those plants that escape the desert climate by racing through a speeded-up life cycle of flowering, fruiting, and going to seed during the cooler, moister months—enduring drought, then sprouting again when the rains come. These include desert wildflowers like poppies, lupine, and verbena.

The third adaptation category consists of those plants that resist the harsh conditions by "sweating it out" during the hot droughts, limiting their activities to simply surviving, then sucking up water when the opportunity arrives. Cacti like the saguaro, barrel, and prickly pear are prime examples—changing little in appearance year-round, but using their shallow, widespread root systems to slurp up the rain water when it hits the ground. They store the precious liquid in their self-expanding succulent stems.

The Magnificent Saguaro

What desert plant can reach a height of 50 feet, weigh over 5 tons, provide housing for birds, mammals, and reptiles in its trunk and root system, and live for 150 years? . . . You guessed it, the giant saguaro—park symbol and identifier plant of the Sonoran Desert. In spring, this spectacular stem succulent displays the beautiful white petals of the Arizona state flower, which ripens into a delectable fruit used by the Tohono O'odam as a food staple.

The Tohono O'odam still make seed flour, jam, syrup, and wine from this bright red-crimson delicacy, respectfully sharing the summertime bounty with birds, insects, rodents, and mammals.

Some of those same hungry desert animals help pollinate the saguaro. The lesser long-nosed bat, the white-winged dove, and the curved-bill thrasher stick their respective snoots and beaks into the flowers, dispersing the pollen among the creamy white blooms.

When the flower matures into a fruit, it may produce more than 2,000 tiny blackish seeds. An average adult saguaro can produce one hundred fruits a year, resulting in an astonishing 200,000 seeds from one plant. But wait, what are the chances that a particular seed will take root? Scientists guestimate one chance in a few million, due to the edibility of the seeds and the precise combination of soil, shade, water, temperature, and luck needed for the seed to sprout.

In addition to food, the saguaro provides temperature-controlled abodes for birds, mammals, reptiles, and insects. The Gila woodpecker and gilded flicker build dwellings by pecking and tearing out holes in the side of the saguaro stems. The cactus then

A western diamondback rattlesnake sleeps at dawn; it eats rodents and birds.

produces a healing compound containing dopamine, which seals off the flesh scars, producing a solid-walled room for its new inhabitant. The woodpecker and flicker raise only one brood in the nest, then abandon it to a succession of critters like cactus wrens, doves, owls, hawks, flycatchers, warblers, starlings, bats, gopher snakes, and hosts of summer insects. Huge beehives have been built in these holes.

And just why are these apartments so popular? Because saguaros can contain up to 90 percent water, insulating the holes to a comfortable 70–80° F during the 110° F summer days. And then when the sun goes down, the interior retains more heat than the outside air, resulting in a comfortable nest for snoozing.

You might think that because of their size, the giant saguaros would grow fast. Just the opposite. Although growth varies according to location, it is very slow. Year-old seedlings weigh less than a pill, and at ten years the mighty saguaro may reach a height of 5 inches. At age 50, the plant might reach up to 6–9 feet. At about age 65, they sprout their first arms and continue sprouting and blooming up to a ripe old age of 150 years, or more.

Saguaro survivability depends not only on the right combination of soil, temperature, and rainfall. It also depends on resistance to disease, consumption by animals, environmental pollution, and residential development. Droughts, freezes, and human saguaro poaching also take their toll.

Scientists are continually studying the long-range adaptabilities of this giant, and are amazed that the plant can survive at all in such a hot, dry environment.

Other Desert and Mountain Plants

Other useful desert scrub plants include cacti like the chain-fruit cholla (edible fruit pods) and prickly pear (purple fruits); desert trees like the paloverde (edible peas), mesquite (sweet edible pods), and ironwood (peanutlike nuts); and shrubs like the creosote (chaparral tea), ocotillo (flower tea), and jojoba (oils for cosmetics).

The Rincon Mountain District (east side) contains habitat for a great many plants in addition to the desert scrub on its west end. The park extends east into the Rincon Mountain chain. The ascending mountain ridges provide increased moisture, cooler temperatures, and changing soil profiles, creating overlapping environments for five other plant communities.

The desert scrub community runs up to about 3,500 feet, gradually changing into the grassland transition community (3,500–4,500 feet), which includes side oats grama, blue grama, and sprucetop grama grasses mixed with a myriad of low-growing plants like turpentine bush, bear grass, snakeweed, sotol, and amole.

The chaparral, pinyon–juniper, and oak–woodland communities blend together from about 4,500 to 7,000 feet, mixing manzanita, scrub oak, Arizona cypress, Arizona sycamore, Emory oak, buckthorn, alligator juniper, Mexican pinyon pine, mountain mahogany, silk tassel, bluegrass, and bull grass.

The coniferous forest community (above 6,000 feet) contains Gambel oak, ponderosa pine, white fir, aspen, Douglas-fir, and snowberry. High-altitude grasses include mountain muhly and pine dropseed. Wildflowers include aster, yarrow, and lupine.

North-facing slopes are colder and wetter, allowing higher-elevation plants to grow at lower altitudes.

Animals

Even though elevation, precipitation, and temperature regulate habitats, wild animals have legs, wings, and claws that allow them to move around and increase their ranges for food, shelter, water, and territory.

By the way, what desert animal can live a lifetime without drinking any water? It's the diminutive and bouncy kangaroo rat. The park visitor might be lucky enough to spot one hopping between ground burrows. By getting up early enough in the morning, the same visitor might spot coyotes, ringtails, kit foxes, jack rabbits, badgers, skunks, cottontails, ground squirrels, javelinas (peccaries), lizards, rattlesnakes, or maybe even mule deer.

These animals inhabit the desert scrub and grassland transition communities, but also amble or crawl up into higher elevations in search of sustenance.

Birds such as the cactus wren (Arizona state bird), curved-bill thrasher, Gambel quail, roadrunner, Gila woodpecker, red-tailed hawk, and mourning dove frequent the desert areas. But they too float up into the higher reaches, when necessary, trying to make a living.

The chaparral, pinyon–juniper, and oak–woodland communities provide habitat for a great number of lizards, snakes, bats, rock squirrels, pocket mice, porcupine, raccoon, bobcat, and white-tailed deer. Birds include Cooper's hawk, prairie falcon, wild turkey, spotted owl, ravens, warblers, and a variety of humming-birds and woodpeckers.

The coniferous forest community (above 6,500 feet) supports the eastern cottontail, Arizona gray squirrel, coati, spotted skunk, and cougar. Birds include zone-tailed hawk, golden eagle, great horned owl, Arizona woodpecker, mountain chickadee, and Mexican junco.

SITES, TRAILS, AND TRIPS

Tucson Mountain District (West Side)

Start at the Red Hills Visitor Center, where you'll find maps, books, and trail and road guides, along with natural history exhibits.

Next, take the short Cactus Garden nature walk to familiarize yourself with the surrounding Desert Scrub vegetation.

Drive northwest toward the *Bajada Loop Drive*, stopping to sample the .5-mile *Desert Discovery Nature Trail*. This short walk provides a better feel for desert life in the context of the total environment, with identification plaques along the route.

Turn right on the Bajada Loop Drive and drive to the *Valley View Overlook Trail*. This 1.5-mile path was built by the Civilian Conservation Corps (CCC) in the 1930s. The route leads to a ridge overlooking the Avra Valley basin.

Continue around the Loop Drive to Signal Hill picnic area where stone ramadas, tables, and cooking grills were built by the CCC in the 1930s. Take the short path over to the Signal Hill pet-roglyphs.

The more adventurous and physically active can consider the longer day hikes that probe the park's desert interior.

The *King Canyon Trail* starts across from the Arizona-Sonora Desert Museum and gradually climbs for 3.5 miles past the Mam-a-gah picnic area and on up switchbacks to the junction with the *Hugh Norris Trail.* Follow that to the top of the 4,687-foot Wasson Peak, highest point in the Tucson Mountain District. The view from this peak takes in the Tucson Basin, the Santa Rita Mountains to the south, and the Santa Catalina and Rincon mountains to the north. Take rest breaks along this trail—take in the smell, sound, and feel of the environment. Listen for bird calls; smell the flower petals; feel the vegetation; involve all your senses in the hiking experience.

The 3.2-mile *Sendero Esperanza Trail* starts across from the Ez-kim-in-zin picnic area. It follows an old mine road for about a mile, then climbs switchbacks to the Amole Peak ridgeline. Views north and south from the ridgeline take in vast expanses of the Lower and Upper Sonoran Desert. The route descends about 1.5 miles to the Mam-a-gah picnic area, where it connects to the King Canyon Trail.

The Hugh Norris Trail angles off Bajada Loop Drive and travels 5 miles across the District, from east to west. The path starts out with switchbacks that angle up to a ridge overlooking the cactus forest that defines the park. This trail goes along a ridgeline to Amole Peak and on to the summit of Wasson Peak.

Drive-in picnic areas include Signal Hill, Sus, and Ez-kim-in-zin. Mam-a-gah is a hike-in picnic area, about 1 mile from the King Canyon Trail trail head.

Rincon Mountain District (East Side)

The Visitor Center has displays, a slide show, books, maps, and trail and road guides. Take the short walk-around path next to the Visitor Center to learn about the local plants.

The scenic 8-mile *Cactus Forest Drive* curves through the forest and provides views of the Rincon Mountain massif. The Mica View picnic area has a popular trail that offers a great introduction to the Uplands Division of the Sonoran Desert. This is one of many loops possible in the Cactus Forest area. The first .75 mile leads across desert lowland and dry washes to Broadway Boulevard. You'll find paloverde, mesquite, whitethorn acacia, creosote bush, desert hackberry, and chain-fruit cholla along the path. The route loops 1.25 miles back to Mica View picnic area.

Next, stop at the .25-mile, paved *Desert Ecology Trail*—open to wheelchairs. Interpretive signs show the visitor how local plants and animals survive. Farther on, the *Freeman Homestead Nature Trail* loops around the old homestead site.

Another turn-out off Cactus Forest Drive goes to the Javelina picnic area. Here, the *Tanque Verde Ridge Trail* starts its upward

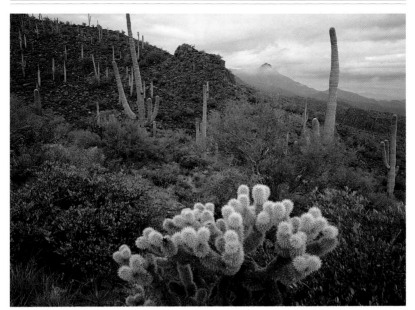

The teddybear cholla looks cuddly, but its barbed spines are severely painful.

climb through five plant communities to Juniper Basin and on to a vast network of mountain backpack trails. This trail offers spectacular views of the Tucson Basin and surrounding "sky island" mountains—the Santa Catalinas, Santa Ritas, and Baboquivari Peak. You can hike as far as you want in one day on this trail, from a half-hour jaunt to a full-day, 7-mile hike to Juniper Basin. There are many superb lunch spots along this gradually ascending route with vistas all the way into Mexico.

Douglas Spring Trail parallels the northern boundary of the new park. From the Visitor Center, leave the park and turn right on Freeman Road. Follow Freeman to Speedway Boulevard. Turn right on Speedway and follow it to the end where the Douglas Spring Trail trail head is located. This route offers great views of the Santa Catalina Mountains along a path that was once burned over. It has revegetated remarkably and provides a visual juxtaposition of the old fire and the new growth. The trail starts by a shady ramada and is level for the first .25 mile, going through a creosote bush forest. You are in the wilderness from the minute you step onto the trail, with no reference to Tucson until you climb higher. You'll cross several drainages with water pools. Look for deer, fox, skunk, javelina, and coyote. You should spot ravens and red-tailed hawks. Continue on to Douglas Spring for a total of 6 miles from the trail head.

ZION

NATIONAL PARK

The Great White Throne is best viewed from the trails in Zion Canyon.

ZION NATIONAL PARK
SPRINGDALE, UTAH 84767-1099
TEL.: (801) 772-3256

HIGHLIGHTS: Great White Throne • Checkerboard Mesa • Weeping Rock • Riverside Walk • The Narrows • Emerald Pools • Towers of the Virgin • Kolob Canyons • Zion Canyon • Temple of Sinawava • Great Arch • Altar of Sacrifice • Watchman • Mountain of the Sun • Beehives • Kolob Arch

ACCESS: From west, take I-15 to Utah 17 and 9, or take exit 40. From east, take U.S. 89 to Utah 9. See map on pages 352–353.

HOURS: All year, 24 hours daily. Zion Canyon Visitor Center, daily, 8 A.M.–8 P.M. in summer; 8 A.M.–6 P.M., spring and fall; 9 A.M.–5 P.M., winter. Closed Dec. 25.

FEES: At entrance, except in winter, and for camping.

PARKING: Facilities crowded, April to October. Plan will be implemented to bar cars from Zion Canyon in favor of shuttle buses.

GAS: In Springdale, St. George, Kanab, Cedar City, Hurricane.

FOOD: At Lion Lodge all year and in above towns.

LODGING: At Zion Lodge year-round and in above towns.

VISITOR CENTER: Near south entrance to park, north of Springdale, and at exit 40 off I-15; offer information and book and map sales; free 12-minute slide show in Zion Canyon.

MUSEUM: In Zion Canyon Visitor Center.

SALES AREA: Offers books, posters, cards, film, and maps.

PETS: Permitted on leash in areas accessible by car, but not in backcountry or on any trails.

PICNICKING: At Grotto Picnic Area; at Kolob Canyons Viewpoint.

HIKING: On designated trails. Check with park rangers for off-trail routes.

BACKPACKING: Permitted with permit, available at visitor centers; fee will be charged beginning in 1996. No ground fires allowed.

CAMPGROUNDS: Camping in designated areas only. Some loops are for tents only. Full hookups only at Zion Canyon Campground in Springdale. No reservations.

TOURS: Daily from late May through October.

OTHER ACTIVITIES: Rock climbing with voluntary permit; limited cross-country skiing; horseback riding; children's program.

FACILITIES FOR DISABLED: Access to restrooms, campsites, parking areas, and most public facilities.

For additional information, see also Sites, Trails, and Trips on pages 365–372, and the maps on pages 352–353 and 368–369.

THE DRAMATIC, HIGH-WALLED ZION CANYON WAS created by Utah's unimposing Virgin River cutting its way through thousands of feet of layered strata, some as old as 200 million years. Within the 147,035 acres of this beautiful park are four major plant zones, extending from an altitude of 3,666 feet to one of 8,740 feet. Amid the eight rock formations that compose this incredible landscape, more than seventy species of mammals and 272 species of birds find a home.

Rangers at Zion National Park advise visitors to remain long enough to see the park, especially when it has been drenched with rain. Then waterfalls cascade from every notch and crack and precipice, and the sun, emerging through a break in the clouds, turns the canyon walls into a kaleidoscope of patterns and colors.

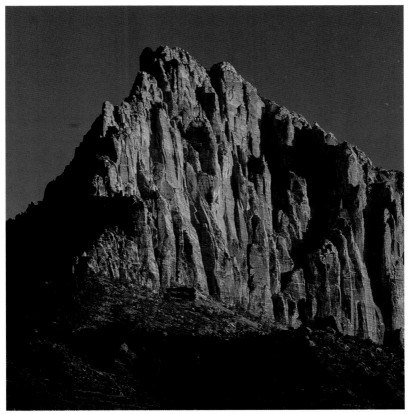

The Watchman rises 6,555 feet at South Entrance. Mormon settlers imagined they could see the face of a watchman at the top of the peak.

ZION
NATIONAL PARK

Ranger Station
Campground
Picnic Area
Parking Area
ROAD
TRAIL

MILES

0 1 2 3 4 6

N

TO CEDAR CITY AND SALT LAKE CITY

15

Taylor Creek

KOLOB CANYONS
LEE PASS

El. 6401'

KOLOB ARCH

TIMBER TOP MTN

Kolob Arch Trail

La Verkin Creek Trail

Timber Creek

Kolob Creek

Kolob Reservoir

(Closed in Winter)

LAVA POINT
El. 7890'

West Rim Trail

Canyon Trail

Wildcat

La Verkin Creek

TO MT. CARMEL JUNCTION, BRYCE CANYON, GLEN CANYON AND GRAND CANYON

CHECKERBOARD MESA

EAST ENTRANCE
El 5700'

WHITE CLIFFS

ECHO CANYON

East Rim Trail

TEMPLE OF SINAWAVA

Riverside Walk

OBSERVATION POINT
El 6508'

East Rim Trail

CABLE MTN

GREAT WHITE THRONE

GROTTO

GREAT ARCH

TUNNEL

CANYON OVERLOOK
El 5124'

TUNNEL

MOUNTAIN OF THE SUN

EAST TEMPLE

Watchman Viewpoint Trail

WATCHMAN
El 6555'

North Fork

WEST RIM
El 7367'

ANGELS LANDING

Zion Lodge
El 4276'

THREE PATRIARCHS

COURT OF THE PATRIARCHS

Sand Bench Trail

ZION CANYON

TOWERS OF THE VIRGIN

WEST TEMPLE
El 7810'

SOUTH ENTRANCE
El 3960'

Springdale

Rockville
El 3760'

Left Fork

Right Fork

COUGAR MOUNTAIN

CRATER HILL

Coalpits Wash

Virgin River

9

North Creek

VICINITY MAP

Panguitch

UTAH
ARIZ.

89

Mt. Carmel Jct.

89

Kanab

9

ZION N.P.

Cedar City

Virgin

59

15

59

St. George

56

INSET SCALE
0 10 20
MILES

TO VIRGIN, ST. GEORGE, AND LAS VEGAS

HISTORY

The Anasazi

The first inhabitants of Zion were nomadic hunters known as the Anasazi (Navajo for "Ancient Ones"). The magnificent ruins of their dwellings, which were built around A.D. 750, are found throughout the Four Corners area—where the states of Colorado, New Mexico, Arizona, and Utah meet. The remains of one large Anasazi settlement were discovered in the Parunuweap Canyon at Zion.

While the Anasazi were farming the southern part of what is now Zion National Park, the northern part was occupied by people belonging to the Fremont Indian culture. But by A.D. 1200, both the Anasazi and the Fremont had begun to decline. Archeological findings suggest that as a sophisticated architecture developed, an increasing number of trees were used for building and fuel, thus destroying the watersheds so vital for crops, game, and forage food. According to this "ecological suicide" theory, the lack of raw materials and food eventually forced a mass exodus, perhaps as many as 700 years ago.

The Paiutes

During the next several hundred years, the region was visited by small bands of Fremont descendants, but Zion was not permanently populated again until the nineteenth century. We know the settlers as Paiutes, a tribe of Native Americans closely associated with some of Zion's great legends—the pranks of Kai-ne-sava, the God of Fire, who set great flames (lightning) atop the West Temple, and the doings of Wai-no-pits, the Evil One, who invaded the Indian camps with disease. So deeply ingrained were these superstitions and the fears that grew out of them that the Paiutes were of little value as guides to the early white explorers.

Early Explorers

Nephi Johnson, a young Morman missionary and interpreter among the Paiutes, was probably the first white to see the glory of Zion. Ordered by Brigham Young in 1858 to explore the upper Virgin River, he persuaded a Paiute to guide him over the rugged escarpment of the Hurricane Cliffs and up the river. But Johnson's guide refused to go any farther than Oak Creek; Wai-no-pits lurked somewhere in the dark shadows of the narrow canyon called Ioogoon, "an arrow quiver," meaning you "come out the way you went in."

Later explorations soon led to the settlement of Zion and Parunuweap canyons. Joseph Black is generally credited with hav-

A cowboy rides his horse on the wet trail through the Virgin River Narrows before the park was established.

ing been the first to explore the upper area of Zion Canyon. In contrast to the early settlers, who viewed the scenery rather calmly, Brother Joseph brought back such glowing accounts of the canyon that it was often referred to as "Joseph's glory."

We owe the name *Zion* to another Mormon, Isaac Behunin. While scraping a living from crops and cattle, Behunin is supposed to have said: "These great mountains are natural temples of God. We can worship here as well as in the man-made temples in Zion, the biblical 'Heavenly City of God.' Let us call it Little Zion."

Although Mormon pioneers farmed and lumbered in and around the canyons, outside expeditions reported Zion's riches to the world. One such expedition was led by the Civil War veteran and surveyor John Wesley Powell, who already was renowned for his exploration of the Grand Canyon. Extending his studies north in 1872, Powell surveyed the Parunuweap ("water that roars") Canyon and Little Zion Canyon, which he named Mukuntuweap ("straight canyon").

Establishment of the Park

Stephen T. Mather, the first director of the National Park Service, was impressed by Zion's beauty and believed the area worthy of national recognition. He and his assistant, Horace Albright, who became the second director of the National Park Service, worked hard to bring it under federal protection. Earlier, on July 31, 1909, President William Howard Taft signed a proclamation creating a small Mukuntuweap National Monument. Nine years later, the National Park Service recommended enlarging the monument and changing its name to Zion. President Woodrow Wilson signed the legislation on March 18, 1918, and the following year Zion National Park was established.

Sedimentary Rock

Sedimentary rocks, deposited between 225 and 53 million years ago and forming what geologists call "a staircase of time," are the building blocks of Zion National Park. Today, this staircase is seen in part as Grand Canyon, Zion, and Bryce Canyon national parks. Other "risers" in the staircase are adjacent to the three parks and are impressive formations in themselves.

The steps of this great stairway are a series of rock formations that differ from one another in thickness and mineral content. The layered rocks that form the walls of the Grand Canyon were laid down first; the higher layers, those of Zion Canyon, were deposited later; the rocks of Bryce Canyon, the highest layer, are of even more recent origin. Most were deposited by vast seas laden with various types of sediments.

Zion's oldest sedimentary rock is the relatively thick Moenkopi layer, which is composed of sandstone and shale. The composition and depth of these rocks indicate that approximately 230 million years ago the Colorado Plateau was covered by a vast, gentle sea. During the Triassic period (225 to 190 million years ago), as the land began to thrust upward, the sea gave way to shallow rivers that steadily increased in velocity and carried away the rocks. Trees toppled, while volcanoes erupted and spewed forth millions of tons of ash. This slow, natural holocaust laid down the Chinle Formation, a remarkable assemblage of shale, sandstone, and petrified wood. The rivers persisted for several million years and, in their wake, left large lakes. Deposits formed the Moenave layer, reddish sandstone in which fossils of fresh-water fish and other creatures are evident, and streams laid down sandstone sediments that would later compose the Kayenta Formation. Dinosaurs plodded through these streams; one track in the Kayenta Formation is displayed in the park Visitor Center.

Late in the Triassic period and early into the Jurassic period (190 to 136 million years ago), the Colorado Plateau became distinctly arid. Sand-laden wind smothered the verdant land and gradually laid the most visible of Zion's formations—the Navajo Sandstone, as much as 2,220 feet thick in some areas of the park. The great temples, towers, and cliffs of Zion Canyon were formed from this sandstone. The Temple Cap Formation is another sandstone layer, some 20 to 200 feet thick, with a high concentration of

Opposite: Checkerboard Mesa is one of the strangest formations in the park. The pattern was created by the weathering of horizontal bedding planes and vertical cracks.

iron oxide that streaks the cliffs red when dissolved by rain.

The most recent mineral layer is the Carmel Formation, deposits of limestone formed by seas that once again flooded the land. Fragments of the Carmel Formation are found high in the canyon on the East Temple and West Temple.

About 13 million years ago, the entire area of southern Utah and northern Arizona began to rise. Pressure on the layered rocks was so great that they broke into great plateaus, seven of which are in southwestern Utah. Two of these are the Paunsaugunt Plateau, of which Bryce Canyon is part, and the Markagunt Plateau, which encompasses Zion.

The uplift caused rivers to run fast and strong; the Virgin River, for example, began to cut into its present bed. A very powerful process of erosion was quite pronounced 1 million years ago.

Erosion

The steep walls of the North Fork of the Virgin River are the result of water cutting into soft sandstone. So soft is this sandstone and so abrasive is the action of the gushing waters and their accumulated particles, that erosion is quick and decisive. Naturalists call the North Fork an "endless belt of sandpaper."

Zion Canyon is still being formed. Erosion by the Virgin River begins on the Markagunt Plateau at an elevation of 9,000 feet, where the river begins picking up sediment. Downstream, the Virgin combines with tributaries and gathers momentum. Its cuts become deeper, and in some places the river drops 80 feet each mile, a fall ten times as great as that of the Colorado River in Grand Canyon National Park. As it leaves the Narrows, the river opens into a broad canyon at the Temple of Sinawava, where it fans out and loses some of its momentum. Continuing on, it flows southwest for 200 miles until it reaches Lake Mead at an elevation of less than 1,000 feet. Occasionally when the river leaves the Narrows, it floods the river bottom, churning sediments and toppling trees in a few awesome moments. In 1954, its volume increased fiftyfold in fifteen minutes, and the Virgin became an enormous force that ripped through the landscape.

Many other valleys and canyons at Zion also have been carved by erosion, but some have not experienced the force of the Virgin River and have been left hanging, so to speak. These "hanging valleys" stand at 1,000 to 1,300 feet above the river; examples are found between the Mountain of the Sun and Twin Brothers.

The *widening* of Zion Canyon is the result of water percolating through the porous Navajo Sandstone until it reaches the imper-

Aerial view of the canyon of Birch Creek, carved in the Navajo Sandstone. The West Temple rises in the distance.

vious shales of the Kayenta Formation. Then the water accumulates and flows laterally, forming a natural watercourse that over time erodes the shales, which support the Navajo layer. Once undermined, the sandstone gives way, and the canyon widens. This process is dramatically illustrated near the Temple of Sinawava, where the Narrows of the Virgin River begin.

The percolating action of water also has been responsible for the formation of the Great Arch of Zion, and the cliff along the Weeping Rock Trail. Stream channels, choked with sand, forced the river to meander, removing shales from the Kayenta Sandstone. Eventually, slabs of undermined Navajo Sandstone gave way, and the arch emerged. These forces are still at work, and one day a patch of blue may appear beneath a semicircular ribbon of vermilion rock.

Overleaf: Temple of Sinawava, named after the Wolf-god, a chief deity of the Paiutes. The "temple" is deep in Zion Canyon, near the lower end of the narrows.

Climate and Precipitation

A satellite view of the American Southwest shows Zion situated between the Rocky Mountains in Colorado and the Sierra Nevadas in California. The Sierra Nevadas intercept the moisture-laden clouds that move east from the Pacific Ocean, thus serving as a barrier that puts most of Utah and much of Zion in a rain shadow. The Coalpits Wash area of the park, which is on the edge of an expanse known as the Great Basin Desert, receives only a few inches of rain a year. Precipitation increases in Zion Canyon (4,000 feet), where as much as 15 to 25 inches of rain may fall annually and where temperatures vary between 115° F and -15° F. The high plateaus of Zion (7,000 to 8,000 feet) receive about 25 inches of rain a year.

The mountain lion once ranged from Canada to the tip of South America, but because of its skill as a predator, human hunters have greatly reduced its numbers.

Flora

Because the elevation rises from 3,666 feet to 8,740 feet in the course of a few miles, Zion's landscape changes from desert to boreal forest.

A variety of flowers dot the canyon floor, their appearance stimulated by Zion's alternating wet and dry seasons. The sand buttercup, chorispora, and Indian paintbrush flourish in March and April. May heralds the violet, orchid, sego lily, and columbine. During the drier July and August, day-blooming plants are replaced by night species, such as white evening primrose and the sacred datura. Reaching a height of 2 or more feet, the datura's trumpet-shaped blossom opens in the evening and then closes in the morning sun.

Where water tables lie near the surface of the canyon floor, groves of box elder, willow, cottonwood, and ash flourish. Beavertail cactus blooms in the late spring in the dry Parunuweap

Ancestors of the fragile dragonfly once possessed wingspans of more than 3 feet.

Ponderosa pines, with their scaly orange bark, grow in the higher elevations.

Canyon, Coalpits Wash, and Huber Wash.

At the higher elevations, nature is not so parsimonious as in the desert, and in some areas plant life is exceedingly luxuriant. Ponderosa pine, pinyon pine, quaking aspen, gnarled juniper, white fir, Douglas-fir, and, occasionally, sage flats predominate. Dazzling leaves of the radiant aspen transform murky waters of the Virgin River to a golden luster in the autumn. Pines and firs also grow in the side canyons, providing food and protection for wildlife.

Fauna

One delightful animal that can be seen throughout much of Zion National Park is the mule deer. It is particularly abundant in the canyons and occasionally can be spotted sloshing through the Virgin River or leaping a fallen log. So abundant is this animal that it is difficult to believe that its numbers were greatly reduced in Zion at two different times: soon after the establishment of the park, when the National Park Service attempted to reestablish native vegetation; and during the 1930s, when the Park Service tried to preserve "good" animals, such as the deer and elk, by eliminating "bad" animals, such as the cougar. Predator control was so effective that deer and elk soon overgrazed their ranges, eating themselves out of house and home. Mass starvation became a critical problem. Today, with improved understanding of Zion's ecological system, the deer and the cougar have returned.

Bighorn sheep have been as much a part of the natural scene as deer, quail, hawks, golden eagles, roadrunners, and kangaroo rats; archeologists know from petroglyphs that bighorn sheep were hunted by Indians. But as years passed, they became extinct at Zion.

Poaching, construction of the Zion–Mount Carmel Highway, and the inability of sheep to cope with the excessive deer population may have contributed to their demise. Whatever the reasons, the last bighorn sighting in the area, until the 1970s, was in 1953. For the next twenty years, there were no sheep in the park, although biologists believed that Zion could well support them; studies showed that the critical winter range could support a band of 100 animals. In July 1973, twelve sheep from the River Mountain area of Lake Mead, Nevada, were released into a huge paddock adjacent to the Visitor Center. Five years later, acclimated to the environment, the new flock was set free. Some were later sighted in various parts of the park, but from 1979 to 1990 few were seen, prompting concern that the experiment had failed. In 1991, a climber on a peak above Zion Canyon saw 25 bighorns, and searchers in a helicopter then found 35. In the mid-1990s, there were about 50 to 75 sheep in the park.

Frederick Fisher, viewing the Great White Throne—Zion's chief landmark—declared:
"Never have I seen such a sight before. It is by all odds America's masterpiece."

The view from the Visitor Center is magnificent—one of the major features of Zion National Park—but you have barely entered the canyon at this point. A wealth of beautiful geological wonders awaits around the next bend.

Mount Carmel Highway

The Mount Carmel Highway, which enters the park from Mount Carmel Junction, Utah, and U.S. 89 to the east, is a breath-taking engineering marvel, to say nothing of the magnificent natural sculptures it passes as it wanders through one of the lesser canyons in the park. The highway approaches the Virgin River, passing Checkerboard Mesa on the left and the White Cliffs on the right—a dramatic entrance to this exciting country. Then the road begins an abrupt descent, leading first through a 530-foot tunnel and then through the Zion–Mount Carmel Tunnel, which is more than 5,600 feet long and 800 feet above Pine Creek. Piercing the tunnel side at intervals convenient for ventilation are five large, gallerylike windows that look out and down onto the canyon below.

These giant windows were cut first during the early construction of the Zion–Mount Carmel Tunnel; rocks blasted from the internal diggings were then thrown into Pine Creek below. In less than a year, flood waters cleared the entire stream of the boulders.

Then, as the highway squeezes through an area less than .25 mile wide, it plunges toward the great canyon below on a 6 percent grade, covering 1 linear mile in 3.5 miles of broad and safe—but thrilling—road. Six switchbacks take the highway past the Great Arch, and simultaneously offer views of the East Temple and the Beehives. Eventually, the highway leads to the Visitor Center and the south entrance, where the magnificent Altar of Sacrifice, the Towers of the Virgin, the Watchman, and the West Temple can be seen.

The Mount Carmel Highway is intersected by a spur road, the Zion Canyon Scenic Drive, .5 mile north of the Visitor Center. If you bypassed this road on entering the park, it is imperative that you retrace your route to the junction. This canyon drive runs parallel to the Virgin River—passing the Mountain of the Sun, Lady Mountain, the Great White Throne, Angels Landing, Weeping Rock, and The Organ—and ends at the Temple of Sinawava. (Parking is scarce from April to October. Under a plan scheduled for implementation in the late 1990s, access to Zion Canyon will be by shuttle bus only during the peak visitor season, March to October.)

Trails

Stopping at overlooks and pulloffs for a view can be an exhilarating experience, but a dozen or so maintained and unmaintained trails covering 165 miles crisscross the park and lead to wondrous, out-of-the-way places that offer a totally different perspective on Zion. Water is scarce, and some trails are steep. But there is nothing fast-paced about exploring the small springs that seep from ledges where Indians once stalked their prey, the sandstone buttes that show millions of years of nature's work, or the isolated pines of a hollow through which have passed bears, mule deer, and bighorn sheep. Stop at the Visitor Center for a free permit if you plan to camp overnight.

East Rim Trail. East Rim Trail is one of Zion's most rewarding—and one of the most strenuous—trails. Beginning at Weeping Rock parking area, it switches back and forth up the face of Cable Mountain, through Echo Canyon, and then up sheer stone walls to the plateau and a pine forest, where it levels out and runs on to Observation Point. The trail is 8 miles round trip; 6 hours, 2,148-foot climb.

Opposite: Water spraying down Weeping Rock from openings high in the Navajo Sandstone brings relief to the visitor on a summer day. Winter transforms the "tears" into icicles.

TRAILS OF ZION NATIONAL PARK

RIVERSIDE WALK: Starts at Temple of Sinawava; ends at end of pavement; 2 miles round trip; 57-foot ascent; views of hanging gardens and Virgin River Narrows; wheelchair accessible with assistance.

WEEPING ROCK TRAIL: Starts at Weeping Rock parking area; ends at Weeping Rock; .5 mile round trip; 98-foot ascent; views of Great White Throne and Zion Canyon; hanging gardens; self-guiding.

EMERALD POOLS TRAIL: Starts at Zion Lodge; ends at Lower Pool; 1.2 miles round trip; 69-foot ascent; views of Heaps Canyon, Red Arch Mountain, waterfalls, and pools; 1-mile trail to Upper Pool is not maintained.

CANYON OVERLOOK TRAIL: Starts at tunnel parking area; ends at overlook; 1 mile round trip; 163-foot ascent; views of Pine Creek Canyon, West Temple, Towers of the Virgin, and Zion Canyon; easy walking to top of Great Arch.

EAST RIM TRAIL: Starts at Weeping Rock parking area; ends at Observation Point; 8 miles round trip; 2,148-foot ascent; views of Zion Canyon, Echo Canyon, Great White Throne, Virgin River Narrows, and Temple of Sinawava; carry water and food.

TRAIL MAP

Ranger Station _____ 🇺🇸
Campground _____ 🏕
Picnic Area _____ 🐻
Amphitheater _____ 📡
Parking Area _____ 🚗
ROAD _____
TRAIL ••••••••••••••••

To Springdale →

SOUTH ENTRANCE El. 3960'

9

South Campground

Zion Canyon Visitor Center

Zion Nature Center

Watchman Viewpoint Trail

△ THE SENTINEL El. 7157'

Sand Bench Trail

North Fork Virgin River

Z I O N

△ BRIDGE MTN El. 6814'

△ EAST TEMPLE El. 7110'

△ MOUNTAIN OF THE SUN El. 6723'

TUNNEL

Canyon Overlook Trail

M   I   L   E   S
0   ½   1

HIDDEN CANYON TRAIL: Starts at Weeping Rock parking area; ends at mouth of canyon; 2 miles round trip; 850-foot ascent; views of Weeping Rock and small arch in Hidden Canyon; canyon is good example of a hanging valley.

WEST RIM TRAIL: Starts at Grotto picnic area; 12.8 miles round trip to the West Rim Overlook; 3,070-foot ascent; leads through Refrigerator Canyon and Walter's Wiggles to view of the canyon systems; footbridge crosses river; continues through Potato Hollow to Lava Point and Kolob Plateau; carry water and food.

ANGELS LANDING TRAIL: Starts at Grotto picnic area; ends at Angels Landing; 5 miles round trip; 1,488-foot ascent; view of Angels Landing and of panorama including Great White Throne and Zion Canyon; footbridge crosses river; last .5 mile strenuous; carry water.

WATCHMAN VIEWPOINT TRAIL: Starts at South Campground bridge; ends at cliff above Watchman Campground; 2 miles round trip; 368-foot ascent; views of West Temple across Zion Canyon and of panorama of Zion Canyon and arch on Bridge Mountain.

SAND BENCH TRAIL: Starts at Court of the Patriarchs; ends under streaked wall; 3.5 miles round trip; 500-foot ascent; views of Three Patriarchs, the Watchman, and Pine Creek Canyon; recommended for winter when horses are not in use.

Note: All overnight trips require a permit.

West Rim Trail, including Scout Lookout and Angels Landing Trail. As spectacular as the East Rim Trail, the West Rim Trail is an even more arduous climb to even greater heights. Backpackers begin with an invigorating pull through Refrigerator Canyon; then, before reaching an intermediate point known as Scout Lookout, the trail grows steeper as it passes along Walter's Wiggles. (This section of the trail was supervised by Walter Ruesch, who was custodian of the park in 1919, when it was still just a "monument." In those days, 21 switchbacks in 600 feet were necessary to reach a shelf on the cliff!) Park rangers point out that "it is the only place in the world where you can see both ends of a horse at the same time."

At Scout Lookout, you can climb to Angels Landing and peer across to Observation Point or down again into Zion Canyon. The climb on to Angels Landing is an exciting 1-hour hike. Steel railings have been installed to ensure that climbers do not accidentally plummet into the chasms below. Or, at Scout Lookout, you can continue hiking for several days through Potato Hollow, Lava Point, and eventually on to the Kolob Plateau. Wildflowers grow in season all along these trails, even emerging from tiny cracks in the walls. This is the true backcountry of Zion and the area most frequently visited by wildlife—black bear, deer, and, occasionally, a migrant elk.

The trail begins at the Grotto picnic area and progresses upward for 3,070 feet to the highest point, known as the West Rim Overlook. From the overlook, hikers must either return 5.5 miles to the picnic grounds or continue into remote Potato Hollow.

Riverside Walk. One of the most popular short trails is along the Virgin River, from the Temple of Sinawava to the beginning of the Narrows. It is something of an introduction to the much longer and more arduous Virgin River Narrows Route. At the end, the river is but a mere ribbon between canyon walls that run together in a dramatic setting as the door to the backcountry. Those who do not go on can listen to the canyon frogs serenading, and watch the antlion, buried in the sand up to its jaws, snap at unwary insects, preferably ants. The trail is 2 miles round trip; 2 hours; 57-foot climb.

The Virgin River Narrows Route. This is the most demanding of the Zion hikes, and hikers must be in good shape to negotiate the grueling 12.5 miles along the Virgin River. There is actually no trail as such, and in some areas, backpackers have to wade through rather deep waters. In places, the canyon walls close until they are little more than 30 feet apart, with a vertical 2,000 feet to the plateau that allows little sunlight to penetrate to the river.

This hike is limited to a fixed number each day. Permits are issued on a first-come basis the evening before the hike. Register at the Visitor Center. Plan the hike only during dry weather; late June and late September are generally best.

Kolob Arch Trail. Kolob Arch Trail is reached from La Verkin Creek Trail. Side trips into Hop Valley or up Willis Creek, two of the most rugged of Zion's backcountry areas, require a 2- to 3-day trip. Days could be spent exploring these canyons and their beautiful scenery. Kolob Arch, the world's largest with a span of 310 feet, is 6.5 miles from the trail head at Lee Pass. About 15 miles later, hikers reach a road that will take them back to their point of origin, now about 40 miles away. Obviously, planning is required as far as logistics are concerned. A trip along Kolob Arch Trail should be planned and then discussed with a ranger at the Kolob Canyons Visitor Center for maximum enjoyment and safety.

Other Trails. Six other trails in Zion National Park lead past waterfalls, canyons, and a myriad startlingly beautiful rock formations. *Weeping Rock Trail* is a lovely, easy, .5-mile walk to a rock that "weeps" with water that has filtered through more than 2,000 feet of Navajo Sandstone. Weeping Rock is the junction at which water

During a thunderstorm and in the spring snowmelt season, waterfalls appear everywhere. The Emerald Pools, with their rich, dark coloring, are fed by several waterfalls.

encounters impervious layers of shale, which forces the water to flow outward. As water proceeds along this course, it dissolves calcium, the cementing agent in the sandstone. Once the particles of sand are released and sections of sandstone collapse, the cliff is enlarged. This self-guiding trail has interpretive labels that describe features along the route.

Leaving from the parking area of the Zion–Mount Carmel Tunnel is another self-guiding nature trail, the *Canyon Overlook Trail*. It terminates in .5 mile at the Canyon Overlook and takes about 1 hour to complete. A fairly steep escarpment leads under an overhang before the trail opens to a broad and exciting panoramic view at the Canyon Overlook. All along this trail are excellent views of Pine Creek Canyon, the East Temple, and the west side of Zion Canyon.

Another trail that begins at the Weeping Rock parking area is the *Hidden Canyon Trail*. This rather steep trail ascends 850 feet in 1 mile and leads to a quiet canyon in which the silence is broken only by the occasional trill of a canyon wren. It is a 2-mile round trip and takes about 3 hours.

An arched metal bridge that crosses the Virgin River at the Zion Lodge is the beginning of the *Emerald Pools Trail*. If you are properly dressed in foul-weather gear, this is an ideal area to visit during one of the park's summer thunderstorms. Rivulets of water surge down from every direction and unite to dramatically illustrate the awesome power of nature when unleashed in its fullest force. When the storm is over and the waters quieted, little pools attract a variety of wildlife. Look in the surrounding sands for paw prints. This is a 2-mile 2- to 3-hour, leisurely round trip.

The *Sand Bench Trail* is a 3.5-mile round-trip walk that starts at the Court of the Patriarchs and provides views of the park's main features. It is recommended for winter hikes when the horse concession is not operating.

Just a short distance from the South Campground is the trail head for the *Watchman Viewpoint Trail*. It will take 2 hours to hike this 2-mile round trip. This trail ascends to an elevation of about 370 feet in 1 mile and provides views of the Watchman, Oak Creek Canyon, and the town of Springdale. From this vantage point, hikers also will be able to see the rather abrupt change in vegetation as it ascends from the parched desert floor to the relatively moist mountain slopes. This is an excellent site to view a sunset.

There is not a single uninspiring trail in Zion National Park. Some are more strenuous than others; all are rewarding.

Opposite: White Arch, created by the forces of erosion and weathering, looks deceptively small from a distance. It is made up of the Navajo Sandstone that is found throughout the park.

ANIMALS & PLANTS

OF THE DESERT SOUTHWEST

This appendix provides a sample of animals and plants commonly found in the national parks of the Desert Southwest. The two-letter abbreviations indicate the parks in which these animals and plants are most often seen.

AR	Arches	CR	Capitol Reef	SA	Saguaro
BB	Big Bend	GB	Great Basin	PF	Petrified Forest
BC	Bryce Canyon	GC	Grand Canyon	ZN	Zion
CC	Carlsbad Caverns	GM	Guadalupe Mountains		
CL	Canyonlands	MV	Mesa Verde		

MAMMALS

BADGER
BB, GB, GC, PF

The nocturnal badger is seldom seen in heavily visited areas. Generally a little over 2 ft. long, including a 5-in. tail, it has a flattish body, with short, bowed legs. Its burrow has an 8–12-in. elliptical opening and is marked by a large mound of earth and debris; the badger can bury itself faster than a person can dig with a shovel. It feeds on rodents.

BAT   BB, BC, CC, GB, GC, GM, MV, ZN

Of the 900 species of bats, the big brown bat and the Mexican freetail bat are the most common in the Southwest. The 5-in.-long big brown bat varies from light to dark brown in color and has a plain nose and a tail that extends only slightly beyond the body; it lives in caves, mines, storm sewers, and buildings. The 3.5–4.5-in.-long Mexican freetail bat is dark brown or dark gray and has narrow wings and a

tail that extends well beyond the body; it has a snub nose and a face that resembles a mastiff's.

BEAVER
BB, BC, CL, CR, MV, ZN

The beaver is North America's largest rodent; it generally is up to 4 ft. long, including a 1-ft., flat, scaly tail, and weighs 45–60 lbs., but can weigh up to 100. Mainly nocturnal, it is seldom seen; but there is evidence of its work in the dams of small streams. The beaver lives in lodges formed by logs; on major rivers, it lives in dens along the bank. The beaver's diet is mainly the bark of trees, although in summer it feeds on water vegetation.

BIGHORN SHEEP

Also known as the "mountain sheep" or the "Rocky Mountain bighorn sheep," it is one of the most spectacular animals in the parks. Rams are 3–3.5 ft. in height, 127–316 lbs., and with a horn

spread of 33 in. (the horns curve up and back over ears); ewes are 4.25–5.25 ft. in height and weigh 74–200 lbs. Color varies from dark brown to pale tan; generally the belly, rump patch, back of legs, muzzle, and eye patch are white. The bighorn's diet is mostly grasses, sedges, and woody plants, and its habitat is alpine meadows and foothills near rocky cliffs.

BLACK BEAR
BB, BC, GC, GM, ZN

The black bear may be a brownish or cinnamon color, but it can easily be distinguished from the grizzly and brown bear by its straight-profiled face, rather than the dished face of the others, and by its comparatively smaller size (3 ft. at the shoulder, 4.5–6.25 ft. long, 203–595 lbs.) and humpless shoulders. The black bear feeds on grasses, buds, leaves, berries, nuts, bark, insects, rodents, the fawns of deer and elk, and fish, particularly salmon; a scrounger by nature, it will forage near campsites. This is a powerful and potentially dangerous animal, despite its clownlike antics; although primarily nocturnal, it is sometimes seen during the day, sometimes "galloping" as fast as 30 miles an hour.

BOBCAT BB, CL, CR, GB, GC, MV, PE, SA, ZN

The bobcat is North America's most common wild cat; because it is nocturnal and secretive, it is seldom seen. It is tawny in color, with indistinct black spots, a pale or white belly, and a short, stubby tail with 2 or 3 black bars. It weighs 14–68 lbs. and measures 2.3–4 ft. long; the males are larger than the females. In the late winter, the male may be heard yowling at night, much like a domesticated cat. Kits are born in a den, usually in thickets or under rocks and logs. The bobcat feeds on rodents and especially ground-nesting birds.

COYOTE AR, BB, CL, GB, GC, GM, MV, SA, ZN

The coyote is the smallest species of wild dog; although resembling a domestic dog, it is often mistaken for a wolf. The coyote is seen fairly regularly in the western parks; its evening "howl" has made it legendary. It weighs about 75 lbs., stands about 2 ft. at the shoulder, and is 3.5–4 ft. long, including a tail of 12–15 in. Its fur is brownish- to reddish-gray—at the lower altitudes more tan and red, at the higher altitudes more gray and black. The coyote has a varied diet of deer, elk, rabbit, rodents, snakes, birds, and insects. A typical den is a wide-mouthed earthen tunnel, 5–30 ft. long, which may be the former residence of a fox or badger.

DEER MOUSE AR, BB, BC, CL, GB, GC, GM, MV, PE, SA, ZN

There are about 100 species of rats or mice in North America, and probably the most common in the Southwest is the deer mouse. A grayish to reddish-brown mouse about 5–8.75 in. long, including a 2–5-in. tail, it feeds on seeds, nuts, small fruits, berries, and insects. It usually burrows in the ground, though some may nest in raised areas or have refuge burrows.

DESERT COTTONTAIL AR, BB, CC, CL, CR, GB, GC, GM, MV, PF, SA

The buff-brown desert cottontail is 13–16.5 in. long and can be seen at night sitting on a stump or log watching for predators; during the day, it scampers about feeding on grass and plants. Cottontails usually hop, but they can leap up to 15 ft., and, like all rabbits, they freeze when threatened and then abruptly change direction and flee.

ELK BC, CC, GC, GM, MV, SA, ZN

The elk is second in size only to the moose in the deer family. Males may weight 600–1,100 lbs. and stand 5 ft. at the shoulders (its graceful antlers may reach another 5 ft.); females weight 450–650 lbs. Mostly nocturnal, elk can be seen at dusk or dawn grazing in meadows on grasses and woody vegetation. Mating season is the fall, at which time occur the legendary fights with clashing antlers.

GRAY FOX AR, BB, BC, CC, CL, CR, GM, ZN

Of the six species of foxes in North America, the gray fox is the most commonly found in national parks; yet, being nocturnal, it is seldom seen. It is gray, with a black stripe running down the top of its tail, stands 14–15 in. at the shoulder, and is 3–4 ft. long, including a 9–17 in. tail.

MERRIAM'S KANGAROO RAT
AR, BB, CC, GB, GM, ZN

Merriam's is the smallest of the kangaroo rats; it is light yellowish-buff and white, and measures 8–10 in., including a 4–6-in. white, side-striped tail. It feeds mostly on seeds. The rat burrows and frequently gives itself a sand or dust bath to keep its fur from matting.

MOUNTAIN LION AR, BB, CL, GB, GC, GM, MV, ZN

Often called cougar or puma, the mountain lion is a most secretive mammal, living mostly in mountainous areas and seldom seen; it is a rather docile cat, rarely attacking humans, but its scream can be terrifying. Yellowish to tawny, with a long, black-tipped tail, it weighs up to 275 lbs. and measures 5–9 ft., including a 2–3-ft. tail. The mountain lion feeds on deer, coyote, beaver, mice, hares, raccoons, birds, and grasshoppers.

MULE DEER
AR, BB, BC, CC, CL, CR, GB, GC, GM, MV, SA, ZN

The mule deer is a fairly common species of the deer family seen in the western parks, particularly in the early morning and late evening. It is characterized by its large, mulelike ears, from which it gets its name, and white rump, although it should not be confused with the white-tailed deer—also seen in some western parks; it weighs up to 400 lbs. and stands 3–3.5 ft. at the shoulder. The male loses its antlers in the late winter and is generally solitary in its roamings. The mule deer eats acorns, berries, cactus fruits, twigs, buds, grasses, herbs, tree bark, and mushrooms.

PORCUPINE
AR, BB, BC, CC, CL, CR, GC, MV, PF, ZN

Contrary to legend, porcupines *cannot* throw or "shoot" their quills, although the quills are rather loosely attached and may shake off if the porcupine threshes its tail about in self-defense. Classified as a rodent, it is the only quilled mammal. About 3 ft. long, 1 ft. high, and 35 lbs., it lives mostly in coniferous forests, but may also inhabit brushy areas of the Southwest. It survives mostly on a diet of the wood directly beneath tree bark, although it also eats buds and twigs from a number of trees and bushes.

PRAIRIE DOG
BC, CL, CR, GC, GM, MV

Four species of prairie dogs live in the national parks—black-tailed, white-tailed, Utah, and Gunnison's; all four are similar and sometimes difficult to identify. The prairie dog varies from 14–16

in. in length, including a 2–4.5-in. tail, and weighs 1.5–3 lbs. The black-tailed prairie dog builds a 1-ft.-high, volcano-shaped burrow of hard-packed earth; the other three species build burrows ranging from level to 3 ft. high. Several thousand may live in "towns" covering 100 acres or more. Most of its diet consists of green plants or grasses in the immediate area of its burrow.

RACCOON
BB, CC, GM, MV, ZN

The notorious "black-masked" raccoon raids garbage cans in national parks, just as it does in the suburbs; nocturnal, the raccoon can be seen around park campgrounds. It is reddish-brown with black above and gray below, and measures 2–3 ft., including a 7.5–16-in. bushy tail with alternating black and brown rings. Its diet includes grapes, nuts, insects, rodents, turtles, frogs, and birds' eggs; dens are usually in hollow trees, caves, rock clefts, or culverts.

RINGTAIL BB, CC, CR, GB, GC, GM, MV, ZN

The ringtail is a member of the raccoon family, but it has no mask around the eyes and is smaller than the raccoon. The ringtail is yellowish-gray above and whitish-buff below, with a catlike body and foxlike face; it measures 2.5 ft., including a 12–17-in. bushy tail with as many as 16 black bands. A better mouser than a cat, it eats rodents, rabbits, snakes, insects, and fruit. Sometimes found about buildings, it generally makes its den among rocks or boulders.

ROCK SQUIRREL
AR, BB, CL, CR, GB, GC, GM, SA, MV, ZN

The rock squirrel is the largest of the ground squirrels, measuring 16–21 in., with a tail of 6–10 in. It lives in rocky areas, where its grayish-brownish color blends naturally with the terrain. The squirrel feeds on acorns, nuts, and seeds of mesquite, cactus, agave, and currant.

STRIPED SKUNK
BB, BC, CR, GB, GC, GM, MV, PE, SA, ZN

The striped skunk is the skunk that is found almost everywhere in the U.S., except Alaska. It has a narrow stripe of white down its nose, and a V-shaped, white configuration down its back; males weigh 6–14 lbs. and measure 20–31 in., including a 7–15-in. bushy tail. The striped skunk feeds on insects, small mammals, amphibians, and eggs of small ground-nesting birds.

BIRDS

AMERICAN KESTREL

AR, BB, CC, CL, CR, GB, GC, PF, SA, ZN

Until recently, this small falcon was known as the "sparrow hawk." The kestrel measures 9–12 in. from bill to tail and has a wingspread of 22–23 in. It has blue-gray wings and head with a buff breast and nape. The kestrel does not build a nest of its own, but lays its eggs without nesting or borrows another bird's nest in tree holes or building niches. It can be seen perched on trees and telephone poles, from where it swoops rapidly upon its grasshopper and rodent prey.

AMERICAN ROBIN

BB, BC, CC, CR, GB, GC, GM, MV, PF, ZN

Best known of all North American birds, once called "robin," the American robin is gray-brown, with puffed-out, red or orange breast, white throat, and blackish head and tail. It measures 9–11 in. The robin feeds primarily on worms pulled from the ground. In cold weather, the nest is built of twigs and mud and lined with fine material in low, densely leafed or needled trees and bushes; in hot weather, the nest is high in maple or sycamore trees.

ASH-TROATED FLYCATCHER

BB, CC, CR, GC, GM, ZN

The ash-throated flycatcher measures 7.5–8.5 in., has a gray-white throat, olive-brown back, and light yellow underparts. It nests in a cuplike construction that usually includes pieces of shed snakeskin, and it feeds on insects.

BROAD-TAILED HUMMINGBIRD

BB, BC, CC, CL, CR, GB, GC, GM, MV, PF, SA, ZN

Distinguished by a unique musical trill from wings in flight, the broad-tailed hummingbird resembles the ruby-throated hummingbird, but the male is rose, not red, and the tail is rounded, not forked. Both sexes are greenish above, white below, and 4–4.5 in. from bill to tail. It feeds on insects and flower nectar.

BULLOCK'S ORIOLE

BB, CC, CR, GB, MV, PF, ZN

The western species of oriole (eastern is Baltimore), the Bullock's oriole measures 7–8.5 in. Male is orange-yellow, with black crown, nape, and mantle, narrow black eye stripe, narrow black bib, and wings with broad white patch and white edges on flight feathers. The oriole nests in a finely woven basket and feeds on insects, seeds, waste grain, fruit, and small aquatic life.

COMMON NIGHTHAWK

AR, BB, BC, CL, CR, GB, GC, MV, PF, SA, ZN

A slim-winged gray-brown bird, with ample tail, large eyes, tiny bill, and short legs, the common night-hawk measures 8.5–10 in. from bill to tail. Male has white throat patch and white subterminal tail bar. It feeds on nocturnal insects, and by day sits on tree limbs in a "dead-leaf" camouflage.

COMMON RAVEN
AR, BB, BC, CL, CR, GC, MV, PF, ZN

Considered to have an intelligence matching a dog's, applying reason to new situations, the raven is the largest of the crows; it is 21.5–27 in. from bill to tail. It is black, with thick bill and wedge-shaped tail. The raven nests in a large collection of sticks, bones, and soft material on a cliff face or in a tree, and feeds on almost anything.

GOLDEN EAGLE
AR, BB, CL, GB, MV, PF, ZN

The golden eagle, the most majestic of North America's birds, is 2.5–3.5 ft. from bill to tail and has a wingspread of 7–8 ft. It is shaped like a hawk, but with a much greater wingspan when flying. Dark brown with a

'golden" nape visible only at close range, its legs are feathered down to the talons. Its nest is generally a large mass of twigs or sticks on a crag or rocky ledge or high in a tree. The golden eagle's primary diet is rodents and rabbits.

GREAT HORNED OWL
BB, BC, CC, GB, GC, GM, MV, PF, SA, ZN

The great horned owl is common to all of North America, from Mexico to the tree line in Canada. It is 1.5–2 ft. from tail to top of head, gray-brown above, with a fine dark-gray horizontal barring below, large yellow eyes, and ear tufts set far apart. It nests in trees, crevices, or cliffs, often in a nest once occupied by a hawk. The owl hunts rabbits, rodents, ducks, crows, and other owls, and it has been seen capturing a skunk.

HAIRY WOODPECKER
GB, GC, GM, MV, ZN

A medium-size woodpecker, but larger than the downy, the hairy woodpecker has a white head with black crown, eyemask, and "whiskers." Male has red patch at base of crown, and black tail with white outer feathers; female has no red patch. Both are 8.5–10.5 in. from bill to tail. It feeds by pecking a hole in tree bark and, with long, flexible tongue, extracting grubs; it nests in tree cavities.

HORNED LARK
BB, CC, CR, GB, PF, ZN

The horned lark is faithful to its birthplace, where it returns after migration. It measures 7–8 in. long and is pale brown, with black bib, yellow sash on throat and face, and black tail feathers with white margins. The lark feeds on seeds and ground insects, and nests in grass-lined depressions in the ground.

KILLDEER
BC, CC, GB, GM, PF

The killdeer is grayish-brown above, white below, with two black breast bands, and a long tan tail, which is evident in flight. It measures

9–11 in. long. It lays its eggs in a scrape on bare ground in plowed field, gravel shore, roadway, or bald spot in pasture, and is conspicuous for its means of distracting predators from young—by dragging itself along the ground, as though it has broken a wing, until it has led danger away. It feeds on worms and insects.

MARSH HAWK
AR, BB, CL, GB, MV, PF

Also called "harrier," the marsh hawk is a specialized mouser in tall vegetation; its owl-like face directs mouse squeaks to its sensitive ears. It measures 1.5–2 ft. from bill to tail, has slim, long wings, tail, and legs, and in flight shows black wingtips and barred tail. Male is light gray above, with underparts of reddish spotting. The marsh hawk roosts on the ground at night, builds grass nests on or close to the ground, and feeds on rodents.

MOUNTAIN CHICKADEE BC, CR, GB, GC, GM, MV, ZN

The mountain chickadee is a small, constantly active insect seeker. It is 5–5.75 in. long, gray, with a black cap, white eye stripe, and pale gray sides. The chickadee nests in a hair- or fur-lined natural cavity or woodpecker tree hole.

MOURNING DOVE
AR, BB, CC, CL, CR, GB, GC, GM, MV, PF, SA, ZN

The mourning dove's name comes from the melancholy cooing of the male, generally "sung" from a prominent perch and followed by a courtship flight. The bird measures 11–13 in. from bill to tail; it is light brownish-gray, with a pale buff chest, darker wings with black spots along the inside edge, and an iridescent, light violet neck shield. The central tail feathers on the male are quite long, with sharply tapered, white-tipped outer feathers. Like other species of doves, it feeds primarily on seeds, and nests in trees and bushes.

ROADRUNNER
BB, CC, GB, GC, GM, SA

One of the most famous birds of the Southwest, the roadrunner is named for its rapid actions when surprised; it runs rapidly on strong feet and seldom flies. It measures 20–24 in. long, is brown with a green sheen, streaked with black and white above, buff below, has brown streaks on breast, and a heavy bill. The roadrunner nests in mesquite bush and large cactus, and feeds on snakes, lizards, insects, scorpions, and rodents.

ROCK WREN
AR, BB, CC, CL, CR, GB, GC, MV, PF, ZN

The 5.25–6.25 in. rock wren has a gray body and rust-colored rump. It feeds on insects, and nests in crevices in rocks and walls. The wren can be identified by a trail of rock chips leading to the nest, a behavior presumed to be "decorating" its territory.

RUBY-CROWNED KINGLET
BB, CC, CR, GM, MV, SA, ZN

A small, Old World warbler, the ruby-crowned kinglet measures 3.75–4.5 in., is olive gray above, shaded white below, with white wing bars, and is conspicuous for its "broken" white eye ring. It nests in small cups in bushes or trees, and feeds on insects.

RUFOUS HUMMINGBIRD
BB, BC, CC, CL, CR, GC, GM, MV, ZN

The male rufous hummingbird is identified by distinctive black throat and white collar below; the female is greenish above, whitish below. Both are 3.5–3.75 in. from bill to tail. It nests in a feltlike cup in shrub or tree, and feeds on insects, spiders, and flower nectar.

SAY'S PHOEBE
BB, BC, CC, CR, GB, GC, GM, MV, PF, SA, ZN

A flycatcher that is about 7–8 in. long, the Say's phoebe has a dusky body, with dark wings and black tail. It feeds on insects and berries, and nests in a cup or bracket of mud, grass, or moss on an elevated ledge, rock wall, or building.

SCALED QUAIL
BB, CC, GM, PF

The scaled quail has a white, cottony topknot, with pale unstreaked gray head, and black-edged bluish-gray feathers on breast and mantle. It measures 10–12 in. from bill to tail. The quail feeds on insects, seeds, buds, and berries, and nests in a grass-lined hollow under a bush.

SCRUB JAY
AR, CL, CR, GB, MV, ZN

A robin-size member of crow family, the scrub jay has a blue head, wings, and tail, a brown back, gray underparts, and a white throat. It measures 11–13 in. The jay nests in a twiggy cup in dense shrub or tree, and feeds on nuts and has been credited with helping regenerate forests—burying more acorns than it eats.

SHARP-SHINNED HAWK
BB, BC, CR, GB, MV, ZN

Recognized by its short, broad, rounded wings and long, thin, cross-barred tail, which is often notched, the sharp-shinned hawk is slate blue above, white below, with rusty cross-barring. It measures 10–14 in. long. The hawk nests on a twiggy platform in dense conifers, and feeds on small mammals, reptiles, and insects.

WESTERN BLUEBIRD
AR, BB, CC, CL, CR, GB, GM, PF, ZN

The male western bluebird has a deep-blue hood and upper parts, and a rust-red breast, to warn off aggressors and rivals and to attract the female; it measures 6–7 in. The bluebird feeds on insects, worms, snails, berries, and fruits, and its grass nest is generally in a tree hole.

WESTERN KINGBIRD
AR, CC, CL, CR, GB, GM, PF

Formerly called the Arkansas kingbird, the western kingbird is found throughout the West. It measures 8–9 in. from bill to tail, and is olive brown above and yellow below, with a light gray breast, dusky wings, and a blackish tail with white margins. The western kingbird nests in trees, bushes, or buildings, and feeds primarily on flying insects.

WESTERN TANAGER
BB, CC, CR, GB, GC, GM, MV, PF, ZN

The male western tanager has a brilliant red head,

bright yellow body, and black back wings and tail; the female is yellow-green above and yellow below. Both measure 6–7.5 in. It makes a shallow saucerlike nest of woven weed stalks, bark strips, and rootlets, usually in the fork of a horizontal branch of Douglas fir, spruce, pine, or oak.

WHITE-CROWNED SPARROW
BB, CC, CL, GB, GC, MV, PF, SA, ZN

The white-crowned sparrow has a crown with alternating 5 white and 4 black stripes; a white stripe over the eye, and a black stripe through the eye; face and nape are grayish, and breast is pearl-gray. It is 6–7 in. long. Its grass nests are on or near the ground, and it feeds on seeds, insects, and small fruit.

AMPHIBIANS, ARTHROPODS, AND REPTILES

BLACK-NECKED GARTER SNAKE
AR, BB, CC, CL, GB, GM, SA

The 1.5–4-ft. black-necked garter snake is olive gray or olive brown, with 2 large black blotches on the neck separated by a stripe down the back that may be wavy and orange in neck region, yellow or cream toward tail. Pale side stripes occupy second and third rows of scales; 2 rows of black spots are between the back and side stripes; and the top of the head is gray. Active during the day, the snake swims on the surface of water and feeds on frogs, toads, and tadpoles.

BLACK-TAILED RATTLESNAKE
BB, CC, GM

The unaggressive black-tailed rattlesnake can be seen during the day basking in the sun. It is 2–4 ft. long, greenish, yellowish, or grayish, with irregular light-edged and light-centered cross-bands, and black tail. The snake feeds on small rodents.

BULLSNAKE
BB, GM, MV, PF, SA

Large and powerfully built, the bullsnake measures 4–8 ft. and has a small head. The yellowish snake has at least 40 black, brown, or reddish-brown blotches on back and sides. Active during the day, it consumes large numbers of rodents.

CANYON TREE FROG
BB, CR, GC, SA, ZN

The canyon tree frog is small, brown or olive-gray, with a blotched or spotted dark-brown or olive camouflage pattern (sometimes no pattern) and a cream belly, grading to yellow on the hind legs. It measures 1.75–2.25 in. and feeds on insects.

COACHWHIP SNAKE AR, BB, CC, CL, GM, PF, SA, ZN

The coachwhip is perhaps North America's fastest snake; when cornered, it will coil and strike out. It is 3–8 ft. long, and a patternless yellow, tan, brown, gray, or pinkish. The coachwhip hunts during the day for cicadas, lizards, grasshoppers, small rodents, and other snakes.

COLLARED LIZARD AR, BB, CC, CL, GC, MV, PF, SA, ZN

The collared lizard is aggressive and will bite. It has a large head, a conspicuous black and white collar across the back of its neck, and a yellow-brown to green body with bluish highlights. It is 8–14 in. long. When fleeing danger, it lifts its body and tail and dashes on its hind legs. The collared lizard feeds on insects and other lizards.

COUCH'S SPADEFOOT TOAD
BB, CC, GM, PF, SA

The Couch's spadefoot is a plump toad, with long, sickle-shaped spades on hind feet, a bright greenish-yellow to brown body, and a white belly; it measures

2.25–3.5 in. The nocturnal spadefoot lays eggs on plant stems in temporary pools, lives in underground holes, and feeds on insects.

CREVICE SPINY LIZARD

BB, CC, GM

The crevice spiny lizard is elusive and hides among stones and in crevices. It is 8.5–11.25 in. long, with large rough scales on its drab olive to reddish body, a prominent white-edged black collar, dark crossbands on tail, and blue patches on its throat and belly. It feeds on insects and occasionally on blossoms.

DESERT TARANTULA

BB, GC, SA, ZN

Despite bad publicity, the tarantula is not dangerous; its venom is no more poisonous than that of a bee, and it is reluctant to attack humans. The male measures 2–2.5 in. and the female, which can live for 20 years, 2–2.75 in. The tarantula's body is gray to dark brown, its abdomen is brownish-black, and its legspan is 4 in.; it nests on the ground and feeds on insects, lizards, and other small animals.

DESERT TORTOISE

BB, GC

An endangered species, the terrestrial desert tortoise has a domed shell and round, stumpy hind legs; it is 9.25–14.5 in. long. Its small head is reddish-tan; upper shell, horn-brown; and lower shell, yellowish. The desert tortoise feeds on grasses in early morning and late afternoon.

GRAND CANYON RATTLESNAKE

GC

The size and color of the Grand Canyon rattlesnake vary. Generally 1.3–5.3 ft. long, it has brownish blotches down midline of back, edged with dark brown or black, and often surrounded by light color. Aggressive, it feeds on small mammals.

GREAT BASIN GOPHER SNAKE

AR, BC, CL, CR, GB, GC, MV, PF, ZN

The 4–8 ft. Great Basin gopher snake is light-colored, with black, brown, or reddish-brown blotches on back and sides, and wide, black blotches on forepart of body. Active during the day, it feeds on rodents.

LEOPARD FROG AR, BB, BC, CC, CL, CR, GB, MV, ZN

The leopard frog is gray or dull-green, with a dorsal pattern of well-defined oval or round dark spots with pale borders; it measures 2–5 in. The frog frequents springs, creeks, rivers, and ponds where there is abundant aquatic vegetation. and feeds on insects.

RED-SPOTTED TOAD

BB, CC, GB, GC, GM, PF, SA, ZN

The small, flat, red-spotted toad is olive to grayish-brown, with reddish warts; it measures 1.5–3 in. It is active at twilight, can be seen as far as 1 mile from water, and feeds on insects.

SIDE-BLOTCHED LIZARD
AR, BB, BC, CC, CL, GB, GC, GM, PF, ZN

The small side-blotched lizard measures 4–6.5 in. It is brown, with blotches, spots, speckles, and stripes on its scaly back, and a single dark blue to black spot on each side behind the foreleg. The lizard feeds on insects.

SOUTHERN PRAIRIE LIZARD
AR, CC, CL, GM, PF, ZN

The terrestrial southern prairie lizard is 3.5–7.5 in. long; color varies according to geography—generally gray to brown or rusty, with wavy, dark crossbars on back and blue patches on belly and throat. The lizard shelters under bushes and feeds on almost any insect, spider, centipede, and snail.

TIGER SALAMANDER
AR, BC, CC, CL, CR, PF, ZN

The tiger salamander is the world's largest land-dwelling salamander; it is 6–13 in. long. It has a broad head and small eyes. Often seen at night after heavy rain, the tiger salamander lives beneath debris near water. It feeds on earthworms, large insects, small mice, and amphibians.

TRANS-PECOS RAT SNAKE   BB

The 3–5-ft. Trans-Pecos rat snake has large "bug-eyes" separated from upper lip scales by a row of small scales. It is yellowish-tan or olive green, with a series of dark-brown, H-shaped blotches. It feeds on small mammals, birds, and lizards.

TREE LIZARD   AR,BB, BC, CL, CR, GC, GM, SA, ZN

The tree lizard spends much time on rocks or in trees, from which it sometimes can be seen hanging head down. It measures 2–2.25 in. and is dark brown, tan, sooty, or gray, with small scales. The tree lizard feeds on insects.

WESTERN SPADEFOOT TOAD
AR, BB, CC, CL, PF, ZN

The western spadefoot is a stout, 1.5–2.5-in. toad, with wedge-shaped spades on hind feet; its body is dusky-olive to brown or gray, with irregular light stripes, random dark blotches, and a white belly. A nocturnal toad, it feeds on insects.

WOODHOUSE'S TOAD   AR, BB, BC, CL, CR, GC, PF, ZN

The Woodhouse's toad is large, with a light stripe down the middle of its back; it is yellow to green or brown, and measures 2.5–5 in. The nocturnal Woodhouse's toad feeds on insects.

FLOWERS, SHRUBS, AND TREES

BLAZING STAR
AR, CL, GB, PF, ZN

This member of the stick-leaf family is called blazing star because of barbed hairs on its leaves that stick to fabric. Many large, starlike blooms are on branches at the top of a stout, satiny, white stem; flowers 2-5 in. wide bloom from June to September; 4-12-in. leaves are very rough, with large, irregular teeth. It grows 1-3 ft. high.

BOX ELDER
AR, CL, CR, ZN

Classed with maples, the small to medium-size box elder has a short trunk and a broad, rounded crown of light-green foliage. It grows to a height of 30-60 ft. and a diameter of 2.5 ft. Its leaves are 2.4 in. long; flowers are 3/16 in. with small, yellow-green calyx of 5 lobes. Plains Indians made sugar from box elder sap.

COLUMBINE
AR, BB, GB, ZN

The columbine is a bushy plant, with white and blue flowers that tip upward at end of stem. The 5-petaled flowers are shaped like sugar scoops, and bloom from June to August.

CLIFF ROSE
AR, BC, CR, GB, GC, MV, PF, ZN

The cliff rose is a stout shrub, with shreddy bark and small, pinnately lobed leaves; its flowers have 5 light yellow or white petals. Its fragrance rivals that of any plant.

DOUGLAS-FIR
GB

This tree is found primari-ly in the loamy soils on mountain slopes, in pure or nearly pure stands. It grows 80-200 ft. tall and the trunk measures up to 10 ft. in diameter. The evergreen needles are about .75-1.25 in. and quite flexible; cones measure 2-3.5 in. long and are light brown and egg–shaped. The foliage is eaten by grouse, deer, and elk; the seeds are eaten by birds and mammals.

ENGELMANN ASTER
AR, CR, GB, GC, MV, PF, ZN

The Engelmann aster is one of a number of tall asters. Stems are leafy; flower heads have a yellow disk about 1.5-2.5 in. around and are surrounded by about 15 rays of white or pinkish petals. It grows to 1.5-5 ft. and is found in open places.

FREMONT BARBERRY
AR, BC, CL, CR, GC, GM, ZN

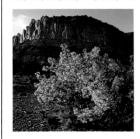

The barberry is a shrub with compound leaves

and clusters of bright yellow, fragrant flowers; the evergreen leaves are spiny. The Fremont grows up to 4 ft. and is frequently seen on dry slopes south and west of Zion.

FREMONT COTTONWOOD
BC, CL, CR, PF, ZN

Named for its discoverer, John Charles Frémont, this cottonwood is a tall tree, with a broad, flattened, open crown of large, widely spreading branches. It is 40-80 ft. high, 2-4 ft. in diameter, with 2-3 in. leaves. The cottonwood grows in wet soil and indicates permanent water. Hopi Indians carve kachina dolls from cottonwood roots.

GAMBEL OAK
AR, BC, CC, GC, GM, MV, SA, ZN

The Gambel is the com-

mon oak of the Rocky Mountains, and abundant in Grand Canyon. A tall tree with rounded crown: 20-70 ft. high, 1-2.5 ft. in diamter, 2-6 in. leaves, egg-shaped .5-.75-in. acorns. Foliage eaten by deer and livestock; wild turkeys, squirrels, and other wildlife, as well as livestock, eat acorns.

INDIAN PAINTBRUSH
AR, BB, CC, CR, GB, GC, GM, MV, PF, ZN

The flower resembles a crimson or scarlet paintbrush, thus the name Indian paintbrush. Usually found in clumps of several stems in sagebrush areas, it grows to 1-3 ft. and flowers from May to September. Indian paintbrush parasitizes other plants through connecting roots.

MONKEY FLOWER
AR, BB, CR, GB, ZN

The monkey flower is a leafy plant ranging from spindly and tiny to large and bushy; it can grow to

3 ft. Its yellow, bilaterally symmetrical flowers measure .5-1.5 in. on slender stalks, and bloom from March to September.

OCOTILLO
BB, CC, GM, SA

The funnel-shaped ocotillo has several woody, spiny, straight stems with a cluster of red flowers at the tip of each branch. It is leafless most of year, with leaves appearing only after rain and then withering when the soil dries; it flowers from March to June. It grows to 2.5 ft.

PENTSTEMON
AR, BB, CR, SA, ZN

The name pentstemon comes from the Greek pente (five) and stemon (thread) and refers to its slender fifth stamen. The

slender, scarlet flower hangs slightly in a long open cluster on sparsely leafy stems that grow to 3 ft.; its 1-1.5 in. flowers bloom from June to September.

PINYON PINE
AR, BB, BC, CC, CL, CR, GB, GC, GM, MV, PF, ZN

The pinyon pine is a slow-growing, small evergreen, with spreading, rounded, gray-green crown; it is often shrubby. The pine is 16-30 ft. high, and 1-1.5 ft. in diameter, with stiff, sharp needles and egg-shaped, dull yellow-brown cones. Large, edible, mealy seeds are sold as pinyon nuts and used as staple food by some Indian tribes.

PONDEROSA PINE
BB, BC, CC, CR, GB, GC, GM, SA, ZN

The most widely distributed and common pine in North America, the ponderosa pine is a large evergreen with a broad, open, conical crown of spreading branches. It is 60-130 ft. high, and 2.5-4 ft. in diameter, with stiff dark-green needles and 2-6 in. cones. It is the most commercially valuable western pine.

PRICKLY PEAR
AR, BB, CC, CL, CR, GB, GC, GM, MV, PF, SA, ZN

The prickly pear is a flat, nearly oval cactus, 3-6 in. high. Its bright yellow or bright magenta many-petaled flowers are 2-3 in. wide and bloom in late spring.

QUAKING ASPEN
BB, BC, GB, ZN

The most widely distributed tree in North America, the quaking aspen grows to a height of 80-100 ft. Its leaves are 1.25-3 in. long and nearly round, shiny green above, dull green beneath, and turn golden-yellow in autumn before dropping; the "quaking" comes from leaves that tremble in the slightest breeze. The bark is the favorite of beaver and rabbits; deer, elk, moose, sheep, and goats feed on twigs and foliage.

RABBITBRUSH
AR, BC, CL, CR, GB, MV, PF, ZN

Rabbitbrush is a shrub found only in North America. Its erect, slender, flexible branches are covered with dense, matted hairs; it has narrow leaves and small yellow flower heads in dense clusters at ends of stems. It grows to 7 ft. Rabbitbrush flowers from August to October, and Navajo Indians use the flower heads for yellow dye.

ROCKY MOUNTAIN MAPLE
GC, GM, MV

This maple is a shrub or

small tree with short trunk and slender, upright branches. It grows to 30 ft., 1 ft. diameter, with leaves 1.5-4.5 in. long, flowers .25 in. wide, with 4 greenish-yellow petals. Deer, elk, cattle, and sheep browse foliage.

SACRED DATURA
AR, BB, CL, CR, GC, SA, ZN

The sacred datura is commonly called jimsonweed, a corruption of Jamestown weed. Its large, trumpet-shaped, white flower blooms at night and is usually withered by morning. It has coarse foliage, with rank-smelling, spherical fruit 1.5 in. in diameter, with a prickly surface. The datura grows to 5 ft. and flowers from May to November.

SAGEBRUSH
AR, BC, CL, GB, PF, ZN

There are several varieties of sagebrush in the western U.S. They are silvery shrubs, with rigid black trunks and persistent leaves, whose heads are small and yellowish when in bloom. Sand sagebrush at Zion is 2-3 ft. tall, with narrow, threadlike silvery leaves.

SQUAWBUSH
AR, BC, CL, CR

Also known as lemonade sumac, squawbush is a rank-smelling, sprawling shrub with greenish flowers.

SUNFLOWER
CC, CL, CR, GC, GM, PF, ZN

The common sunflower is a tall, coarse, leafy plant with a hairy stem that grows to 2-13 ft. Its flower head has a central maroon disk surrounded by many bright yellow rays; it flowers from June to September.

UTAH JUNIPER
AR, CL, CR, GB, GC, MV

Junipers are also called cedars. This short tree, with upright trunk, low spreading branches, and rounded open crown, is 15-40 ft. high and 1-3 ft. in diameter; the leaves are 1/16-in. long. It grows slowly and becomes contorted with age. Indians used juniper bark for cordage and sandals.

YUCCA
AR, BB, CC, CL, CR, GC, GM, MV, PF, SA, ZN

Of the several species of yucca, the banana yucca is the most common. It has rigid, spine-tipped leaves in 1 or several rosettes, and a long cluster of large whitish flowers on a stalk; flowers are 2-4 in. long in spring. The yucca grows to 5 ft. Baked fruit of banana yucca tastes like sweet potato.

PHOTO CREDITS

322: © Roy Murphy
324-325: © Russ Finley/
Holiday Films
327: © David Muench
329: © Russ Finley
331: © Russ Finley/Holiday
Films
332: © Jeff Foott
335: © Laurence Parent
338, 341, left: © George H.

Huey
341, right, 343: © Fred
Hirschmann
347: © Laurence Parent
348: © Jeff Gnass
351: © Ed Cooper
355: New York Public Library
Picture Collection/
Photograph by Eyre
Powell

357: © David Muench
359: © Collier/Condit
360-361: © Jeff Gnass
362: © Dr. E. R. Degginger
363, left: © Sonja Bullaty;
right: © Stephen Trimble
365: © Ed Cooper
367: © Michael Collier
371, 373: © Jeff Gnass

Appendix of Animals and Plants Photo Credits

376, col. 1, top: © Roy
Murphy, bottom: © R. C.
Simpson/Tom Stack &
Assoc.; col. 2, top: © Larry
Thorngren/Tom Stack &
Assoc., bottom: © G. C.
Kelley/Tom Stack & Assoc.;
col. 3: © Roy Murphy.
377, col. 1, both: © Roy
Murphy; col. 2: © Joe
McDonald/Tom Stack &
Assoc.; col. 3, both: ©
Roy Murphy.
378, col. 1, top: © Bob
McKeever/Tom Stack &
Assoc., center: © Stephen
Trimble, bottom: © Roy
Murphy; col. 2: © Rod
Planck/Tom Stack &
Assoc.; col. 3, top: ©
William R. Eastman III/Tom
Stack & Assoc., bottom:
© Robert C. Gildart.
379, col. 1, top: © Roy
Murphy, bottom: © C.
Summers/Tom Stack &
Assoc.; col. 2, top: © Phil
& Loretta Hermann/Tom
Stack & Assoc., bottom:
© Robert C. Gildart; col. 3:
© Joe Branney/Tom Stack
& Assoc.
380, col. 1, top: ©
Christopher Crowley/Tom
Stack & Assoc., bottom: ©
Stephen Trimble; col. 2,
top: © John Gerlach/Tom
Stack & Assoc., bottom: ©
Stephen Trimble; col. 3,
top: © Anthony Mercieca/
Tom Stack & Assoc., bot
tom: © John Shaw/Tom
Stack & Assoc.
381, col. 1, top: © G.C.
Kelley/Tom Stack & Assoc.,
bottom: © Joe Branney/

Tom Stack & Assoc.; col.
2, top: © Stephen Trimble,
bottom: © Rod Planck/
Tom Stack & Assoc.; col.
3, top: © Anthony
Mercieca/ Tom Stack &
Assoc., bottom: © Rod
Planck/Tom Stack & Assoc.
382, col. 1, top: © Keith H.
Murakami/Tom Stack &
Assoc., bottom: ©
Anthony Mercieca/Tom
Stack & Assoc.; col. 2,
both: © Roy Murphy; col.
3, both: © Anthony
Mercieca/Tom Stack &
Assoc.
383, col. 1, top: © Alan G.
Nelson/Tom Stack &
Assoc., bottom: © G. C.
Kelley/Tom Stack & Assoc.;
col. 2, both: © G. C.
Kelley/Tom Stack & Assoc.;
col. 3, top: © Robert C.
Simpson/Tom Stack &
Assoc., bottom: ©
Anthony Mercieca/Tom
Stack & Assoc.
384, col. 1, top: © Anthony
Mercieca/Tom Stack &
Assoc., bottom: © Larry R.
Ditto/Tom Stack & Assoc.;
col. 2: © Anthony
Mercieca/Tom Stack &
Assoc.
385, col. 1, both: © Bob
McKeever/Tom Stack &
Assoc.; col. 2, top: © C.
Summers/Tom Stack &
Assoc., center: © Stephen
Trimble, bottom: © Steve
Elmore; col. 3, top: ©
Stephen Trimble, bottom:
© Bob McKeever/Tom
Stack & Assoc.
386, col. 1, top: © Wayne A.

Lea/Tom Stack & Assoc.,
bottom: © Bob McKeever/
Tom Stack & Assoc.; col.
2, top: © Michael Collier,
center: © Stephen
Trimble, bottom: © Bob
McKeever/Tom Stack &
Assoc.; col. 3, both: ©
Stephen Trimble.
387: All © Bob McKeever/
Tom Stack & Assoc.,
except col. 3, bottom: ©
J. Cancalosi/Tom Stack &
Assoc.
388, col. 1, top: © Rod
Planck/Tom Stack &
Assoc., bottom: © Stephen
Trimble; col. 2, top: ©
Frank Mendonca/Tom
Stack & Assoc., center:
©Donald Young, bottom:
© Stephen Trimble; col. 3,
top: © Stephen Trimble,
bottom: © Roy Murphy.
389, col. 1, top: © Roy
Murphy, bottom: © Jeff
Gnass;
col. 2, top: © Roy Murphy,
bottom: © Michael
Collier, col. 3, top: © Roy
Murphy, bottom: ©
Stephen Trimble.
390, col. 1, both: © Stephen
Trimble; col. 2, top:©
Michael Collier, bottom: ©
Tom Stack/Tom Stack &
Assoc., col. 3, top:
© Stephen Trimble, bot
tom: © Ed Cooper;
391, col. 1, top: © Michael
Collier, bottom: © Stephen
Trimble, col. 2, both: ©
Stephen Trimble; col 3,
top: © Stephen Trimble,
bottom: © Ed Cooper.

393

INDEX

Numbers in italics indicate illustrations.